# BRITAIN & IRELAND

# BRITAIN
# & IRELAND

## *A Visual Tour of the Enchanted Isles*

ROBIN CURRIE

NATIONAL GEOGRAPHIC

WASHINGTON, D.C.

# [ CONTENTS ]

*Opposite:* A solitary figure atop the chalk cliffs in East Sussex—a favorite spot for the writer Lewis Carroll, who vacationed in nearby Eastbourne. The cliffs are part of the South Downs that look out across the English Channel.
*Previous pages:* Thousand-year-old Corfe Castle rises above the morning mist on the Isle of Purbeck in Dorset.

[ I ]

# THE BRITISH ISLES

Shetland
Islands

• Lerwick

0 _____ 150 Kilometers
0 _____ 100 Miles

Orkney Islands
• Kirkwall

ATLANTIC OCEAN

Outer Hebrides

The Minch

Sea of the Hebrides

Inner Hebrides

• Inverness

• Aberdeen

SCOTLAND

GREAT

NORTH SEA

Dundee

Firth of Forth

• Glasgow    ★ Edinburgh

North Channel

Londonderry •
NORTHERN
IRELAND
Belfast ★

UNITED KINGDOM

BRITISH

• Newcastle

IRELAND

Douglas • • Isle of Man

IRISH SEA

ISLES

Leeds •

BRITAIN

Ouse

• Galway

Dublin
(Baile Átha Cliath) ⊛

Liverpool •   Manchester •   • Sheffield

IRELAND

Shannon

Waterford •

St. George's Channel

Cardigan
Bay

Aberystwyth •

Birmingham •

ENGLAND

• Norwich

Trent

Cork
(Corcaigh) •

WALES

Severn

Bristol •

Thames   ⊛ London

Swansea •
Cardiff ★

BELGIUM

Bristol Channel

• Dover

Strait of
Dover

CELTIC

SEA

Portsmouth •

EUROPE

Plymouth •

ENGLISH CHANNEL
(LA MANCHE)

FRANCE

Guernsey
CHANNEL ISLANDS

Jersey

For many readers, "the British Isles" will seem like the right collective term to describe Britain and Ireland. It is, after all, the geographic term that is generally used when referring to the archipelago of the two main islands and hundreds of surrounding smaller islands and islets that lie just off the northwest coast of the European continent.

One of the main islands is Great Britain, which comprises England, Scotland, and Wales. At more than 80,000 square miles—about the size of Kansas or half the size of France—it is the biggest island in Europe. The other is Ireland, made up of the Republic of Ireland and Northern Ireland. It is more than 30,000 square miles—about the size of Maine—and is the third largest island in Europe (with Iceland coming in at number two).

"The British Isles" is the usual way to refer to this part of the world. It is the term used by National Geographic and the one that will be used in this book. But as with many things related to Ireland and Britain, the term is somewhat controversial, a little more complicated than it first seems. So let's back up a bit first, just to make sure we have our terminology straight.

Most people know that the British Isles is not the same as the United Kingdom, which comprises Great Britain (England, Scotland, and Wales) and Northern Ireland. The Republic of Ireland is not within the United Kingdom but is a completely independent country. Sometimes simply referred to as Southern Ireland, it used to be part of the British Commonwealth of nations, like Australia, Canada, and India. It has a long shared history with the neighboring larger island, some of it happy, some of it not. But today, the Republic and the UK are separate countries, both equal members of the European Union.

The British Isles and the United Kingdom are not synonymous, then: One is a geographical expression, the other a political one. However, some people maintain that "British Isles" is not a purely geographical term. The people in question generally come from the Republic of Ireland. To them, it is inaccurate to consider all of the islands as part of the British Isles, because British they are not. It is incorrect, they argue, to apply what they see as a political term like "British" to a geographical region.

These issues surfaced during the negotiations that led up to the Good Friday Agreement of 1998. Signed at Castle Buildings, Stormont, just outside Belfast, the agreement sought to bring an end to the Troubles, as the sectarian and ethnic conflict in Ireland has long been known. In doing so, the Protestants and Roman Catholics of Northern Ireland worked to negotiate the ways in which they could best share power

**RULE BRITANNIA**
Flanked by a cannon and, in the distance, a Royal Navy ship, the union-flag-clad figure of Britannia stands on the shores of Britain. The White Cliffs of Dover, to her left, have historically been the first view for travelers to the island kingdom. *Previous pages:* A small coastal town in the Orkney Islands.

between them. The political settlement that took place between the Protestant Unionists, who seek to maintain their union with Great Britain, and the Catholic Nationalists, who prefer for Northern Ireland to be unified with the Irish Republic, was the most important aspect of the Good Friday Agreement. At that time, the various parties also endeavored to establish agreement on a whole range of relationships: those between the two parts of Ireland; between Ireland and Britain; and among Northern Ireland, the Republic, Scotland, and Wales.

> ### IN SCOTLAND
>
> The size of the Inner Hebrides island of **Iona**—only 3.5 miles long and 1.5 miles wide—belies its significance as a spiritual center of the British Isles since St. Columba arrived here in A.D. 563. Iona Abbey is now an ecumenical church, one of the best-preserved buildings from the early Middle Ages.

During this new dispensation in Irish-British history, new terms were coined. "Islands of the North Atlantic," or "IONA" was one. It is a term at once ancient and modern. As former Irish prime minister Bertie Ahern declared, "We are, ourselves, very mindful of the unique relationships that exist within these islands—islands of the North Atlantic, or IONA as some have termed them."

IONA is without question a purely geographical term and is therefore preferred by some Irish nationalists. But Iona is also the name of a tiny island off the west coast of Scotland, a hauntingly beautiful place in the Inner Hebrides known in Gaelic as Ì Chaluim Chille, or "Saint Columba's Island."

Columba is a name revered by the Scots and the Irish alike. The saint was born in County Donegal, and is known as the founder of Derry, Northern Ireland's second city, where he established a monastery. In 563, the Irish monk was exiled from his homeland in Ulster. According to tradition, he had become involved in a dispute over a psalter that

**ROPE TRICK**

Visitors gingerly make their way across the Carrick-a-Rede rope bridge near Ballycastle on Northern Ireland's Antrim coast. The bridge leads to a salmon fishery on the nearby island, though today the span is traversed more by tourists than by fishermen.

**LOVELY IONA**

A Celtic cross stands against the evening sky on the Hebridean island of Iona. The monastery at Iona has long been a draw for pilgrims, past and present. The grim skeleton on the page opposite adorns a plaque in Norwich Cathedral.

eventually escalated into a pitched battle in which many men lost their lives. Columba was held responsible for their deaths, and as a result was banished from Ireland. With great sadness, he set off across the sea to Scotland, vowing to work as a missionary and to save as many souls as had been killed in the battle that he had caused.

The distance across the sea was—is—a short one. Scotland's Portpatrick lies little more than 20 miles across the North Channel from the small Irish port of Donaghadee, and from various points in northeast Ireland the coast of Scotland is clearly visible. The Irish coast is visible from the other direction, too, of course, a fact that was only too apparent to the departing monk. Columba is said to have sailed farther and farther up the western shore of Scotland until he landed at Iona, the first place where he could no longer look back and see the land of his birth.

Ireland's loss, so to speak, was Scotland's gain. On little Iona—just 3.5 miles long and 1.5 miles wide—he founded a monastery. And from there he began to convert the pagans of Scotland and northern England to Christianity.

In time, Iona became renowned as a place of learning and pilgrimage, a holy island where kings of Scotland and Ireland would be buried, among them a certain Macbeth, King of Scots. Columba was buried here, too. But these waters were prowled by Viking raiders, and after a series of Viking attacks on the island and its monastery, Columba's relics were removed and, fittingly, divided between Scotland and Ireland. Today, Iona Abbey is an ecumenical church. The island is home to the famous Iona Community, which is made up of Christians from different traditions and is an important force in the movement for Celtic Christian revival.

Tiny Iona, larger Ireland, and still larger Great Britain, then, are all part of the islands of the North Atlantic. So are the Isle of Man, perched in the middle of the Irish Sea between Ireland and Britain; Anglesey off the northwest coast of Wales; the Shetlands, Orkneys, and Hebrides off the north and west coasts of Scotland; the Isle of Wight to the south of England; and the Channel Islands, just miles off the coast of France.

Later chapters of this book will examine the various parts of these "British Isles," showing the particular characteristics that distinguish them. But this chapter will reveal what unites them and makes them distinct from the rest of Europe. As the story of Saint Columba shows, the history of the islands is intertwined and elaborate. The Christian faith that Columba spread to Scotland had originally come to Ireland from Britain more than a century earlier, brought by a Roman Briton named Saint Patrick and other Latin-speaking missionaries. Over and over, the history and cultures of Ireland and Britain overlap.

As the map on page 8 shows, the most obvious thing that sets the British Isles apart is their isolation from the European mainland. Originally, the islands would have been attached to the rest of the larger landmass. But after the end of the last ice age, warming temperatures caused glaciers to melt and sea levels to rise. By around 6000 B.C., with temperatures close to what they are today, a channel had opened, cutting off what is now southern England from today's northern France. The waterway became the English Channel (though the French insist on calling it La Manche, which means "the sleeve").

When recorded history began—it being written by the victors, as one of history's most famous Englishmen, Winston

## [ British Isles Basics ]

**1** **Total Area** 121,376 square miles, approximately the size of Connecticut.

**2** **Highest Mountain** Ben Nevis, in the Highlands of Scotland, at 4,406 feet.

**3** **Longest River** The Severn, at 200 miles long; it rises in central Wales and flows through Shrewsbury, Worcester, and Gloucester in England to the Bristol Channel.

**4** **Largest Lake** Lough Neagh, in Northern Ireland, at 153 square miles.

**5** **Deepest Lake** Loch Morar, in the Highlands of Scotland, at 1,017 feet deep.

**6** **Highest Waterfall** Eas a'Chual Aluinn, from Glas Bheinn, in the Highlands of Scotland, with a drop of 660 feet.

**7** **Deepest Cave** Ogof Ffynnon Ddu, Powys, in Wales, at 1,010 feet deep.

Churchill, would say two millennia later—the people who were living in this part of the world were the ancient Britons. Their chroniclers, those who had defeated them in battle, were the (equally ancient) Romans.

Although the sun-accustomed legionnaires stationed there would likely have disagreed, the land they called Britannia enjoyed a temperate climate. The shores of the British Isles may not have been lapped by the waters of the Mediterranean, but they were insulated in winter by the North Atlantic Drift, the ocean current that originates in the Gulf of Mexico. As if knowing the islands need help, the Gulf Stream doggedly makes it all the way across the Atlantic to take the chill off the British Isles during the colder months. And the islands do need help, for they lie farther to the north than many people realize. London, for example, is on the same line of latitude as Calgary, Alberta, and Edinburgh lies as far north as Moscow. But Londoners and residents of Edinburgh experience none of the bitter temperatures endured by their Canadian or Russian counterparts.

Yet even if they don't get the snow their latitude "deserves," the British Isles do get more than their fair share of rain. And the west tends to get more rainfall than the east. Manchester has long had the reputation of being the wettest city in Britain. The wettest place, however, is actually in Snowdonia, Wales, which receives nearly 120 inches of rain each year.

Across the British Isles, the land shows the same lack of extremes as the climate. The ice sheets that moved across the land during the last ice age eroded the mountains, leaving the highest point, Ben Nevis in the Highlands of Scotland, at just over 4,400 feet.

The Highlands are largely composed of ancient rocks, from the Cambrian and Precambrian eras, while the youngest rocks in Britain are in the southeast, near London. The best agricultural land also tends to be in the south and the east, and the most rugged and mountainous territory in the north and the west. The population densities reflect

**TREASURES OF WILTSHIRE**

The polished gneiss mace head above was found in a grave near Stonehenge, and the chalk White Horse at right adorns one of the county's hillsides.

this divide, with the highest concentrations of people around London. The more sparsely populated parts of the British Isles are Wales, Scotland, and Ireland, the so-called Celtic fringe.

## Britain Before the Romans

So who were the ancient Britons, the people the Romans found when they crossed the Channel to Britannia and started recording their history? They were the Celts. These people had come from Europe about 500 years before Julius Caesar arrived in 55 B.C., not far from the White Cliffs of Dover.

---

**IN WESTERN BRITAIN**

**The Severn Way Long-Distance Path,**
Britain's longest riverside path meanders through a stunning range of landscapes along the River Severn from its source at Pumlumon in the Cambrian Mountains of Wales through Shropshire, Worcestershire, and Gloucestershire to Bristol. Along the way it intersects many other river paths.

---

During the first millennium B.C., the Celts spread throughout much of Europe, moving from their homeland north of the Alps. Eventually, like so many Europeans later would, they made their way across the sea to the British Isles.

We know little about the indigenous inhabitants of the islands, a mysterious people who predate the Celtic migration. One recent study on the genetic ancestry of these people analyzed blood groups, oxygen traces in the teeth, and DNA samples from skeletal remains. It concluded that despite subsequent waves of invasion and migration—by the Romans, Anglo-Saxons, Vikings, and Normans—the genetic makeup of white Britons remained remarkably unchanged up through modern times.

In fact, the study argues that around 80 percent of the genetic characteristics of most white Britons have been passed down from a few thousand hunter-gatherers who arrived after the last ice age. These

**TOMBSTONES**

A modern visitor pays his respects to an ancient forebear at the Pentre Ifan megalith in West Wales. Such prehistoric monuments are not an uncommon sight throughout the British Isles.

earliest settlers were later isolated as rising sea levels cut Britain off from mainland Europe. Their most visible genetic characteristic is red hair: There are more redheads in Scotland and Wales than in any other part of the world. And the most visible reminder of their presence is the great circle of standing stones that they raised at Stonehenge, in what is now southern England.

The Celts who arrived in Britain were a spiritual people. Their priestly class was the druids, who are often wrongly credited with building the pre-Celtic Stonehenge. In fact, the druids chose less monumental settings for their holy places, preferring to locate their shines in oak groves, where they worshipped the moon and made sacrifices. Some tribes on the continent practiced such rites as human sacrifice, but it is believed that this was not the case among the Celts of Britain.

They were also warriors. The Celts rode into battle on war chariots, wielding iron swords and shields. Often they fought naked, their bodies painted with blue dye. This is what awaited Julius Caesar when he crossed from Gaul and tried to land at what is now Dover. Little over a decade later, during the reign of the emperor Claudius, the Romans were back. This time they came in force. The imperial legions occupied the land and added their latest province, home to some five million people, to the growing Roman Empire.

THE ROMAN RULE did not extend the entire length of Britain, though. The newcomers occupied the lowland regions, abandoning the mountainous north and west (in what is now present-day Scotland and Wales) to the fierce tribesmen who lived there.

Roman writer Dio Cassius gives an account of the weapons carried by the Pictish warriors of the north: "Their arms are a shield and a short spear, in the upper part whereof is an apple of brass, that, while it is shaken, it may terrify the enemies with the sound, they have likewise daggers. They are able to bear hunger, cold, and all afflictions."

So it was that the Romans never conquered Scotland. Though it was not for want of trying.

Over the years, the story of the "lost legion" has arisen. It's a tale told in the popular children's book *The Eagle of the Ninth* by British writer Rosemary Sutcliff, a work of fiction based on the disappearance of Rome's Ninth Legion from the historical record. According to the story, the 4,000 or so soldiers of the Ninth Legion marched north to conquer Scotland around A.D. 117 and were never seen again. The entire legion vanished without a trace.

The heretofore all-conquering Romans would not make the same mistake twice. After the disappearance of the Ninth, they would take up a defensive stance behind the mighty fortifications of Vallum Aelium, or Hadrian's Wall.

## [ Roman Sites ]

**1 Bath** The Georgian splendor of Bath should not obscure the fact that it also features some of Britain's best preserved Roman remains, legacy of the town of Aquae Sulis, founded around A.D. 44. The most striking are the baths, one of the world's finest such monuments, along with the remains of a temple to Sulis-Minerva and other bathhouse remnants.

**2 Fishbourne Palace** Discovered by construction workers in the 1960s, this is the largest known Roman residence in Britain, a once lavish building probably created for a Romanized local king around A.D. 75. The complex includes replanted Roman gardens, a hypocaust, foundations, and an outstanding floor mosaic depicting scenes from Roman mythology.

**3 Hadrian's Wall** Emperor Hadrian commissioned this 73-mile monument to Roman engineering and endeavor, built between A.D. 122 and 128. It ran from coast to coast, from the Solway Firth in the west to close to the mouth of the River Tyne in the east. Still remarkably well preserved in places, it was built to mark a border, rather than as a defensive barrier between the Picts to the north and the subdued Britons under Roman rule to the south.

**4 St. Albans** An otherwise quiet suburban town, St. Albans—founded as Roman Verulamium in A.D. 43—is celebrated for five majestic mosaic floors preserved in the Verulamium Museum. Parts of a Roman theater, basilica, walls, and bathhouse also survive close by.

## Legacies of Rome

The Romans stayed for 400 years. What did they bring to Britain? Or as John Cleese's character asks in the Monty Python film *The Life of Brian*, "What have the Romans ever done for us?" The answer is probably similar to what he comes up with: Nothing . . . "apart from the sanitation, the medicine, education, wine, public order, irrigation, roads, the fresh-water system, and public health."

Among many ruins and archeological dig sites throughout Britain, the most visible evidence of the Roman occupation is, indeed, Hadrian's Wall. Made from stone, turf, and timber, much of the wall still exists today, and its entire length can be followed on foot. Established as a barrier against raids by the Picts, it was the most heavily fortified border in the Roman Empire.

But the Romans did bring one more enduring legacy to Britain: the Christian faith that they had once persecuted in the Colosseum and elsewhere. When Constantine the Great became the first Christian emperor of Rome and proclaimed religious toleration throughout the empire, the new religion spread with Rome's advancing legions. Roman Britain became Christian Britain. And from there the missionary St. Patrick—Patricius—would set out to take the Gospel message to the people of Ireland.

Columba, founder of the Christian settlement on Iona, would be one of those who benefited from the work of Patrick and other British missionaries, eventually taking the Christian message from Ireland to northern Britain to the still pagan Pictish tribes of Scotland. The narrative would come full circle.

By the early years of the fifth century A.D., however, the Romans were pulling back their legions, which were desperately needed at home to defend against the increasing attacks by barbarians to the north. When they left, southern Britain lay open to barbarian invasion itself, and the Christianity brought by the Romans went into decline.

Concerned about Britain's spiritual state, Pope Gregory I later dispatched a Benedictine monk named Augustine on a missionary journey to the island. Augustine landed in the southeast in 597, where he established the ecclesiastical capital of Canterbury and became its first archbishop. Augustine's followers began to take the faith of Rome north again, even as the followers of Columba in Scotland were spreading a Celtic version to the south.

The two major points of difference between the traditions may seem trivial today: an agreed date for the celebration of Easter and the accepted form of tonsure for monks. But these hid more profound differences in approach to the faith, with the Celtic church's mysticism and spiritualization of the natural world a marked contrast to Rome's drive for uniformity and order.

The two "movements" met at Whitby, in what is now Yorkshire. There, a synod of learned men declared in favor of the Roman church, which then began to dominate. Some of the Celtic clerics accepted the ruling; others did not. They left Whitby still clinging to their customs and practices, and returned to the tiny Hebridean island that has played such a big role in the history of the islands of the North Atlantic—Iona.

**IN BRITAIN**

Talking about the weather is said to be a national pastime in Britain. **British weather** is rarely extreme but fluctuates from gray skies to light rain to sunshine year round. Carry an umbrella. The British are fond of saying, "There is no such thing as bad weather, only bad clothes."

**BEYOND THE CAPITAL**
A solitary loon swims the water in the shadows of a riverside church. Sights like this await tourists who venture out of London and upriver on the Thames.

English Origins

There'll always be an England, and England shall be free," sang Dame Vera Lynn during the dark days of World War II.

The Scots, Welsh, and Northern Irish were similarly involved in the struggle against Nazi Germany. For that reason, the popular singer might well have chosen to perform the more inclusive "Rule Britannia!" which declares that "Britons never, never, never shall be slaves." But to bolster the patriotic fervor of her fellow countrymen and women, the singer known as the Forces' Sweetheart made her moving appeal to the English.

Others have done the same. During the First World War, the English poet Rupert Brooke wrote the following lines before heading off to serve— and die for—his country:

> *If I should die, think only this of me:*
> *That there's some corner of a foreign field*
> *That is forever England.*

And the Irish writer William Butler (W. B.) Yeats called Brooke himself "the handsomest young man in England." Where Yeats ranked Brooke among the young men of *Britain,* he did not say.

Even Shakespeare, the great Bard himself, seemed to use the terms "Britain" and "England" interchangeably. In *King Richard II,* he incorrectly refers to "this royal throne of kings, this scepter'd isle, this earth of majesty, this seat of Mars . . . This blessed plot, this earth, this realm, this England."

Of course, England only covers approximately half of the "scepter'd isle," with Scotland and Wales occupying the rest. Lynn, Brooke, and Yeats may or may not have meant to include the greater isles in their description of England. But what Shakespeare was referring to was, to borrow the title from a popular BBC comedy series, *Little Britain.*

## Angles, Saxons, and Others

Vera Lynn may have hoped that there would always be an England in the future, but there was not always an England in the past. At least, not as long as there had been a Britain. The beginnings of England can be traced to the period when the Romans began to leave Britain. Called back to defend Rome against barbarian attack, they abandoned the ancient Britons, the Celts, to their fate.

The "void" left by the Romans did not take long to be filled. As one former invader departed, others arrived. From northern Germany came the Angles and Saxons, from Denmark the Jutes, and from the Low Countries the Frisians. Over the course of the next two centuries, wave after wave of these Germanic tribes arrived. King

**SUTTON HOO**
This ceremonial whole-face helmet is one of the prize parts of the Sutton Hoo treasure. Dating from the early seventh century, the treasure was discovered in East Anglia in the 1930s and is today one of the many draws of the British Museum. *Previous pages:* The village of Snowshill in Gloucestershire.

# ENGLAND

**GETTING YOUR BEARINGS**

England takes up about half of the landmass of Great Britain. It stretches from Land's End in the southwest to the Scottish border in the northeast, and from Wales in the west to East Anglia in the east.

SCOTLAND

Holy Island (Lindisfarne)

Tweed
Cheviot Hills
Rede
N. Tyne
Liddel
Alnwick
Morpeth

Hadrian's Wall
Tyne
Newcastle

Solway Firth
Carlisle
Eden
Durham
Stockton-on-Tees
Hartlepool
Redcar
Middlesbrough

Derwent Water
Ullswater
Darlington
Northallerton
Cleveland Hills
North York Moors

St. Bees Head
Cumbrian Mts.
977
Lake District
Scafell Pike
Swale
Ure
Rye
Derwent

Flamborough Head

Isle of Walney
Morecambe Bay
Aire
Ouse
York

IRISH SEA
Blackpool
Ribble
Beverley
Humber
Kingston upon Hull

Preston
Blackburn
Wakefield
Scunthorpe
Grimsby
Spurn Head

Manchester
Barnsley
Lincoln Wolds

Liverpool
Mersey
Warrington
Peak District
Don
Sherwood Forest
Lincoln

Widnes
Chester
ENGLAND
Matlock
Lincoln Heights
Fen Country
The Wash

Stoke on Trent
Nottingham
West Bridgford
The Broads

Dee
Derby
Trent
Norwich

Stafford
Shrewsbury
Telford
Glenfield
MERCIA
Oakham
Leicester

WALES
Severn
Birmingham
Nene
Peterborough
East Anglian Heights
Waveney

Avon
Worcester
Warwick
Northampton
Cambridge
Framlingham

Hereford
Wye
Milton Keynes
Bedford
Ipswich
Orford Ness

Black Mts.
Gloucester
Cotswold Hills
Great Ouse
Luton
EAST ANGLIA
Stour

Aylesbury
Hertford
The Naze

Thornbury
Thames
Oxford
Chiltern Hills
Epping Forest
Mersea I.
Chelmsford

Bristol
Bath
Swindon
Maidenhead
Slough
London
Southend-on-Sea
Foulness I.

Bristol Channel
Avon
Kennet
Reading
Grays
River Thames
Isle of Sheppey

Newbury
Wokingham
Bracknell
Rochester
Thanet

Mendip Hills
Trowbridge
Guildford
North Downs
KENT
Shakespeare Cliff

Barnstaple Bay
Salisbury Plain
Winchester
Maidstone
Dungeness
Strait of Dover

Lundy Island
Exmoor
WESSEX
SUSSEX
The Weald
Ashdown Forest

Hartland Point
Taunton
Yeo
Avon
South Downs
Lewes
Beachy Head

Bude Bay
Bournemouth
New Forest
Southampton
Chichester
Brighton

Trevose Head
Bodmin Moor
Dartmoor
Exeter
Dorchester
Poole
Portsmouth
Selsey Bill

St. Ives Bay
CORNWALL
Torbay
Lyme Bay
Bill of Portland
The Solent
Newport
Isle of Wight

Gara Cornwall
Truro
St. Austell Bay
Dodman Point
Bolt Head
Durlston Head
St. Alban's Head

Isles of Scilly
Land's End
Mount's Bay
Lizard Point
Start Point

ENGLISH CHANNEL

0        100 Kilometers

0        75 Miles

## [ Ancient Sites ]

**1** **Callanish, Isle of Lewis**  Avebury is larger, Stonehenge more famous, but this Scottish stone circle is one of Europe's most complete—and eerily evocative—ancient monuments. Thirteen gneiss pillars surround a central monolith, with 40 smaller stones arranged in a complementary cross. The site is between 3,800 and 5,000 years old—older than the Pyramids—but its purpose is unknown.

**2** **Offa's Dyke**  King Offa, an eighth-century king of the ancient kingdom of Mercia, ordered the building of this dyke (wall and ditch) to mark the border between his kingdom and Wales, to the west. Large parts of the earthwork are still visible—they form the basis of a popular long-distance hiking trail—and still more or less follow the border between England and Wales.

**3** **Skara Brae, Orkney**  A storm in 1850 blew away the dunes that had covered and preserved this haunting Neolithic village, inhabited for 600 years and probably abandoned at about the time that Egypt's Great Pyramid was being built. Stone beds, hearths, and large parts of the dwellings survive, along with a fully reconstructed house.

**4** **Tara, County Meath**  The sacred center of Irish myth and legend, home to the ancient Celtic mystic priest-rulers of Ireland, and then the ceremonial capital of 142 high kings, who ruled until the arrival of Christianity in the sixth century.

**HOUSE TOUR**
The Neolithic Skara Brae settlement contains the best preserved prehistoric dwellings in northern Europe. "The Heart of Neolithic Orkney" was declared a UNESCO World Heritage site in 1999.

Arthur, whose deeds are legend, battled these newcomers, but the warlike invaders overwhelmed all resistance, pushing many of the Celts to the west and the north. And unlike the Romans, these foreigners had come to stay. The Angles, Saxons, Frisians, and Jutes would become the English, and they would give their new home a new name: Angle-land.

The Saxons, as they became collectively known, in time adopted the Christianity brought by Augustine and began to parcel the land into a series of adjoining kingdoms: Wessex in the southwest, Kent in the southeast, Mercia in the Midlands, East Anglia in the east, and Northumbria in the northeast.

But while the Saxons were dividing up the land, others were casting their greedy eyes on the riches that lay within easy reach along the coasts. In their dragon-prowed longships, Viking raiders from Denmark and Norway plundered settlements and monasteries throughout the islands, making little distinction between Celtic booty and Saxon treasure.

The attacks that began in the late eighth century continued for the next 300 years. By that time, the Vikings, or "Norsemen," had made England their home, too. A compromise emerged between the Vikings and the Saxons after Alfred the Great, the King of Wessex, won a great victory over the Danes in 878. In the wake of their defeat, the Danes consolidated their power in the north and east of England, the so-called Danelaw, where Norse influence and strength was strongest.

### The Norman Conquest

There are many key dates in English history, but one stands out more than most: the year 1066. It was then that England was invaded again, albeit for the last time. No would-be conqueror of England has succeeded since the Normans did so more than a millennium ago.

On October 14, 1066, William I, Duke of Normandy, landed near Hastings on the south coast of England with an army of 8,000 men. There, he defeated the English King Harold and proceeded to subdue the land.

The Normans left a most enduring mark. The first castles they built were of the motte and bailey type—strongholds on mounds with walled garrison enclosures

**DEEPEST ENGLAND**

An aerial shot of Framlingham Castle and surrounding Suffolk countryside shows the appeals of rural East Anglia.

made of wood. None of these early castles have survived. But many of their later squat, turreted stone castles still dot the land, enduring symbols of Norman power. Such notable examples include Framlingham in Suffolk, Rochester in Kent, Alnwick in Northumberland, and Caernarfon in north Wales.

The "body language" of these key fortifications spoke volumes: They boasted a portcullis, murder holes, and offset entrances, and eventually curtain gatehouses and fortified courtyards known as barbicans. The Normans were ready for anything.

Once they conquered England, the Normans set about counting their conquests. In 1085 they began the wonderfully named Domesday Book survey, with a mandate and an efficiency of which Her Majesty's Revenue and Customs can only dream. According to the *Anglo-Saxon Chronicle*—Old English annals that began with Alfred the Great and were updated into the 12th century—William "sent men all over England

. . . to find out . . . what or how much each landholder had in land and livestock, and what it was worth."

By now the Saxon landlords were under assault on many fronts, their powers eclipsed by that of Norman barons and bishops. Their language, Old English, was under assault, too, giving way to the Old French of their conquerors. With Latin as the language for all matters ecclesiastical, English was rapidly relegated to third place as the language of England.

The language would make a comeback, of course, as its speakers incorporated the lexicon of those languages that threatened its very existence. In addition to the English word "pig," they would add the French word *porc* ("pork"). To "cow" they would add *boeuf* ("beef"). To "sheep" they would add *mouton* ("mutton").

Hidden beneath these linguistic evolutions was the reality that under the new feudal system established by the conquerors, it was the Saxon English who did the labor (ironically, an Old English word) and the Norman French who did the feasting (appropriately, a French-derived word). But in the process, the English language was being enriched, filled with shades of meaning to become a hybrid that would be England's gift to the world. Today, only Mandarin is spoken by more people.

THE NORMAN BARONS who had so successfully usurped the power of the Saxon landlords eventually began to make plans to usurp the power of their Norman king. From William the Conqueror to Henry II to Richard the Lionheart, the Normans had given England powerful and capable rulers. But when the hapless John ascended the throne, these power-hungry barons saw their chance and made ready to pounce.

In 1215 they did so. The barons laid before the outmaneuvered monarch a list of demands he was in no position to refuse. The document he signed at Runnymede, the Magna Carta ("Great Charter"), included the writ of habeas corpus, which allowed for appeal against unlawful imprisonment, and the right to a trial by a jury of peers. Magna Carta laid one of the great foundations of constitutional law and, along with the development of common law, would become another one of England's great gifts to the wider English-speaking world.

**BOOK OF RECORD**

An 11th-century "tourist guide" to the wonders of England, the Domesday Book was commissioned by William the Conqueror and today is housed at the National Archives in Kew, London.

## England and the Welsh, the Scots, and the Irish

The particular gift of Edward I (1239–1307) to his neighbors was much more likely to be that of English invasion. At six feet two inches tall, Edward "Longshanks" led troops against his uppity nobles in the so-called Barons' War and against Muslims in the Holy Land during the Eighth Crusade. He conquered much of Wales and in 1284 made it subject to the English crown. And had it not been for William Wallace and Robert the Bruce, King Edward—the so-called Hammer of the Scots— may well have succeeded in doing the same to Scotland.

On the way back from one of his campaigns in the north, Edward did carry off the Stone of Scone, or the Stone of Destiny as it is also known. (According to legend, this ancient coronation stone of Scottish kings is the pillow stone used by the biblical patri- arch Jacob.) In doing so, Edward was declaring that the destiny of the Scots was now in the hands of the King of England. Edward had the stone fitted into a wooden throne in Westminster Abbey, and nearly every English king and queen has been crowned upon it since. In 1996, the Stone of Scone returned to Scotland, where it resides in Edinburgh Castle. With England's expansion west into Wales and north into Scotland, its transition into what is now Britain had begun.

NORMAN INVOLVEMENT in Ireland had come about in fits and starts. Back in 1155, Pope Adrian IV had encour- aged Edward's great-grandfather, King Henry II, to invade Ireland in order to straighten out what he saw as ongoing abuses in the Irish church. Henry had also been entreated to do so by Diarmait, one of the provincial kings of Ireland who had been driven from his throne by rivals and had come to Henry's court for help in get- ting his throne back.

But the English king was preoccupied with matters at home, including the need to suppress the growing assertiveness of his barons (which he did), and a feud with Thomas Becket that would have unhappy consequences for all.

Henry declined the request of Diarmait, King of Leinster, to lead an army to Ire- land. But he did grant the Irishman leave to raise a force himself.

This the deposed king promptly did, rallying a group of Norman knights whose land ambitions had been frustrated in Wales and who were seeking pastures anew. The Norman knights crossed the Irish Sea and landed at Bannow, in the southeast corner of the island not far from Waterford. With the support of these mercenaries, Diarmait managed to fight his way back onto the throne. Their appetites whetted, the knights then made plans to set themselves up as powerful barons, and were encour- aged to do so by King Diarmait, who needed their continued support to ensure he stayed in power.

## NEWGRANGE MOUND

mound of stones and turves

cruciform central chamber

remains of stone circle surrounding mound

front retaining wall of quartzite stones

orthostats lining interior passage

**CRUCIBLE OF HISTORY**

The Boyne Valley in Ireland is home to the Newgrange Mound (above), a megalithic grave older than Stonehenge in England and the Great Pyramid of Giza. Nearly five millennia after it was built, a Protestant English king, William III, defeated a Catholic English King, James II, on the banks of the nearby River Boyne.

**LORDS OF THE DANCE**

Quintessentially English, a group
of Morris dancers performs a
May Day celebration at Ickwell
Green in Bedfordshire.

Back in England, Henry quickly saw the dangerous turn that events were taking in Ireland. What his barons had tried to do in England, these upstarts were now threatening to do across the Irish Sea—establish their own independent fiefdoms that, under the right conditions, could threaten his own power and that of Ireland's other provincial kings. Henry finally sailed to Ireland with an army in 1171. At a ceremony in Dublin, six Irish kings paid homage to him, as they would to any high king. Some see in this the beginning of the loss of Irish freedom. The Irish kings, however, saw it as a solution to their own problems with the increasingly ambitious Norman barons.

From this point on there would "always be an England." But it would be an England whose destiny and actions would constantly intersect with its smaller neighbors to the north, to the west, and on the far side of the Irish Sea. By the 1500s, the Welsh were sending members of Parliament to London, and they began to play a shared role in government. And the Scottish issue was "solved" to some extent in 1603, when King James VI of Scotland also became King James I of England, uniting the two crowns. This was followed a century later by the Treaty of the Union of Parliaments. Now the

Scots, like the Welsh, could elect representatives to Parliament in London, which had become the Parliament of Great Britain.

The "Irish problem," however, proved more intractable—and bloody. The issue ultimately led the island to be partitioned at the beginning of the 20th century. It wasn't until the Good Friday Agreement was finally pursued at the end of the century that there existed a peaceful means to resolve political differences among previously hostile parties.

In the meantime, England had much history of its own to play out. Some would take place within the confines of the country itself, and some would occur on the world stage, across which England would stride like an imperial colossus.

## Growing Ambitions

From the beginning, the Norman kings had governed England while keeping an opportunistic eye trained across the English Channel on territories in France. In 1337, the seemingly never ending struggle between England and France began. The Hundred Years' War actually lasted longer than a hundred years, and it saw English troops conquer great swathes of French territory on battlefields that still resonate strongly in the English psyche: Crécy, Poitiers, Agincourt. The latter is particularly revered, a battle in which the outnumbered English foot soldiers scored a historic triumph over the heavily armored French knights in 1415. Few speeches stir the hearts of the English as much as the rousing pre-battle address of Shakespeare's Henry V, even when delivered onscreen by the Belfast-born actor Kenneth Branagh:

**ROYALTY PAST AND PRESENT**

Crowds gather at Windsor to watch a Garter ceremony at the Castle, held every June. Not far from here, spectators of a different kind—the power-hungry barons of early 13th-century England—watched King John use the seal above to endorse the Magna Carta.

*For he to-day that sheds his blood with me*
*Shall be my brother; be he ne'er so vile,*
*This day shall gentle his condition;*
*And gentlemen in England now-a-bed*
*Shall think themselves accurs'd*
*   they were not here,*
*And hold their manhoods cheap*
*   whiles any speaks*
*That fought with us*
*   upon Saint Crispin's day.*

Iconic victories notwithstanding, the English advances in France were eventually reversed. Inspired by the example of Joan of Arc, the Maid of Orleans, the French pushed the invaders back to the coast, and by 1453 the English had little more than a toehold left on the continent, at the Channel port of Calais.

Despite the reverses, the English at least did not suffer the humiliation of invasion by the French. But during the long struggle between the two countries, a deadly killer did manage to cross the English Channel from the continent and proceeded to wipe out more English men and women than the French ever did: Between 1348 and 1349, the Black Death, also known as the bubonic plague, ravaged the population of England, reducing it by a third.

The year 1455 marked the official end of the Hundred Years' War—and launched the outbreak of the so-called Wars of the Roses, when the English began to fight each other. This civil war was a struggle for the English throne between the House of Lancaster and the House of York. After thirty long years, the Lancastrian Henry Tudor won a decisive victory at Bosworth Field and was crowned there. King Henry VII, as he was now, united the Houses of Lancaster and York through marriage.

Under the Tudors, England would undergo radical change—particularly during the reign of Henry's son, Henry VIII, next in line to the throne of England.

## Reformation and a New Golden Age

Only nineteen years old when he became king, Henry VIII was a man used to getting what he wanted. When he failed to get the son and heir that he desired, he proceeded to look for another wife (and another and another, all the way up to number six, who outlived him). This brought him into conflict with the pope, who refused him the right to divorce. Rebuffed by the church in Rome, Henry set up a church in England—the Church *of* England.

Henry's motives for establishing a church were one thing. Those of the new church leaders were another. Inspired by the ideas of the Reformers that were challenging Catholicism all across the continent, they seized the opportunity to remake the church in England into a reformed and Protestant church. Parliament supported the break with Rome. Henry became head of the new church and began to dissolve the old one, pillaging its treasures along the way.

## [ Royal Residences ]

1 **Buckingham Palace** England's most famous palace was originally built for the Duke of Buckingham in 1803, and only became a royal residence in 1837, replacing the nearby St. James's Palace. The monarch is in residence when the red, yellow, and blue Royal Standard is flying.

2 **Clarence House** Built between 1825 and 1827 for Prince William Henry (later William IV). It was home to Princess Elizabeth following her marriage in 1947, then the residence of the Queen Mother until 2002. Today, it is the official home of Prince Charles and the Duchess of Cornwall and Princes William and Harry.

3 **Sandringham House** The monarch's country estate, near King's Lynn in East Anglia, was bought by Queen Victoria in 1862 for her son, the future Edward VII.

4 **Windsor Castle** Windsor is the world's oldest and largest occupied castle. One of the few defendable points in the Thames Valley, it has been a royal residence since 1070 and the reign of William the Conqueror.

England would endure several more turbulent periods before returning to ecclesiastical equilibrium. When the throne passed to Mary Tudor—Henry's *daughter* and heir, despite all of his machinations—she brought Catholicism back as the official religion in England. "Bloody" Mary's reign is remembered as one of oppression and turmoil, when Protestant leaders were burned at the stake. It was with relief the English people welcomed the 1559 coronation of Henry's other daughter, Elizabeth.

Vowing not to "make windows into men's hearts," the new queen sought to restore order to England as she reestablished the Church of England. The country entered a golden age. Commerce and industry flourished, William Shakespeare wrote plays for the ages, and explorers tracked the far reaches of the globe and brought back treasures to England.

Of course, England continued to face dangers—political, military, and religious. None were greater than those that came in the form of the Spanish Armada, which sailed into the English Channel in the summer of 1588. But even that vast invasion

**CROWNING GLORY**

The crown-topped royal coat of arms opposite adorns the oldest stained glass window in the Tower of London, where the English crown jewels are kept. They aren't the only crown jewels in Britain, however. Above, the crown jewels of Scotland are carried into the new Scottish Parliament building in Edinburgh in 2004.

force proved no match for the island's plucky defenders. Among them was Sir Francis Drake, the first sea captain to successfully circumnavigate the world. When the Spanish fleet loomed into sight, Drake was playing lawn bowls on Plymouth Hoe, near where a statue of the mariner stands today. Displaying what is now

regarded as characteristic English aplomb, Drake is said to have received the news with the following words: "There's time to finish the game and beat the Spanish, too."

And beat the Spanish they did. Assisted by a storm that wrecked many of the enemy's big ships, they drove the others off into the North Sea and round to the Atlantic Ocean. In this, the English saw the favor of a benevolent and protective God who had sent "the Protestant wind" to destroy the invaders and deliver England.

## Tudor Turns to Stuart

When Elizabeth died unmarried and without an heir (the Virgin Queen considered herself betrothed to England alone), she was succeeded by her nearest relative, James VI of Scotland. James, who became the first of the Stuart kings of England, believed in "the divine right of kings." So, likely, did all of his predecessors. But the ineffectual Scot seemed particularly less able to fit the bill of regal sovereignty than those who had gone before.

The mood of the country was also changing. Parliament, which had been growing steadily in power and prestige, was keen to flex its muscles. At first, James was still able to at least maintain royal prerogatives and made a number of contributions that had long-lasting significance. For instance, his coronation had united the crowns of England and Scotland. He also gave England and the English-speaking world a new authorized version of the Bible, which was published in London

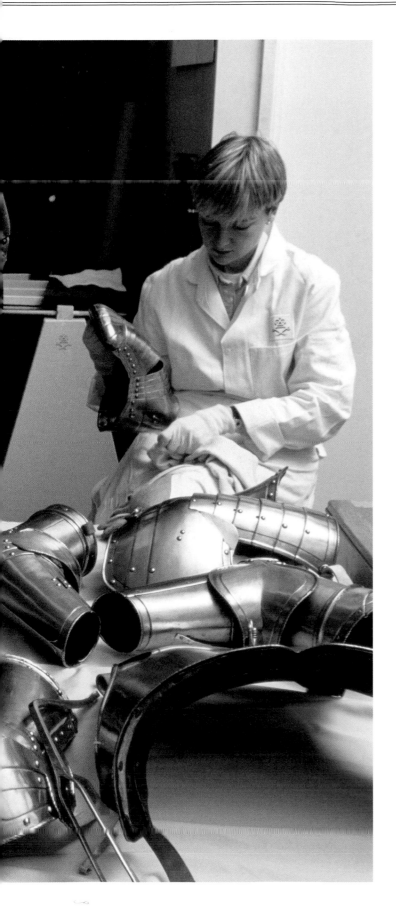

**A COMBATIVE KING**
One of the top tourist attractions in London, the Tower of London is also home to these suits of armor (shown being waxed), which once belonged to Henry VIII. The king, shown above, famously broke with the Church of Rome to establish the Protestant Church of England.

in 1611. And he established the first English settlement in North America, named in his honor, at Jamestown, Virginia, in 1607.

At the same time, James launched "the plantation of Ulster," which granted land in northern Ireland to Lowland Scots. English rule in Ireland had long been based in Dublin and the surrounding "Pale." The province of Ulster—the most Catholic and Gaelic part of the island—had always been the most rebellious and troublesome. By "planting" it with loyal Presbyterian Scots, it was thought that the province could be pacified. Now, four hundred years later, that most troubled of regions in the British Isles may finally be finding peace.

### IN ENGLAND

**English Gardens** were designed as an antidote to the formal, symmetric gardens of Europe and have influenced gardeners throughout the world since the 18th century. They are marked by a more relaxed, romantic ambiance, often with a bridge to a pond; small, classical buildings; and a natural, welcoming mix of flowers, plants, and trees.

## Parliament Versus King

The power and ambition of Parliament had been rising since Tudor times. And while its leaders had stayed their hand during Elizabeth's reign, they had been less inclined to do so during James's. James may have "dodged a bullet," but his son, Charles I, was unable to escape the ax.

When Charles tried ruling without Parliament, both sides mobilized their armies, launching an outright war. The English civil war culminated in the beheading of the king in 1649 and the establishment of an English republic. The new ruler of the republic, or Commonwealth, was Oliver Cromwell. The Lord Protector, as he was known, imposed English dominance over both the Scots and the Irish.

Not long after the death of Cromwell—and little more than a decade as a republic—the English welcomed their executed king's son

**ENGLISH GARDENS**

A path makes its way through Trentham Gardens, a popular English landscape park near Stoke-on-Trent in Staffordshire.

back to the throne as Charles II. The Restoration years were a more relaxed time in England, but short lived: When Charles died, his Catholic brother, James II, tried to steer the country back toward Rome. Parliament would have none of it and invited James's Protestant daughter, Mary, to take the crown along with her Protestant husband, the Dutch-born Prince William of Orange. But in doing so, Parliament asserted its pre-eminence over the monarchy in what is known as the Glorious Revolution.

James fled to Ireland and raised an army. But William followed him and decisively beat him on the banks of the River Boyne in 1690. Jacobite pretenders to the throne would continue to raise rebel armies and stake their claims, especially in Scotland, where support for the cause remained strong. But in England, the royal succession was assured, and Parliament became the true driver of political change.

The 1707 Act of Union merged the Parliaments of England and Scotland to create a unified Parliament of Great Britain. England had morphed into Britain (though some might suspect it was the other way around).

## A Revolutionary Century

The 18th century was a remarkable time of achievement and progress for England—and for Britain. Even before it began, Isaac Newton, considered the father of modern physics, had been conducting experiments with light and had built the first reflecting telescope. By the middle of the century, the great engineer James Watt was working on a commercially viable engine that harnessed steam power. By the end of the century, the industrial revolution had turned England into "the workshop of the world" and the richest nation on earth.

Not that the 18th century was without conflict. Revolutions raged, with

**TUDOR APPEAL**

The charms awaiting visitors to Mermaid Street in the town of Rye, East Sussex, are much as they would have been when Elizabeth I, shown above, visited in 1573.

one prizing Britain away from its colonies in North America and another killing the King of France, putting an emperor on the throne, and plunging the countries of Europe into a continent-wide war. Britain emerged as one of the victors of that war, though, and thanks to the Duke of Wellington's victory in 1815 over the French, the expression "meeting your Waterloo" passed into common usage.

Many of the soldiers serving under Wellington during the Napoleonic Wars were Irish. Since the 1800 Act of Union, their native country had formally become part of the United Kingdom of Great Britain and Ireland. Indeed, the "Iron Duke" himself was Irish-born, though Wellington downplayed its significance, attributing his place of birth to a mere happenstance of geography. "Being born in a stable," the future prime minister of the United Kingdom is said to have quipped, "does not make one a horse." Wellington was equally derisive about the soldiers serving under him, Irish, Scottish, and English alike, calling them "the scum of the earth."

At the Congress of Vienna, which convened in 1814, statesmen from Britain and its continental allies set about redrawing a map of Europe that would largely remain unchanged—with the exception of the borders around a steadily expanding Germany—for the next 100 years.

Just as surely, Britain also set about rearranging the boundaries of countries all around the globe. The victory over France had removed any serious international competitor, and Britain began to carve out its empire. On world maps, British territorial possessions have traditionally been shown in pink, and during this "imperial century" the pink began to spread like no other color in the imperial palette. India became the Jewel in the Crown. During the reign of Queen Victoria, a country on which the sun rarely shines had forged an empire "on which the sun never sets." According to one wag, "That's because God doesn't trust the British in the dark."

## Challenges of a New Era

An Englishman standing at the dawn of a new century in 1900 would have looked to the future with confidence. And with good reason. Britannia undoubtedly ruled the waves, and throughout much of the world *Pax Britannica* reigned on land. However, a hundred years later his English counterpart would have gazed on the world with markedly different eyes—with equal pride, perhaps, but from a very different viewpoint, and as a citizen of a very different country.

The statesmen who had gathered at the Congress of Vienna in 1814 to

**LORD PROTECTOR**
The statue of Oliver Cromwell stands watch at the Palace of Westminster, where he led the political opposition to King Charles II before taking up arms against him.

**PERENNIAL PARADE**

The annual Quit-Rents parade
wends its way through a London
street. Among the oldest of
English legal ceremonies, it has
been held since 1211 and is open
to the public.

congratulate themselves on beating Napoleon and to restore order in Europe all had one overriding concern: maintaining the balance of power on the continent. They were determined that no single European nation should again be allowed to grow so strong that it could threaten the rest of them. The Germans, however, had other plans—and began acting on them. By 1914 they had amassed the strongest army on the continent and were intent on using it. That summer the "Guns of August" began to roar.

Britain entered the Great War, as it was initially known, when the Germans invaded tiny Belgium, which lay between them and their prize of Paris. The British Expeditionary Force was duly dispatched, a nod to the island nation's commitment to its major continental allies, France and Russia.

Britain had fought wars on the continent before with the help of allies. But it had always done so by relying on a small professional army that was backed up by the might of the Royal Navy. Though few people knew it at the time, this war would be different. The Great War would involve great sacrifice, and Britain began to send unprecedented numbers of young men to fight it out in the trenches of Flanders.

The slaughter on the Western Front stunned the nation, and the anguish it generated inspired some of the world's most tragically beautiful poetry. Like his countryman Rupert Brooke, the poet Wilfred Owen died on a foreign field—killed a week before the end of the war in November 1918. By the time news of his death reached his hometown of Shrewsbury, church bells were

---

**IN LONDON**

One of the world's most beautiful botanical gardens, **the Royal Botanic Gardens, Kew,** (usually referred to simply as **Kew Gardens**) also has the world's largest collection of living plants. Its mission is "to inspire and deliver science-based plant conservation worldwide, enhancing the quality of life."

---

ringing out the peace. Many of Owen's poems, like "Anthem for a Doomed Youth," were published posthumously:

> *What passing bells for those who die as cattle?*
> *Only the monstrous anger of the guns.*
> *Only the stuttering rifles' rapid rattle*
> *Can patter out their hasty orisons.*
> *No mockeries now for them; no prayers nor bells;*
> *Nor any voice of mourning save the choirs,*
> *The shrill, demented choirs of wailing shells;*
> *And bugles calling for them from sad shires.*

The First World War had a profound impact on the nation. And its memory continues to haunt the land. Every November 11, on Remembrance Day, the British people stop to honor the dead, particularly those of the Great War. All across the country, their poppies proudly displayed, Britons collectively pause for two minutes—at the eleventh hour of the eleventh day of the eleventh month, the time when the Armistice was signed in 1918.

A number of empires disappeared in the war's wake: the Russian,

**HOTHOUSE**

The Waterlily House is the hottest and most humid environment at the Royal Botanic Gardens, Kew.

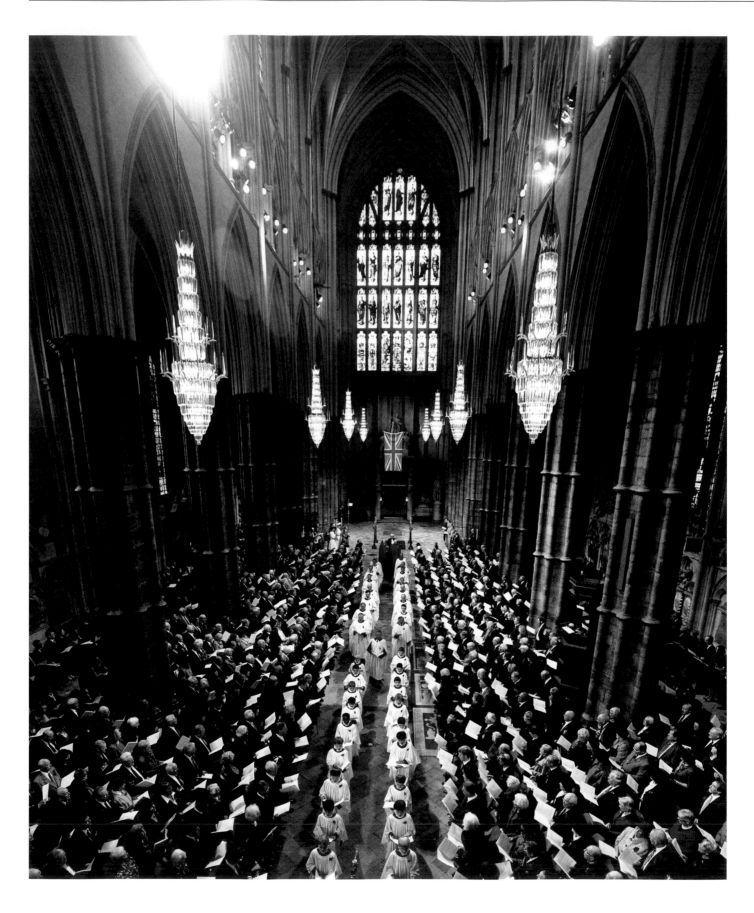

Ottoman, German, and Austro-Hungarian. The British Empire survived to fight another world war that century, again battling a rising Germany. As they had in the Great War, Britain's colonies responded to the call and sent soldiers to the front lines. But in the wake of the second war, colony after colony began to peel off from the empire, forming in its place a British Commonwealth of independent nations.

## Postwar Nation

The United States emerged as the great power after World War II, while a greatly weakened Britain became the more junior player. The two *pays anglo-saxon,* as the French refer to them, enjoyed a continuation of their so-called special relationship in the postwar years.

Meanwhile, Britain maintained its ties and trade with the Commonwealth nations. It was from these countries—India, Pakistan, the West Indies—that Britain drew workers during the 1950s and the boom years of the 1960s, encouraged by the British Nationality Act that was passed after World War II, which granted Commonwealth citizens entry to Britain. The result was the biggest influx of people into the country since the Norman Conquest.

By the Swinging Sixties, the British were finally able to let their hair down. Postwar rationing had lasted throughout much of the 1950s, and the surging 1960s economy led to growth in all areas of life. England led the world in music, birthing bands like the Beatles and the Rolling Stones and forging the "British Invasion" of North America. Groups such as Cream, with guitarist and vocalist Eric Clapton at the helm, were breaking new musical ground. "Clapton is God" declared a famous graffito spray painted on a wall in north London.

The Union Flag became a symbol of all that was cool and hip, made only more popular when England won the World Cup in 1966. The Mini Cooper charmed the world. If movies like *Alfie,* starring Michael Caine, summed up the self-confidence of the upwardly mobile, TV series like *The Avengers* typified the swagger of the era. (Later, during the 1990s, the term "Cool Britannia" would come to represent a

[ The First English UNESCO World Heritage Sites ]

1 **Durham Castle and Cathedral** (1986*) Glorious Anglo-Norman church and castle built in 1072. The former contains, among other things, the tomb of the Venerable Bede, an eighth-century monk whose writings form the basis for much of our knowledge of early Christian Britain.

2 **Ironbridge Gorge** (1986*) The cradle of the industrial revolution, site of the world's first iron bridge, and home to the Darby family, who first mass-produced iron by smelting it with coke.

3 **Studley Royal Park** (1986*) A beautiful park in Yorkshire created in the 19th century to enhance the picturesque ruins of Fountains Abbey, built around 1135.

4 **Stonehenge, Avebury, and surrounding sites** (1986*) Two majestic prehistoric stone circles and a wealth of minor burial mounds and other archeological treasures.

5 **Bleinheim Palace** (1987*) Immense stately home (built between 1705 and 1722) close to Oxford. Constructed with funds and on land donated by the crown to John Churchill, Duke of Marlborough, for his achievements on the battlefield. One of the duke's descendants, Sir Winston Churchill, was born here in 1874.

6 **City of Bath** (1987*) This city in southwest England contains some of the country's finest Georgian architecture.

7 **Hadrian's Wall** (1987*) A 73-mile fortification, much of which survives, built by the Romans between A.D. 122 and 128 to defend their northern border.

8 **The Palace and Abbey of Westminster** (1987*) Contains the Houses of Parliament, which date largely from 1840, but the oldest part of the palace, celebrated for its immense wooden roof (added between 1394 and 1401), Westminster Hall, was built in 1097. The nearby abbey is where virtually every monarch since William the Conqueror in the 11th century has been crowned.

* year of designation

**ARMISTICE DAY**

A memorial service takes place in Westminster Abbey on November 11, 2009, for the war dead from World War I. Each year on that day at 11 a.m.—the hour the armistice was signed the nation collectively pauses for two minutes of silence.

similar period of national optimism and contentment, this time under the rule of Tony Blair's New Labour Party.)

Despite its special relationship with America, Britain eventually began to realize that its future was not so much across the Atlantic as across the Channel. But the British have always been reluctant Europeans. By the time they belatedly sought admission to the European Economic Community (now known as the European Union), the French and the Germans had asserted their dominance. In response to British applications for membership

**IN SOUTHERN ENGLAND**

Although not England's longest river, the **River Thames** is the most famous because of associations with London. Walking the Thames is now possible on the **Thames Path National Trail,** from its source in the Cotswolds through historic villages, then London, and finishing at the Thames Barrier near Greenwich.

in the 1960s, General Charles de Gaulle had what amounted to a one-word response: *Non.*

In 1973, four years after the end of de Gaulle's presidency—and veto—the United Kingdom of Great Britain and Northern Ireland joined the EEC. Eurosceptics continue to voice their reservations, and the country has still refused to adopt the euro in place of the pound, now the oldest continually used currency in the world.

Today, three of the UK's constituencies have their own legislative assemblies—Scotland, Wales, and Northern Ireland. That leaves England without its own elective body. But the English can console themselves with the fact that, by dint of their population, they dominate the British Parliament.

Few travelers from London, Cornwall, or Yorkshire will describe themselves as "Britons." They have never really gotten used to the somewhat awkward term.

**THE TRANQUIL THAMES**
Far from the madding crowd, the Thames meanders through farmland in the English countryside. Here, a pleasure craft leisurely makes its way along the famous waterway.

The words of Vera Lynn resonate more strongly. "There'll always be an England," sang the Forces' Sweetheart. And the English, by and large, will settle for that.

# Sites and Sights in England

The **River Thames** is not England's longest river, but it is the most famous for its dominant presence and many associations with London. Walking the Thames is now possible on the **Thames Path National Trail**—from its source in the Cotswolds through historic villages, then London, and finishing at the Thames Barrier near Greenwich.

**Greenwich**, on the south bank of the Thames in southeast London, has been the site of a royal palace; a resort with many grand houses; and since 1997, a World Heritage site honored for its maritime history, architecture, and legacy. It is best known for its associations with timekeeping and as the namesake of Greenwich Mean Time, the universally agreed-upon time. The **Old Royal Naval College Visitor Centre** offers an overview of Greenwich's history, attractions, and important role in timekeeping.
*www.greenwich2000.com*

The Thames passes through the beech woods of Cliveden Reach in the heart of the Berkshire countryside near the opulent **Cliveden House**, where the "Cliveden Set" of 1920s

and 1930s politicians and glitterati gathered to chatter and arrange the world with Lord and Lady Astor. Although it is now a luxury hotel, it is still set on its original 376 magnificent acres of gardens and parkland.
*www.clivedenhouse.co.uk*

**English Gardens** were designed as an antidote to the formal, symmetrical gardens of Europe and have influenced gardeners throughout the world since the 18th century, offering a more relaxed, romantic ambiance, often with a bridge to a pond; small classical buildings; and a natural, welcoming mix of flowers, plants, and trees.

One of the world's most beautiful botanical gardens, the **Royal Botanic Gardens, Kew** (usually referred to simply as **Kew Gardens**), also has the world's largest collection of living plants. Its mission is to "inspire and deliver science-based plant conservation worldwide, enhancing the quality of life."
*www.kew.org*

The **Channel Tunnel** (known as the Chunnel) connects London with Paris and Brussels via high-speed Eurostar trains beneath the English Channel at the Strait of Dover. Designated one of the seven wonders of the modern world, it has the longest undersea portion of any tunnel in the world.
*www.raileurope.com/train-faq/ european-trains/eurostar/index.html*

The idiosyncratic ring of **beaches and beach towns** circling England include elegant Victorian resort towns, craggy coastlines, and hidden coves. Geologists note that the patterns in the stunning cliffs of the Jurassic Coast World Heritage site reveal an ancient desert that had ample sand dunes.

**Monk's House**, in the charming village of Rodmell near Sussex, was the country home of Virginia and Leonard Woolf until Leonard died in 1969. Now owned by the National Trust, it is furnished with many of their belongings, including portions of Virginia's diaries and other work and photographs of family and friends, including T. S. Eliot, E. M. Forster, and other members of the Bloomsbury Group, who frequently visited.
*www.nationaltrust.org.uk/main/w-monkshouse*

Robert Cecil, first Earl of Salisbury, was probably the most influential man in the kingdom when he started building the spectacular **Hatfield House** in Hertfordshire in 1607. Elizabeth I spent much of her rather lonely childhood at the adjacent Hatfield Palace (known today as the Old Palace), which was mostly demolished by Cecil in 1607 to make way for his much grander house.
*www.hatfield-house.co.uk*

On Hampshire's south coast lies **Portsmouth,** the Royal Navy's home port during the centuries that Britain ruled the waves. Today it makes for a delightful visit. At the Historic Dockyard visit the **D-Day Museum** and the **H.M.S. *Victory***, where Admiral Lord Nelson was killed in 1805 in the Battle of Trafalgar. Also nearby is the **Charles Dickens Birthplace Museum**.
*www.charlesdickensbirthplace.co.uk*

Northamptonshire's best known estate is the Spencer family's **Althorp House**, an 18th-century remodeling of a Tudor country house on 14,000 acres. Diana, Princess of Wales, lies buried on an island in the lake, called the Round Oval, on the grounds here. The estate is open on a limited basis for tours of the house and an award-winning exhibition, "Diana: A Celebration," about the princess's life and work.
*www.althorp.com*

London double-decker bus

**Sissinghurst Castle Garden** was created in the 1930s in and around the ruin of a moated Elizabethan mansion in the Wealden countryside in Sussex by Vita Sackville-West and her husband, Sir Harold Nicolson, members of the Bloomsbury Group. Together they created gardens that reflected their different personalities—his formal and classically designed spaces, and her romantic gardens in wild profusion.
*www.nationaltrust.org.uk/main/w-vh/w-visits/*
*w-findaplace/w-sissinghurstcastlegarden*

The long peninsula that forms the southwest corner of Britain is a land of dairy pastures, moors, woodlands, and gentle hills. The coasts of these counties grow craggier, bleaker, and more dramatic the farther west and south you go from **Somerset** to **Devon** to **Cornwall**. Devon is known for its picturesque thatched cottages.

One English indulgence not to be denied is afternoon tea. There is formal tea, farmhouse tea, high tea, and **cream tea**, which is tea taken (ideally in **Devonshire**) with scones, strawberry or raspberry jam, and yellow clotted cream. Substitutes such as whipped cream or butter (or worse, low-fat options) may be offered for the latter—but when in England, insist on Devonshire clotted cream.

Three great moors lie at the heart of the southwest peninsula—**Bodmin**, **Dartmoor**, and **Exmoor**. Daphne du Maurier was inspired by yarns spun to her when she stayed on Bodmin Moor in 1930 at the pub called Jamaica Inn. The inn made famous by her novel of the same name is no longer lonely or as evocative, but it is still worth a stop for its grim, slate-hung aspect and atmospheric interior.

**Dartmoor National Park** is a bleak landscape covering more than 300 square miles of granite tors, heathery cleaves (valleys), and lonely bogs. The third moor is Devon's light and airy **Exmoor National Park**, which has none of Dartmoor's oppressive grimness. The warmth of the underlying sandstone

seems to pervade the moor. England's largest herd of wild red deer roams freely here.
*www.dartmoor-npa.gov.uk*
*www.exmoor-nationalpark.gov.uk*

**The Eden Project** is a complex of large greenhouses, or biomes, located in an old slate quarry designed to experiment, learn about, and educate visitors about ecology and plant life around the world. Various climates—such as tropical and Mediterranean—are reproduced inside each biome along with the specific plant life of that climate. This site is especially popular with families and school groups.
*www.edenproject.com*

Bury St. Edmunds Cathedral, Suffolk

Narrow roads shadow the paths to **Fowey,** a charming little gray stone town set on a winding estuary in Cornwall. American ships were positioned in Fowey Harbor for months before the D-Day invasion.
*www.fowey.co.uk*

One of the great country houses of England is the Georgian **Sandringham House**, best known as the vacation hideaway of the royal family since 1862. The 20,000-acre

estate includes a museum of field sports and a collection of vintage royal vehicles, but the main attraction is the opportunity to touch (figuratively) the hem of the robe of the House of Windsor.
*www.sandringhamestate.co.uk*

**Bury St. Edmunds** is Suffolk's spiritual capital, where a shrine for the body of St. Edmund was built. Medieval houses are incorporated into the striking west front of the 11th-century abbey ruins. The Cathedral of St. James, begun in 1438 and completed in 2004 with a new tower, stands next to the abbey in beautiful gardens. Charles Dickens's Mr. Pickwick stayed here on Angel Hill, reached from the abbey through a 14th-century gateway.
*http://www.burystedmunds.co.uk/*

**The Blackpool Tower,** on Blackpool's Golden Mile, is a long-standing famous English seaside landmark. It opened to the public in 1894, inspired by the Eiffel Tower, which debuted at the Great Paris Exposition of 1889. Today Blackpool is a huge enterprise, with an aquarium, a circus, a ballroom with dancing, and a tram to link it all together. The tower is still a big draw for its views, though its propensity to sway slightly deters many.
*www.theblackpooltower.co.uk*

**Ironbridge** on the River Severn was the cradle of the industrial revolution. A range of fascinating museums tell the story, and from a number of footpaths you can view the graceful, semicircular bridge of 1779, the world's first cast iron bridge. Today it is a World Heritage site, the jewel in the crown of a rural village that once found itself the center of the world.
*www.ironbridge.org.uk*

Beatrix Potter bought her beloved 17th-century Lake District farmhouse, **Hill Top**, with the royalties from her first books and wrote many of her others here. Nearby in Sawrey village is the **Beatrix Potter Gallery** in the former office of the writer's husband.
*www.nationaltrust.org.uk/main/w-hilltop*

W hen a man is tired of London," Samuel Johnson famously declared, "he is tired of life; for there is in London all that life can afford."

Dr. Johnson's statement is as true today as it was in the past. The London of his day, the 1700s, was the capital of a powerful nation and the heart of a growing empire. Today, the city still dominates England—not to mention Britain and the British Isles—in a way that few national capitals do.

Washington, D.C., may be the capital of the United States, but the country's financial center is New York, and its entertainment hub Los Angeles. Ankara is the capital of Turkey, but Istanbul is its most populous center. The same is true for Brasília and Rio de Janeiro in Brazil, for Abuja and Lagos in Nigeria. Russia has had alternating capitals during its long history, Moscow and St. Petersburg. South Africa has three capitals: Pretoria for the executive branch, Bloemfontein for the judicial, and Cape Town for the legislative. Amsterdam is the capital of the Netherlands, but its seat of government is in The Hague.

London is different. The nation's executive, judicial, and legislative branches are all there, in a city that divides its powers with no one. London is the capital city of the present-day United Kingdom of Great Britain and Northern Ireland—and shows, in many ways, that it was also the "capital" of the globe-spanning British Empire. It is the financial center not only of the United Kingdom but also of Europe. It is by far the biggest and most populous city in the British Isles: a port, a tourist magnet, and a center of industry and commerce, media and fashion. London is the entertainment and arts mecca of the country and a cultural treasure of the world.

There is, indeed, a lot packed into that one city. Most of its inhabitants and visitors will not grow tired of London itself. But they certainly quickly tire of making their way through its main airport (Heathrow is the busiest international airport in the world and perhaps the most "dysfunctional") and of commuting to work from increasingly farther and farther afield.

In a way, however, it has always been so. People have been coming to this settlement on the banks of the River Thames for two millennia.

## Londonium

T he Romans were the city's early arrivals, founding a settlement where the Thames was narrow enough to build a bridge but deep enough to sail their ships at high tide. That point is close to where London Bridge is located today, and it is the site at which the base of a huge Roman pier was discovered in 1981.

**CALLING CARD**
The classic British red phone booth—a familiar, though somewhat less common, sight on the streets of London. *Previous pages:* The River Thames, London Bridge, and Tower Bridge beyond.

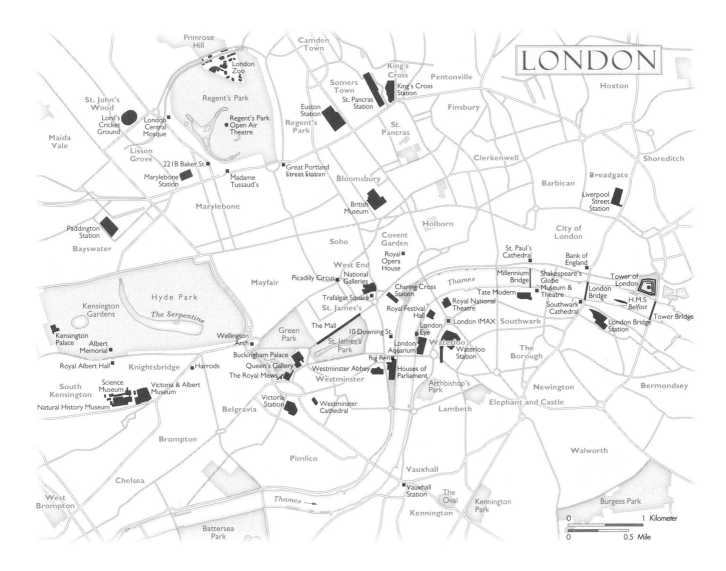

Tourists often confuse London Bridge with the more elaborate Tower Bridge, which spans the river farther downstream. They're not the only ones to make that mistake. In 1967, when the London city council decided to sell the bridge, an American entrepreneur bought it, presumably sight unseen, believing that he was actually buying Tower Bridge. His disappointment notwithstanding, he disassembled London Bridge and then had it reconstructed at Lake Havasu City in Arizona. It is now the state's second most popular tourist attraction, the Grand Canyon being the biggest draw.

The original Roman bridge was a big draw, too. North of the bridge, the Romans established Londinium, carving out an area bounded by the river on one side and defensive walls on the other three. The London Wall, along with the better known Hadrian's Wall in the far north of England, was one of the Romans' biggest construction projects in Britain. Portions of the London Wall can still be seen around Tower Hill.

**GETTING YOUR BEARINGS**

Divided by the great looping bend of the River Thames, this map of central London extends from the Tower of London in the east to Kensington Gardens in the west, and from Primrose Hill in the north to Southwark in the south. Many of the main tourist attractions are indicated, as are districts like Westminster, Kensington and Chelsea, Mayfair, and the City.

The Roman city covered about a square mile and remained that size for the first thousand or so years of its history. Today this area, known as "the City," is probably home to fewer Londoners than ever before, even as the greater city of London has grown by leaps and bounds all around it. For the City is now London's financial district, abuzz by day but virtually deserted by night. Air travelers flying over London after sundown will notice that this part of the city is noticeably darker than the rest, illuminated by streetlights but little else. It is home to the Bank

---

**IN THE CITY**

The sleek steel suspension **Millennium Bridge** (for pedestrians only) was famously wobbly when it first opened in 2000. Closed for nearly two years, it is now stable and well traveled, linking St. Paul's Cathedral with the Tate Modern across the River Thames.

---

of England, Lloyds of London, the London Stock Exchange, and other financial institutions—all built on Roman ruins.

To the south of London Bridge is Southwark, where the magnificent Southwark Cathedral dominates the skyline. The cathedral was mentioned in the Domesday Book of 1086 and sits on a site that has had a place of worship since 606. It was from Southwark, at the Tabard Inn, that Geoffrey Chaucer's pilgrims set out for that other great cathedral in *The Canterbury Tales*. Today, Southwark Cathedral is sunk several feet below London's current level. All that remains to indicate the site of the inn itself is a historical marker plaque.

Shakespeare lived in this part of the city, south of the river, where the famed Globe Theatre stood. The Globe burned down in 1613, during a performance of the Bard's *Henry VIII*, and was rebuilt a year later. The theatre was closed in 1642 when the English civil war broke out, and then destroyed by order of the puritans, who gained control of London shortly thereafter. A modern reconstruction of the theatre opened in 1997, about 750 feet from the original site.

**LONDON, NEW AND OLD**
The Millennium Bridge carries foot traffic from the south bank of the city toward St. Paul's Cathedral, which is one of the great iconic images of London.

To the north of London Bridge rises a fluted Doric column that marks the site of a key event in London's long history. Designed by Sir Christopher Wren, the Monument soars 202 feet, the tallest freestanding stone column in the world. If you pushed it over its urn would land where the Great Fire of London began on September 2, 1666. A plaque on a modern office building along Pudding Lane now indicates the spot.

## Fire in the City

For some time prior to the outbreak of the Great Fire, the weather in London had been unusually dry. When the blaze started, an easterly wind sent the flames racing toward the classical-style "Old St. Paul's" Cathedral. The cathedral sat on Ludgate Hill, the highest point in the city. Said to have been the site of a temple to the Roman goddess Diana, the cathedral had been the seat of a bishop since Roman times. In addition, there were at least three cathedrals on the site before it. Old St. Paul's was under repair at the time of the fire, and its surrounding scaffolding acted like kindling. The edifice had six acres of leaden roof, which melted and crashed to the floor. The building was destroyed.

The diarist John Evelyn recorded the day's events: "[The fire] burned both in breadth and length, the churches, public halls, Exchange, hospitals, monuments and ornaments, leaping in a prodigious manner from house to house and street to street, at great distance from one another, for the heat had even ignited the air."

People took to boats and watched the fire from the Thames, among them another famous diarist, Samuel Pepys. His entry for September 2 reads:

*So I down to the water-side, and there got a boat and through bridge, and there saw a lamentable fire. Poor Michell's house, as far as the Old Swan, already burned that way, and the fire running further, that in a very little time it got as far as the Steeleyard, while I was there. Everybody endeavouring to remove their goods, and flinging into the river or bringing them into lighters that layoff; poor people staying in their houses as long as till the very fire touched them, and then running into boats, or clambering from one pair of stairs by the water-side to another.*

To stop the fire, King Charles II ordered that the houses in the path of the flames be blown up. The fire raged for four days in all, destroying four-fifths of the tightly

## INSIDE ST. PAUL'S CATHEDRAL

ball and lantern
(355.5 feet tall)

Golden Gallery

Stone Gallery

Whispering Gallery

apse

south portico

organ and quire

west-end clock tower

main entrance

**WREN'S MASTERPIECE**
The majestic interior of St. Paul's, shown in the cutaway above, is the venue for select concerts in the capital. Opposite, Russian conductor Valery Gergiev leads a rehearsal by the London Symphony Orchestra in the summer of 2009.

## Westminster Walk

A walking tour of Westminster includes some of the most iconic sights of the British capital. The walk is two miles long and should take half a day.

❶ **The Palace of Westminster** is the great Gothic fantasy built between 1837 and 1860 by Sir Charles Barry and Augustus Pugin to accommodate the House of Lords and the House of Commons.

❷ **Westminster Abbey** has been the scene of 38 coronations since that of William the Conqueror on Christmas Day 1066.

❸ **The Cabinet War Rooms** are where Winston Churchill and his staff planned the Allied conduct of World War II.

❹ **The National Gallery**, with its great portico fronting onto Trafalgar Square, is the city's premier art gallery.

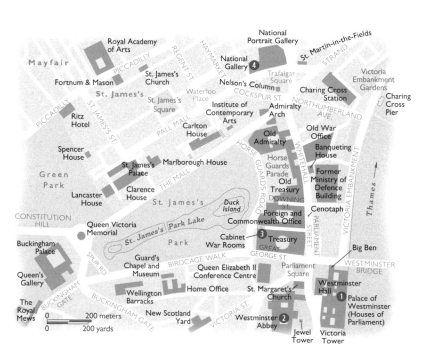

packed housing within London's old walls. Remarkably, only three lives were lost—a relief considering that in the previous year, the Great Plague had killed a quarter of London's inhabitants.

The man in charge of rebuilding the city was Sir Christopher Wren. The great architect drew up ambitious plans, inspired by continental designs, with splendid avenues converging on circular open spaces for the city, wide streets, and huge piazzas. But you won't find that in London today, because the plan was never put into effect. Only Wren's design for the new St. Paul's was utilized. For inspiration, he again looked to the continent—to St. Peter's in Rome. When the baroque cathedral was completed in 1710, it was the third biggest dome in the world and the tallest building in London.

Now crowded by taller skyscrapers, Wren's masterpiece—the crown jewel of the 52 churches he designed—still dominates the London skyline and looms large in the imagination of Londoners. The photograph of the smoke-shrouded cathedral taken during the Blitz of 1940 remains among the most evocative images of London at war.

Although most royal weddings take place at Westminster Abbey, St. Paul's was the venue for the 1981 wedding of Prince Charles and Lady Diana Spencer, which was watched on television by millions of people around the world. The dead buried there are like a who's who of the great and the good. They include T. E. Lawrence, Florence Nightingale, the Duke of Wellington, Lord Nelson, and Dr. Samuel Johnson, who compiled the 1755 *Dictionary of the English Language.*

Sixteenth-century poet and preacher John Donne is there, his ashes buried under a statue that was one of the few monuments from "Old St. Paul's" to survive the Great Fire; the scorch marks are still visible. Sir Christopher Wren is there as well. On his tomb are the following words: "If you seek his monument, look around you."

## An Expanding City

Once the city burst beyond its walls in the late Middle Ages, London began to spread. Following the river, it reached west toward the village of Westminster, where another bridge stretched from bank to bank. One fall morning in 1802, half a century after the Westminster Bridge was built, the poet William Wordsworth, more used to finding beauty in the English Lake District, composed the following lines on the bridge:

*Earth has not anything to show more fair:*
*Dull would he be of soul who could pass by*
*A sight so touching in its majesty:*
*This City now doth, like a garment, wear*
*The beauty of the morning; silent, bare,*
*Ships, towers, domes, theatres, and temples lie*
*Open unto the fields, and to the sky;*
*All bright and glittering in the smokeless air.*

In 1967, the Kinks released the hauntingly beautiful song "Waterloo Sunset," set
on the banks of the same "dirty old river." In it, Ray Davies sings about a young couple named Terry and Julie who meet every Friday night at Waterloo Station before
crossing the Thames. Dubbed the "Anthem of London," the song was only denied
the top slot on the UK pop charts by the Beatles' "All You Need Is Love."

Westminster, on the north bank, has long been the residence of kings and queens,
and is still the site of the government of the United Kingdom. The Victorian Gothic
spires of the Palace of Westminster dominate the river here—especially the main

## WORTH A VISIT

Located on the banks of the Thames, the Palace of
Westminster is London's great Gothic Revival masterpiece.
Public tours include the Commons and Lords debating chambers
and the Queen's Robing Room. Visitors can also watch
debates on current issues from the vantage of the public galleries,
with Prime Minister's Question Time in the
Commons a particular favorite.

Victoria Tower and the clock tower that holds Big Ben (which is the name of the bell, not the bell tower).

Known as the mother of parliaments, Westminster is the biggest Gothic palace in the world, where the great debates of the centuries have taken place in its two chambers, the Commons and the Lords. The House of Commons in particular is where the arts of oratory and debate have flourished over the centuries. Here, the government and opposition benches are significantly spaced two sword lengths apart. Members of the public today can watch proceedings from the safety of the "Strangers Gallery," which for security reasons is now separated from the Commons chamber by a glass screen. The Union Flag is flown over the bell tower when the chamber is in session.

In the House of Commons, Oliver Cromwell delivered a speech in 1648 that propelled England into a civil war that would end with the execution of King Charles I. (Thirteen years later, Charles II had Cromwell's head spiked on the roof in revenge for his father's execution.) In 1789, William Wilberforce delivered his famous abolition speech in the Commons, and in 1836, Daniel O'Connell, the Liberator of Ireland, delivered a call for equal justice for the Irish. It was here that, more recently, Margaret Thatcher spoke out against the labor unions, the Europeans, and the Argentines—and where, in 1982, her great admirer Ronald Reagan delivered his "evil empire" speech.

Winston Churchill made the House of Commons the setting for his most memorable orations. On June 4, 1940, at the height of the Battle of Britain, when the island nation stood alone against Nazi Germany, he told the assembled members of Parliament: "We shall fight on the beaches, we shall fight on the landing grounds, we shall fight in the fields and in the streets, we shall fight in the hills; we shall never surrender."

The annual State Opening of Parliament is a spectacle of symbolism and pomp. During the preparation, the Yeomen of the Guard carry out a ceremonial search of the cellars of the Palace of Westminster to prevent a repeat of the 1605 Gunpowder Plot. That year, Guy Fawkes and a group of English Catholics planned to blow up Parliament and kill the sovereign of the day, the Protestant James I. Today, James's descendant Queen Elizabeth II arrives at the palace in the Irish State Coach, an enclosed carriage drawn by four horses, and escorted by her Household Cavalry. The Union Flag is then lowered from Victoria Tower and the Royal Standard flown in its place.

**BEEFEATERS ON TOUR**
Yeomen Warders, opposite, chat while on duty at a commemorative service outside Westminster Abbey for the 500th anniversary of the death of King Henry VII.

Surrounded by Officers of State and led by the heralds, the Queen proceeds to the House of Lords, where the peers of the realm await her bedecked in ermine-edged robes and coronets. There, she summons the Commons to join them. The Gentleman Usher of the Black Rod proceeds to the chamber of the Commons, but as he approaches, the doors are slammed in his face, in symbolic defiance of the monarch. At this, Black Rod strikes the door three times and is admitted, the Commons' independence now asserted.

The members of the lower house then progress to the Lords' chamber, chatting and joking on the way. With all the members assembled, the Queen reads a speech prepared for her by the government. Delivered tonelessly, it sets forth the government's legislative agenda for the year ahead.

Near Parliament stands a monument to an earlier queen who was less given to the niceties of protocol: Queen Boudicca, a Celt who launched an attack on the Roman settlement 20 or so years after its founding, slaughtered the inhabitants, and set it ablaze. It was not the last time that the city would be burned to the ground and not the last time that it would, like a phoenix, rise from the ashes. The bronze statue at Westminster, right on the Thames Embankment, shows Queen Boudicca riding into battle in a chariot, spear in hand and arms raised as if urging on her warriors.

## On Through Westminster

A short walk north from the Houses of Parliament is Number 10 Downing Street, perhaps the most famous front door in the world. This is the heart of the executive side of the British government. The townhouses on Downing Street were first built in 1682, and Number 10 has been the official residence of Britain's prime ministers since 1733. Next door, at Number 11, resides the Chancellor of the Exchequer, or Minister of the Treasury. Beyond it, near the entrance to Downing Street, stands the Cenotaph, Britain's national war monument.

Just west of the Victorian Gothic spires of the Houses of Parliament are the Gothic spires of Westminster Abbey. This is the traditional venue for royal coronations—which have

**REMEMBERING A PRINCESS**

This aerial shot shows the oval stream bed that surrounds the Princess Diana Memorial Fountain in Hyde Park, opened by Queen Elizabeth II in July 2004. Three bridges provide access to the fountain.

taken place since 1308 upon King Edward's Chair—and royal funerals. Enemies in life, Elizabeth I and Mary Queen of Scots both lie here. In Poets' Corner are monuments to the capital's literary greats: William Shakespeare, Alfred Lord Tennyson, Lord George Byron, Charles Dickens. The cathedral commemorates ordinary Londoners, too, containing a manuscript with the names of all those who died during the Blitz. Each day, one of the pages is turned.

Farther west, at the end of the tree-lined Mall, is the royal family's London residence, Buckingham Palace. This has been the home of the reigning monarch since the accession of Queen Victoria in 1837. It is said that the current royal family doesn't care much for the palace, preferring the charms of Windsor or Sandringham, or the remoteness of Balmoral in Scotland. (Of course, they would never say so.) Tourists, however, have no such reservations. They flock to Buckingham Palace for the daily Changing of the Guard ceremony, which takes place every other day in fall and winter. When the crowds see the Royal Standard flying, they know the Queen is at home.

## The Lungs of London

Still moving west, past the triumphal Wellington Arch (commemorating Britain's victories in the Napoleonic Wars), are Hyde Park and the adjoining Kensington Gardens. The royal parks are one square mile of green and two of London's best loved. For Londoners, these are places of great escape, filled with lawns, trees, bridle paths, statues, and regimental bandstands. There is even a lake (the Serpentine) in Hyde Park for rowboats to share with a wide variety of wild fowl that call the park home, from the small but aggressive—and territorial—coots to the great grey herons.

During the reign of Queen Victoria, Sir Joseph Paxton erected the Crystal Palace in Hyde Park, the biggest glass structure the world had ever seen. It was built to house the Great Exhibition of 1851, but countless sparrows also took up residence there and began to destroy its precious exhibits. When Queen Victoria consulted the Duke of Wellington about how to get rid of the birds, the victor of the Battle of Waterloo had a simple but effective solution: "Sparrow hawks, ma'am."

At one end of Hyde Park stands the rotunda of Royal Albert Hall, famous for staging the patriotic Promenade Concerts, and beside it the elaborate Albert Memorial, commissioned by Victoria in memory of her beloved husband. On this side of the park next to Kensington and Knightsbridge—the so-called heavenly

**ROYAL ESCORT**
The Queen, opposite, makes her way from Buckingham Palace to the Palace of Westminster for the State Opening of Parliament on December 3, 2008. She makes the journey in the Irish State Coach and is escorted by members of the Household Cavalry.

## [ Six Famous London Cemeteries ]

**1 Brompton** One of London's largest and most impressive Victorian-era cemeteries, with countless graves of the famous—from Samuel Cunard, founder of the Cunard cruise line, to Henry Cole, inventor of the Christmas card.

**2 Bunhill Fields** Holds the graves of writers, artists, and religious nonconformists, including the poet William Blake; John Bunyan, author of *Pilgrim's Progress;* and Daniel Defoe, best known for *Robinson Crusoe.*

**3 Highgate** This large, spooky north London cemetery is most famous for the grave of Karl Marx.

**4 Kensal Green** Last resting place of many eminent writers, including Victorian novelist Anthony Trollope and the playwright Sir Harold Pinter.

**5 St. Paul's Cathedral** Tombs and memorials to some of Britain's most noted men and women, including Lord Horatio Nelson, the country's greatest naval commander.

**6 Westminster Abbey** The nation's pantheon, with the tombs of many of kings and queens over hundreds of years, and a wealth of other greats. Some of the best known, including Geoffrey Chaucer, author of *The Canterbury Tales,* are found in Poets' Corner.

twins—are two of the city's smartest shopping districts, where Harrods and Harvey Nichols can be found. The Victoria & Albert (V&A) is here too, the self-proclaimed "world's greatest museum of decorative arts," as is the Science Museum and the Natural History Museum.

At the other end, right on the edge of the upmarket Mayfair district, is Speakers' Corner. Here, people can step on their soapbox and hold forth on any subject. Riots broke out at Speakers' Corner in 1855 when the government tried to outlaw buying and selling on Sundays, the only day of the week when working people had time off. Karl Marx, who lived in London at the time, thought the riots marked the beginning of an English revolution. And while the revolution never came, Hyde Park has long been a staging ground for mass demonstrations, from the women's suffrage movement in the last century to the anti-war protests of today.

No other major capital can boast so much open space. The capital's expanses of greenery are considered the "lungs of London," providing easy escape from the bustle of the city. Speakers' Corner, for example, is located next to one end of Oxford Street, said to be the world's longest shopping thoroughfare at nearly a mile, and one habitually jammed with red double-decker buses and black London cabs.

North of Hyde Park, through the district of Marylebone, is Regent's Park. Several characters from film and literature lived near the park, including the Dearlys and their dogs in Walt Disney's *101 Dalmatians,* and Sherlock Holmes. The great detective, created by Sir Arthur Conan Doyle, lived nearby at 221B Baker Street. One of the most famous addresses in the world, it is now home to a finance company.

The London Underground station at Baker Street is the oldest subway station in the world, and opened in 1863. The first section of the Tube, as it is known because of the system's deeply bored tunnels, ran from here to Great Portland Street. Today, the system has 270 stations, most of them above ground, and its trains run along some 250 miles of track, making it the largest in

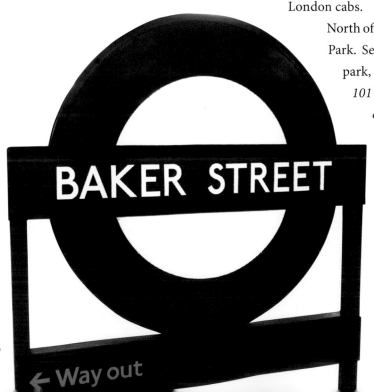

the world. The London Underground map is considered a classic of design and has been imitated by many other subway systems.

A more recent landmark is the crescent-topped golden dome and minaret of the London Central Mosque, which rise on the edge of the park. The property was donated to the Muslim community by King George VI in return for the land on which the Anglican cathedral in Cairo sits. Farther to the northwest, amid the red-brick suburbs, is the magnificent Neasden Temple, the largest Hindu temple in the world outside India. Both buildings testify to the city's growing immigration rates, particularly from the Asian subcontinent.

London is ever a study in contrasts. Minutes away from the London Central Mosque is a place more associated with London's traditional past—Lord's Cricket Ground, often regarded as the Home of Cricket. The first match played at Lord's for which there are records was on June 22, 1814, between Marylebone Cricket Club and Hertfordshire.

Just below Regent's Park is Portland Place, where the BBC, the world's largest broadcaster and a cherished institution, is headquartered. The celebrated CBS journalist

**MARKET FORCES**

Christmas shoppers throng the historic Apple Market at Covent Garden. A "fruit and veg" market has been held in this part of central London since the 1600s, and today it continues to be a popular destination for locals and visitors alike.

Edward R. Murrow broadcast from the roof of Broadcasting House in Portland Place during the Battle of Britain, often to the accompaniment of air raid sirens and explosions. Americans could hear, in real time, London being bombed. "Just overhead now," he reported, "the burst of the anti-aircraft fire . . . and the searchlights now are feeling almost directly overhead. Now you'll hear two bursts a little nearer in a moment . . . *[Boom, boom].* There they are . . ."

A selection of Murrow's reports was published in 1941, under the title *This Is London,* to educate Americans on what

---

**IN BLOOMSBURY**

The **British Museum** is a massive trove of treasures with more than 4 million objects ranging from prehistoric bones to 21st-century pills, from whole Assyrian palace rooms to exquisite gold jewels. It covers 13.5 acres, employs 1,200 people, and hosts more than 6 million visitors a year.

---

Britain was enduring during the Blitz. Night after night, Londoners would trek down into the Underground to take cover from the explosions. In all, 30,000 of the city's inhabitants died in the bombings.

## The West End

Continuing clockwise, east from Regents Park, is the fashionable residential area of Bloomsbury, with its elegant Georgian houses surrounding manicured green lawns. Among the enclave's most famous residents were the so-called Bloomsbury Group of writers and artists in the early 20th century, a circle of free thinkers "who lived in squares and loved in triangles." The group included Virginia Woolf, John Maynard Keynes, E. M. Forster, and Lytton Strachey, who were drawn here by the area's proximity to book publishers, London University, and the British Museum.

The British Museum is home to impressive collections of antiquities from all across the ancient world. Among the most visited artifacts are the Elgin Marbles

**GREAT ROOM**
The Queen Elizabeth II Great Court in the British Museum is Europe's largest covered public square. At its center is the world-famous Reading Room.

from the Parthenon in Athens, the relief frieze that Lord Elgin, the British ambassador to Greece, brought to London in 1801 and which the Greek authorities have been trying to get back ever since. Also here is the celebrated Rosetta Stone, a great dark stone inscribed with a decree by a council of priests in 196 B.C. The decree is written in three different scripts—hieroglyphic, demotic, and Greek—with the last two providing the key to unlocking the meaning of the first.

The British Museum has elements of two of the Seven Wonders of the Ancient World: the Temple of Artemis at Ephesus and the Mausoleum at Halicarnassus, both in Asia Minor, or modern-day Turkey. But it also contains exhibits like the Sutton Hoo treasure, which includes a ceremonial whole-face helmet, iron sword, lyre, and scepter excavated from a Saxon chief's ship burial in Suffolk, East Anglia.

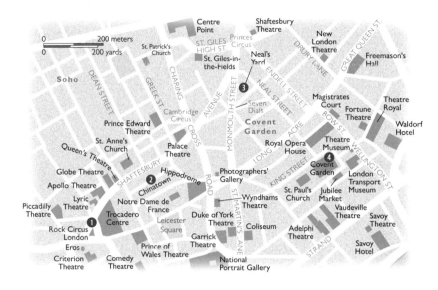

The museum's Reading Room was a favorite haunt of Mahatma Gandhi and George Bernard Shaw. Karl Marx came here, too. Every day, he would sit at a desk in the Reading Room from 10 a.m. to 7 p.m., working on *Das Kapital*.

South of Bloomsbury is lively Covent Garden, home to the Royal Opera House and innumerable retail outlets, and to the chic—though still somewhat seedy—Soho. This is where many Protestant Huguenots settled after fleeing religious persecution in France, followed by other new arrivals from eastern and southern Europe, and more recently, the Chinese from Hong Kong. World-famous Carnaby Street is in the Soho district. In the Swinging Sixties, music clubs here drew the likes of the Rolling Stones and The Who. Boutiques offered the latest fashions, including the daring miniskirt, popularized by supermodel Twiggy. "The impact of Carnaby Street is becoming worldwide," wrote American journalist John Crosby. "Tony Curtis wears Carnaby Street clothes. So do Peter Sellers and the Beatles."

Moving down Shaftsbury Avenue, the city's main theatre thoroughfare, brings us to Piccadilly Circus, with its famous statue of the Angel of Christian Charity (which Londoners, perhaps a touch irreverently, just call Eros). Nearby are Leicester Square, where Britain's film premieres are held, and the stately Trafalgar Square. This is London's most famous public square. It has long been a place for democratic expression and protest, and continues to be a favored venue for demonstrations and rallies. It's the site of the city's Christmas tree-lighting ceremony and other annual events on the cultural calendar—from Chinese New Year celebrations to St. George's Day festivities to the Muslim festival of Eid. This part of London is the heart of the

## Covent Garden and Soho Walk

This four-hour, mile-and-a-half walk takes you through two of the most colorful areas of London, both of which have seen great changes in the past couple of decades.

❶ **The Rock Circus** is upstairs in the London Pavilion; there, among other things, you can get your picture taken alongside a waxwork rock star.

❷ **Chinatown** is marked by bilingual street names and a colorful ceremonial archway across Gerrard Street.

❸ **Neal's Yard** is a little triangular oasis of New Age shops, "therapy rooms," alternative remedy emporia, and inexpensive eateries.

❹ **The Covent Garden Market**, a beautiful 1833 hall of iron and glass, shelters very chic restaurants, cafés, craft stalls, and stores, with entertainment provided by street musicians and jugglers.

**CARNABY STREET**

Under a poster of the newly released Sgt. Pepper album, customers thumb through boxes of records at a sidewalk stall in September 1967.

West End, although it's not really west London. It is west of "the City," or financial district, but it is east of the seat of power at Westminster, so the term "West End" is really synonymous with central London.

Dominating Trafalgar Square (named after the Royal Navy's great victory over Napoleon's fleet in 1805) is a 185-foot column topped by Admiral Lord Nelson (the victor at Trafalgar). A hundred thousand people flocked to the square for the statue's unveiling 38 years after the naval battle. Behind Nelson's Column stands

> **IN BRITAIN**
>
> More than 800 shops in Britain have a
> **Royal Coat of Arms** fixed above the door,
> indicating that the business holds a royal warrant to
> supply "by appointment" to the royal family.
> A coveted marketing tool, this honor and tradition
> began in the Middle Ages.

St. Martin-in-the-Fields, famous for its free lunchtime concerts, and the National Gallery, with more than 2,300 paintings, one of the greatest collections of Western European paintings in the world. But the admiral gazes steadfastly the other way, south, toward the English Channel, as if still watching out for the French. Should he shift his eyes to the right, he would almost be looking straight down Pall Mall.

If anywhere is the heart of the English establishment, this is it. Pall Mall is the elegant thoroughfare where London's clubs are found, the kinds of places you expect to see Bertie Wooster—a member of the fictional Drones Club in P. G. Wodehouse's *Jeeves* stories—dashing down the steps and hailing a cab. These institutions date back to the late 1600s. Not all the clubs attract the same kinds of members. Writers, for example, have long preferred Savages, and bishops the Athenaeum. All would-be members must be proposed and then seconded by existing members before being voted on by a committee of members. The latter do this by slipping a ball into a bag: a white

**TRAFALGAR TREASURE**
One of the chief attractions of Trafalgar Square is St. Martin-in-the-Fields. In addition to religious services, the church offers a brass rubbing center, art gallery, "Café in the Crypt," and free lunchtime concerts on Mondays, Tuesdays, and Fridays.

ball for "yes," a black ball for "no." A single black ball results in rejection, the origin of the expression "to blackball."

Turning east toward the city takes us first along the Strand—originally a sandy beach on the bank of the Thames and now the location of the Royal Courts of Justice—and then Fleet Street. Fleet Street is where the serial-killing barber Sweeney Todd is said to have lived, the so-called Demon Barber of Fleet Street. It is also traditionally the home of Britain's newspaper industry. In the 1980s, the nation's popular tabloids and serious broadsheets left Fleet Street, however, bringing to an end the presence of an industry that had flourished since 1500, when a printing press first began operations there.

Fleet Street is now more associated with the British legal profession. To the south of the thoroughfare lies the Temple, which in earlier times was the headquarters of the Knights Templar, and is today where law students train for the bar exam. The east end of the street is where the River Fleet flowed up against the ancient walls of the city—and this brings us back to the place where London began.

## [ Seven Historic London Pubs ]

1 **French House**, 49 Dean Street. A Soho institution that was the unofficial headquarters of the French Resistance in London in the Second World War.

2 **George Inn**, 77 Borough High Street. Preserves the charm that appealed to Charles Dickens, among others, and is known for the nearby plaque that marks the point from which the pilgrims departed London in Chaucer's *The Canterbury Tales*.

3 **Mayflower**, 117 Rotherhithe Street. Known as the Shippe when the *Mayflower* set sail from its quayside steps in 1620.

4 **Spaniard's Inn**, Hampstead Heath. Dates back to 1585 and the reign of Elizabeth I, when this northerly heath land was still outside the city limits.

5 **White Hart**, 191 Drury Lane. Reputedly first licensed in 1216, and patronized by many notorious figures, including the highwayman Dick Turpin.

6 **Ye Olde Cheshire Cheese**, 145 Fleet Street. Beloved of lawyers and journalists, and rebuilt in 1667 after the Great Fire of London, but has much older roots: The cellar is part of a 13th-century monastery.

7 **Ye Olde Mitre**, 1 Ely Court. Established in 1546, but part of a much older palace mentioned by Shakespeare in his plays *Richard II* and *Richard III*.

## East to Cockneyland

Like a sentry determined never to leave his post, the Tower of London stands on the far side of London. It has been here since 1078, when William the Conqueror selected it as a perfect defensive site, resolved that he would be the last one to conquer the kingdom. So far, no one else has.

In addition to serving as a fortress, and since 1303 as the home of the United Kingdom's crown jewels, the Tower has also been a royal prison and a place of execution. The Tower's famous inmates include Sir Thomas More and Anne Boleyn, both sent there by Henry VIII; Sir Walter Raleigh, ordered to the Tower by Queen Elizabeth I, who had spent time there herself; and Guy Fawkes, who oversaw the Gunpowder Plot.

Tourist maps of London often end here, their eastern limit marked by the Tower of London and the Tower Hill subway station, their western limit by Kensington Gardens. London, of course, continues east, to districts that saw much industrial development and trade centered around the Port of London. The true Londoner, the Cockney, is said

to be one who was born within the sound of the Bow Bells, the bells of St. Mary-le-Bow Church, east of St. Paul's Cathedral.

In the English folktale "Dick Whittington and His Cat," a poor boy sets out with his feline companion to make his fortune in London, where the streets are supposedly paved with gold. But Dick encounters only discouragement and eventually decides to leave. As he climbs Highgate Hill on his way out of the city, he hears the Bow Bells and believes they are calling him back. He returns, embarks on a series of adventures, and ends up as mayor of the city.

The East End is the realm of the Cockneys. Or at least it was. Now it is as much the home of immigrants—or the sons and daughters of immigrants—from the former empire, as it is for traditional Cockneys. Many of the original East Enders have moved farther out to Essex, parts of which have been called "London over the border." To find the original Cockney, we must travel to the past.

The word "Cockney" itself is an unusual one, and its derivation is not entirely clear. Some say "cockney" originally meant a misshapen egg. It was likely a term

**CHEERS, MATE!**
Eyes trained on the overhead television, customers at the Winston Churchill pub keep close to the bar and their drinks. Pubs continue to be an important social center and a great place to meet the locals.

Tower Bridge is one of the city's much-loved symbols, perhaps the most famous bridge in the world. For many, it marks the eastern limits of tourist London, together with the Tower of London and the nearby H.M.S. *Belfast*. Visitors come to enjoy the view from the top of the towers and to watch the lifting of the bridge.

of disrespect employed by provincials to describe the streetwise Londoner. In any event, it has been in use since before the Great Fire.

So what characterizes the Cockney? First and foremost, Cockneys tend to live in tightly knit communities, squeezed into neighborhoods in numbers that seem almost unnatural. The Bible says that a man must leave his father and mother and cleave to his wife. Over the generations, Cockneys may have cleaved, but they generally didn't leave. Relatives lived nearby, perhaps even next door or a few streets away. And in these compact communities they developed their own distinctive accent.

The most famous "stage Cockney" is the flower girl Eliza Doolittle in George Bernard Shaw's *Pygmalion* and its musical version, *My Fair Lady*. As Eliza showed in her pronunciation of her mentor's name, Henry Higgins—'enry 'iggins—Cockneys often drop their *h*'s when speaking. But what's most distinct about their language is their use of rhyming slang.

The rhyming words generally have nothing to do with the word being rhymed. For example, instead of saying "your mouth," a Cockney might say "your north and south." And instead of saying "your wife," he or she might say "your trouble and strife." To complicate things further, he or she often shortens the rhyme. Thus, "your head" can go from "your loaf of bread" to simply "your loaf." By the same process, "a look" can become "a butcher's," a shortened form of "a butcher's hook."

By the Victorian era, the Cockneys had expanded beyond their original home in the city. The Whitechapel area, just east of the original city walls, was the haunt of Jack the Ripper. The character Fagin had one of his hideaways here in Charles Dickens's *Oliver Twist*. And it was at 272 Whitechapel Road that William Booth founded the Salvation Army in 1878.

## [ Five Famous London Prisons ]

**1** **The Clink**. England's oldest recorded prison, dating from at least the 12th century, and feared for the brutality of its regime until its closure in 1780. "In the Clink" is still a colloquial expression meaning to be in jail.

**2** **Newgate**. London's most notorious prison, opened in 1188. Site of London's gallows and public executions after 1783. Closed in 1902, its site now the home of London's best known court, the Old Bailey.

**3** **Tower of London**. Founded as a castle, but later also a prison whose inmates included some of the most famous names in British history, including Guy Fawkes, Sir Walter Raleigh, Sir Thomas More, and Anne Boleyn, one of the two wives of Henry VIII executed here.

**4** **Wormwood Scrubs**. London's best known working prison, a somber Victorian edifice begun in 1874 using convict labor. Lord Alfred Douglas, companion of Oscar Wilde, and Keith Richards of the Rolling Stones are just two of its past inmates.

**5** **Pentonville**. London's other major working prison was built in 1842 and served as the model for 54 prisons elsewhere in Britain and many hundreds of jails across the British Empire. It was the city's place of execution after 1902. The last hanging, of 21-year-old Edwin Bush, took place on July 6, 1961.

The population of this part of London began to swell further with the arrival of immigrants, particularly Irish in the 18th century and Jews from Eastern Europe in the 19th. Cockneys also spread south across the river to districts like the wonderfully named "Elephant and Castle." The origin of the name is not known for certain. According to one story, it is derived from a vision that a local had while standing on London Bridge, of an elephant with a castle on its back. Not surprisingly, its residents—who have included Charlie Chaplin and Michael Caine—just call their district "the Elephant."

Today, many of the original inhabitants of Cockneyland have moved well beyond earshot of the Bow Bells, and have taken their dropped *h*'s and distinct dialect with them. Their original neighborhoods, pummeled by Hitler's Luftwaffe, were redeveloped by urban planners who took little account of the Cockney way of life. Soulless housing developments and high-rise apartment buildings, or flats, rose in their place.

Today, much of the East End is being transformed by newcomers from the subcontinent, as well as from Africa and the Caribbean, who began to arrive in the 1960s. London is one of the most cosmopolitan cities in the world: More than 300 languages are spoken in the capital, but the highest concentrations of non-native English speakers live in the East End.

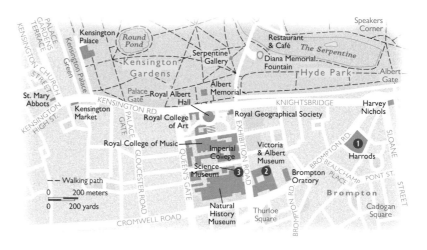

The German bombers that rained so much destruction upon London followed the course of the river from the sea, which provided a flight path right to the Docklands of the East End. Today, business executives have replaced stevedores in the Docklands, which is now a financial center that rivals the square mile of the old City itself. Just where the Luftwaffe pilots would have noticed the great downward bending loop in the Thames, around the Isle of Dogs, modern-day air travelers now see Canary Wharf. Built on the site of the former West India Docks, Canary Wharf contains the city's three tallest skyscrapers.

## An Eye on the Future, an Eye on the Past

The East End is undergoing its latest iteration as London prepares to host the Olympic Games in 2012—which will make it the only city in the world to do so three times. Events for the 2012 Summer Olympics will be held all over the British capital in venues such as Wembley Stadium, Wimbledon, and the Millennium Dome, built across from Canary Wharf to house the "Millennium Experience." But new facilities and infrastructure will also be built, much of it in the East End, which will be home to the Olympic Park.

Of course in London, despite the new buildings and plans for the future, the past is never far away. It is there, perhaps, to remind its people of the former empire that they once ruled.

The great empire poet was Rudyard Kipling. Born in British India, he is famous for the children's stories *The Jungle Book, Rikki-Tikki-Tavi,* and *Kim.* The first English Nobel laureate for literature, Kipling has always been a somewhat controversial

## Knightsbridge and Kensington Walk

A walk around this part of London includes three great museums, two famous stores, two great parks, and the royal residence of Kensington Palace. A good plan would be to allow a full day for the two-and-a-half-mile walk, and to select just one of the three museums, leaving the other two for another day.

**❶ Harrods** is a fairy-lit emporium whose lavishly decorated Food Halls are well worth a visit.

**❷ The Victoria & Albert Museum** proclaims itself "the world's greatest museum of decorative arts," then sets out to prove it.

**❸ The Science Museum** boasts more than 1,000 interactive displays, making it a favorite for all members of the family.

figure, and his writings are perceived as increasingly out of sync with the modern, multicultural world: His poem "The White Man's Burden" (1899) is something of a hymn to imperialism. In Kipling's writings, some see the essence of Victorian character. The virtues of unflappability and stoicism are captured in one of his earlier poems, "If," which was voted Britain's favorite in a 1995 BBC poll.

One line of the poem adorns the wall of the players' entrance at the All England Lawn Tennis and Croquet Club at Wimbledon, a suburb in the southwest of London, as an exhortation to good sportsmanship: "If you can meet with Triumph and Disaster and treat those two impostors just the same. . . ." (For those unable to get a tournament ticket to see the players coming through the famous entrance, Wimbledon does offer tours as well as a museum.)

THE EMPIRE MIGHT be gone, but there is one part of the city that still shows Londoners that they remain very much at the center of the world. Just south of the Isle of Dogs, on the far side of the Thames, is Greenwich. Greenwich first became prominent as the site of a royal palace, where Henry VIII was born, as was his daughter Elizabeth I (doubtless to the great disappointment of the son-obsessed king). The original palace fell into disuse and was eventually rebuilt by Sir Christopher Wren.

An architectural masterpiece, Greenwich Palace is now the home of the Royal Naval College, and is one of London's four UNESCO World Heritage sites (the others being the Tower of London, the Palace of Westminster/Westminster Abbey, and the Royal Botanic Gardens at Kew in the suburb of Richmond to the southwest).

Most famously, Greenwich has given its name to the Greenwich Meridian, location of the Prime Meridian, or 0° longitude. The Prime Meridian passes through the Royal Observatory here. Visitors can stand astride the line so that one foot is planted in the western hemisphere, the other in the eastern. It's appropriate for a country with such a rich history. In London, there's always a sense that you have one foot in the present, one foot in the past.

**ARCHITECTURAL PICKLE**

Saints of a different sort— the 30 St. Mary Axe skyscraper, better known as "the Gherkin," towers behind the 13th-century St. Helen's Bishopsgate in the heart of the financial district.

# Sites and Sights in London

A great introduction to London is the bird's-eye view of the **London Eye**, the largest Ferris wheel in Europe. On a clear day Windsor Castle is visible (25 miles away). One revolution takes about 30 minutes, turning so slowly that passengers easily walk around the "pods" and can disembark and board without the wheel having to stop. *www.londoneye.com/*

The **Thames River Cruises** are popular for good reason. They are a delightful and dramatic introduction to London, floating along the River Thames through the heart of London with views of St. Paul's Cathedral, the Houses of Parliament, the Tower of London, and the commercial hub. *www.citycruises.com*

For the traveler set on really exploring London, The **London Pass** is a bargain. It includes entrance to 55 attractions including the Thames River Cruise, a guidebook, transportation, discounts at many venues, and priority access to sites (no waiting in queues)—a feature that itself is worth the price during peak travel months. *www.londonpass.com*

The **London Underground**—officially called the Underground and, colloquially, the Tube—is the world's first and longest underground railway, with the largest number of stations. The color-coded Tube map is considered a design classic and has influenced subway maps around the world. *www.tfl.gov.uk/*

The sleek steel suspension **Millennium Bridge** for pedestrians only was famously wobbly when it first opened in 2000. Closed for nearly two years, it is now stable and well traveled, linking St. Paul's Cathedral with the Tate Modern across the River Thames and offering outstanding views of London.

Massive and iconic, **St. Paul's Cathedral** is a perfect respite for prayer or contemplation and awe. While here one can ascend to the Whispering Gallery and hear even the softest conversations of those on the opposite side of the vast dome. Steeper steps lead to the open-air Stone Gallery. Finally, a narrow spiral staircase, not for the fainthearted, leads to the Golden Gallery and stupendous views. *www.stpauls.co.uk*

The London Eye

**The Museum of London** holds an astounding collection. London's local museum, its mission is to tell the story of the commercial and political capital of Britain from prehistoric times to the present. Treasures on display include a wealthy Roman's floor mosaic, a medieval merchant's counting table, a model of the Tudor and Stuart sovereigns' lost Whitehall Palace, and dresses made of Spitalfields silk. London's glories, atrocities, and failures are all represented here. *www.museumoflondon.org.uk*

**Westminster**, the nation's political and royal hub, has a totally different atmosphere from that of the commercial City. Unlike the densely packed "Square Mile," this is an area of palaces and large open spaces, of public buildings and public spectacle, of national politics, and unfenced royal estates.

**Westminster Abbey** is not only the largest and loveliest Gothic church in London but very evidently the point where the religious, political, and monarchical lives of the nation come together. This site has been the scene of 38 coronations since that of William the Conqueror. At the east end are the Royal Chapels, where the monarchs rest. Poets' Corner, on the south side, holds monuments to William Shakespeare, Lewis Carroll, Charles Dickens, Thomas Hardy, and D. H. Lawrence, among the many esteemed literary giants of Britain. *www.westminster-abbey.org*

The Victorian Gothic riverside **Palace of Westminster,** with its landmark Big Ben clock tower, is better known as the Houses of Parliament. It has long dominated both the landscape and the day-to-day life of the area. This great building has 1,200 rooms, two miles of corridor, 100 staircases, and a stunning river facade that stretches 320 yards long. *www.parliament.uk*

**10 Downing Street**, the legendary traditional home of the British prime minister, lies behind massive gates in Parliament Square. Although the residence is not open to the public, the official website features a virtual tour. *www.number10.gov.uk/tour*

The maze of underground **Cabinet War Rooms**, Prime Minister Winston Churchill's bunker and headquarters during World War II, are still furnished and open to the public, as is the adjacent Churchill Museum, which illuminates the man, his life, and his legacy. *http://cwr.iwm.org.uk*

The imposing **Buckingham Palace**, the sovereign's London home, is a focal point of the capital. Outside the railings, people gather on momentous occasions to cheer the Queen and the royal family, who come out onto the balcony between the great central columns.
*www.royal.gov.uk/TheRoyalResidences/BuckinghamPalace/BuckinghamPalace.aspx*

The **Changing of the Guard** ceremony outside Buckingham Palace, adjacent to St. James's Park, is held daily throughout the summer months at 11:30 a.m. During the rest of the year it takes place every other day.
*www.changing-the-guard.com*

One of the world's most impressive national museums in the world, the **National Gallery** is home to a collection of about 2,000 paintings that tell the story of European painting from the 13th century to the 19th.
*www.nationalgallery.org.uk*

**Piccadilly Circus** is the lively and famous circular open public space in London's West End in Westminster connecting Regent Street with the major commercial Piccadilly Street.

More than 800 shops in Britain have a **royal coat of arms** fixed above the door, indicating that the business holds a royal warrant to supply "by appointment" to the royal family. This honor and tradition, which is a coveted marketing tool, began in the Middle Ages.

Once one of London's raunchiest and scariest sections, **Soho** today has become a favorite neighborhood for locals and visitors alike. The maze of narrow streets, passages, and courts, once filled with seedy bars and prostitutes, is not exactly pristine, but it's a great area in which to wander. It also offers interesting restaurants, sleek bars, and fun and fashionable shops.

The **British Museum** is vast and daunting to visit, the home of the Rosetta Stone, the Elgin Marbles, prehistoric bones, whole palace rooms, and the beloved and legendary Reading Room, among many treasures.
*www.britishmuseum.org*

The Rosetta Stone, British Museum

Drawing some of the largest crowds in London, **Madame Tussauds** waxwork temple to the famous, infamous, and sometimes unremarkable opened in 1835. The motley collection includes British prime ministers and U.S. Presidents; members of the British royal family; Vladimir Lenin; and a wide range of well-known entertainers, politicians, and other characters.
*www.madametussauds.com/London*

**Harrods**, the world's largest and most famous store, sprawls over seven floors and 20 acres. Every day, 4,000 staff serve 35,000 customers and take in nearly three million dollars.
*www.harrods.com.*

**The Tate** Britain houses the national collection of British art from 1500 to the present day—the foremost collection of its kind—in renovated and expanded buildings on the north bank of the Thames. A century after it opened in 1897, the Tate split into two. The modern international collection is now housed in the separate Tate Modern

building in Southwark on the south bank. Visitors there enter the building on a ramp and descend into the Turbine Hall, which is a "covered street," and proceed through a series of top- and side-lit galleries into the other areas of the building. The top level is worth a visit if only for the stunning views of the river and the rest of London. The Tate Boat plies between the two buildings. The Tate also has two outposts: one in Liverpool and the other in St. Ives, Cornwall.
*www.tate.org.uk/britain*

**The Tower of London,** Britain's most perfect surviving medieval fort, is tucked behind the sleek City towers. It is forgotten by most Londoners but perpetually popular with visitors. It's not only a tower; it contains a palace, prisons, an execution site, chapels, museums, and the Beefeaters, the entertaining guides who are officially, if only ceremonially, the guardians of the crown jewels.
*www.hrp.org.uk/toweroflondon*

One of the most recognizable bridges in the world, **Tower Bridge** is Gothic in style but was extremely modern when it was completed and dedicated in 1894. Elevators take visitors to the Tower Bridge Experience, an exhibition about the bridge and the Engine Rooms, whose coal-fired boilers drove the hydraulic system until electrification in 1976.
*www.towerbridge.org.uk/TBE/EN*

London's **South Bank** is known for its excellent entertainment venues—museums for design, modern art, war, and underwater life are interspersed with theaters, concert halls, restaurants, and a fine cathedral.

**Shakespeare's Globe Theatre** reopened in 1997, 200 yards from the original location. The designers used contemporary illustrations and archaeological evidence, together with traditional materials and techniques, to re-create the Tudor theater: a polygonal building of 20 three-story wooden bays with a thatched roof.
*www.shakespeares-globe.org*

## 4

Southern England

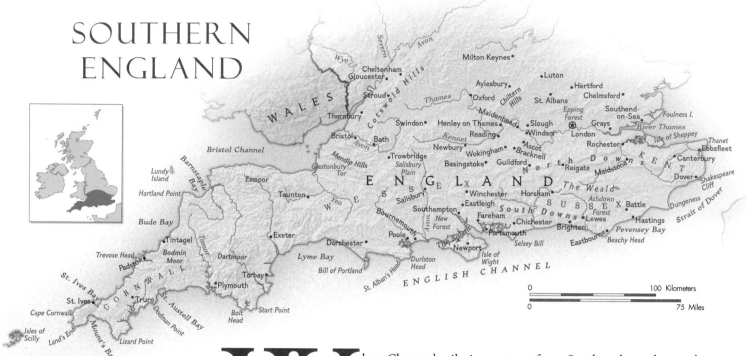

# SOUTHERN ENGLAND

**GETTING
YOUR BEARINGS**

Southern England stretches from
Kent in the east to Cornwall
in the west, and includes the
offshore Isle of Wight and Scilly
Isles. The region's long southern
coastline looks across the English
Channel toward France. To its
north lies Wales, the Midlands,
and East Anglia. *Previous pages:
The Seven Sisters, East Sussex.*

When Chaucer's pilgrims set out from Southwark on the south bank of the River Thames, they were bound for Canterbury, 60 miles to the southeast. There stood the great cathedral, in the county of Kent.

Kent is one of the "home counties" that surround London, and is considered the Garden of England. It is also the closest part of England to the continent (even sharing a border of sorts with France in the middle of the Channel Tunnel).

It is in Kent, at the Strait of Dover, where the English Channel narrows to just 21 miles and cross-Channel swimmers endeavor to swim to France. It is also where Frenchman Louis Blériot became the first pilot to fly from France to England. At 4:35 a.m. on July 25, 1909, Blériot lifted off from the Pas de Calais. Thirty-six minutes later, the white cliffs of Dover flashing beneath him, he touched down in England. But although the distance is short and it is quick to traverse, the Strait of Dover has held at bay some of the world's great powers. Adolf Hitler was never able to cross it. Napoleon Bonaparte was similarly unsuccessful.

The ancient Romans, of course, made the crossing to Britain; Kent was where they first stepped ashore. Believing that the Britons had been abetting their Celtic cousins, the Gauls, Julius Caesar traversed the Channel in 55 B.C. and again a year later. But it wasn't until A.D. 43 that they arrived in force, during the reign of Emperor Claudius. After establishing a beachhead on the south coast, they began to move inland. The era of Roman Britain had begun.

Just as Britain was changing, Rome itself was being transformed. The practice of Christianity had begun to spread in the empire during Claudius's day, though believers would soon undergo a long period of persecution. Things finally changed when the emperor Constantine issued the Edict of Milan in 313, which proclaimed religious toleration throughout his vast realm.

Changes in Rome would have a dramatic impact on the islands off the northwest coast of Europe. Although Christianity had first come to Britain with the Roman legionnaires who were stationed there, hundreds of years later, in 595, Pope Gregory the Great decided the Holy See should send a missionary to the island to spread the faith. According to the Venerable Bede, the eighth-century author of *The Ecclesiastical History of the English People,* Gregory had seen fair-haired slaves from Britain in Rome's slave market one day and determined that the church should evangelize the land. The man Gregory chose for the mission was Augustine—not the great church father Augustine of Hippo, who was long since dead, but Augustine the Benedictine monk, the prior of a monastery in Rome.

Pope Gregory sent Augustine specifically to the kingdom of Kent. In 597, he and a band of around 40 monks and other followers set off from Rome. Daunted by the prospect of their mission, however, some got cold feet on the way—and not just at the thought of the chilly northern climates that lay ahead. These monks eventually prevailed upon Augustine to return to the pope to seek his permission to call off the expedition. But Gregory was determined that the mission to Britain should proceed: He sent Augustine back to the party with letters of encouragement. The journey resumed, and the little band finally arrived at Kent. Today, a stone cross stands in the village of Ebbsfleet to mark the spot where, according to tradition, Augustine came ashore (next to the appropriately named St. Augustine's Golf Club).

Once on terra firma, as Augustine and his Latin-speaking brothers would have no doubt called it, the band made its way inland to the biggest town in the region, Canterbury. Here, Augustine served as bishop, and later as archbishop, sending out missionaries to other parts of southern England. At first, he worked from the relatively modest St. Martin's Church, the oldest church in England, where the local rulers worshipped. Queen Bertha was already a believer when Augustine arrived; thanks to Augustine's efforts, the conversion of her husband, King Ethelbert, would follow quickly thereafter.

## [ A Quartet of Cathedral Towns ]

1 **Exeter** The cobbled streets of Devon's main city, which grew rich on the export of wool in Tudor times, contain Roman, Saxon, Norman, Georgian, and many more historical monuments, none more impressive than the glorious Gothic cathedral, begun in 1140, but built on a site whose religious significance dates back to at least the fifth century.

2 **Salisbury** The spire of the 13th-century Salisbury Cathedral—the highest in England—dominates what has been a pivotal provincial center for over 1,000 years. The city began life as Old Sarum, initially an Iron Age fort and one of the most important settlements in southern England, now an impressive set of ramparts two miles from the present town.

3 **Wells** Wells is England's smallest city (generally defined by the presence of a cathedral and bishopric) and is little visited, even by the English. But it is home to one of the country's most beautiful medieval ensembles, dominated by the moated Bishops' Palace and the cathedral church of St. Andrew (begun in 1108) and its 13th-century west front, adorned with more than 300 sculpted figures.

4 **Winchester** Ancient capital of Wessex and the Saxon kings, including Arthur the Great (who reigned from 871 to 899), Winchester has always been one of the most important cities in England. It was here that William the Conqueror claimed the English throne, and where, in 1085, he commissioned local monks to draw up the Domesday Book. The Normans' majestic cathedral, one of the great buildings of southern England, still dominates the city.

Near this church Augustine founded a cathedral, which has been rebuilt and enlarged over time to become what it is today. Canterbury early became a center of pilgrimage. Over the centuries, many came to visit Augustine's shrine. But Chaucer's pilgrims made the journey not to venerate the Roman-born archbishop but another, later archbishop of Canterbury: Thomas Becket.

## Murder at the Cathedral

Becket was archbishop of Canterbury during the reign of King Henry II. Monarch and cleric, the onetime friends often argued over the privileges and independence of the church. After Henry learned that Becket had excommunicated a number of bishops who supported the king in his dispute, he is said to have exclaimed, "Who will rid me of this turbulent priest?"

**STAINED GLASS DEATH**

This depiction of the murder of Thomas Becket, the archbishop of Canterbury who ran afoul of his king, Henry II, is just part of Canterbury Cathedral's wealth of stained glass.

Within earshot of the king were several knights who were more than prepared to do so, and in the process, they hoped, win Henry's favor. Four days after Christmas 1170, they made their way to Canterbury, where they found the "turbulent priest" in his own cathedral. They confronted him, swords in hands, and struck him down. In the aftermath, Beckett was venerated as a martyr and canonized by the pope. Filled with remorse, Henry undertook a humiliating display of public penance. It was not the first or the last time that an English ruler would have a dispute with an English archbishop.

Becket suffered rough treatment at the hands of the royals even after his death. His shrine at the cathedral was destroyed at the order of another Henry, Henry VIII, at the time of the Dissolution of the Monasteries. Today, a lit candle marks the place of the shrine and an altar commemorates the spot where Becket was martyred.

The Romans had originally brought Christianity to Britain. Why then did Pope Gregory later feel the need to send missionaries back to the island? What had happened in the interim? In a word—invasion.

The slaves in Rome that had so moved the heart of Gregory were not Celtic Britons. Nor were Augustine's new parishioners in Canterbury. They were newcomers—English. And the English were, or had been, pagans.

When the Romans pulled out of Britain at the end of the fourth century, they left the country open to attack. The Picts and the Irish threatened from the un-Romanized far north and west, and Germanic tribes from across the sea were poised to pounce to the east. The Britons managed to repel a number of incursions, but the country looked increasingly vulnerable. By the early years of the fifth century, the Saxons had gained a foothold, and once ashore, they created their own settlements.

More and more Saxons joined them, as did increasing numbers of Angles, Jutes, and Frisians. The warlike newcomers pushed the Britons—and their Christianity—to

**PLACE OF PILGRIMAGE**
Canterbury Cathedral has drawn pilgrims since Chaucer's time and beyond. Today's visitors can get there with a two-hour train ride from London's Victoria Station.

the north and the west. In the south of Britain the invaders set up their own kingdoms that would merge to become the English nation. The name "Angle" endures in the word "England," while "Saxon" survives in the Gaelic term *Sassenach*, now mostly used by Scots as a term of disparagement for the English.

The county names in the south of England likewise reflect the changes brought about by the Anglo-Saxon invasion. Sussex, the next county over from Kent, comes from the Old English for "South Saxons." And it was here that the next invaders would land, on the Sussex coast near the town of Hastings.

## Battle at Hastings

As the year 1066 began, Harold Godwinson was worried. He had just ascended the throne of Anglo-Saxon England after the death of King Edward the Confessor. But a rival had emerged: William, Duke of Normandy, who hailed from the French side of the English Channel. William, a cousin of Edward, claimed that the old king had promised the throne to him—and he decided to press his claim. William assembled an army of Europe's best foot soldiers, prized archers, and cavalrymen. They were transported to England by a fleet of around 700 ships, and landed at what is now known as Normans Bay, not far from Hastings.

Upon hearing about William's arrival, King Harold set off from London with his own army, determined to show that he could hold on to the crown that he had so recently acquired. He took up a position on high ground that barred the way north to the capital and waited for the Normans to come.

**NORMAN CONQUEST**
Armed horsemen move across the Bayeux Tapestry, which commemorates William the Conqueror's victory over the English at the Battle of Hastings. The tapestry is not to be found in England, however, but in a special museum in the town of Bayeux in Normandy.

Come they did. But the Saxons, safe behind their interlocking shields, were hard to move. Only when the Normans started to pull back, and the Saxons—sensing victory—abandoned their defensive positions atop the hill, did the battle begin to change. In the midst of the fighting, William ordered his archers forward. They fired volley after volley of arrows into the Saxon ranks, one of which struck Harold in the eye. As the English ranks thinned, Norman foot soldiers surged forward. William and his cavalrymen followed, one of them finishing off the wounded Saxon king. Their leader dead, most of the English army turned and fled the field. The way to London lay open. The Norman conquest of England had begun.

Today, the small town of Battle sits on the site of the Battle of Hastings. The high altar of the town's Abbey church once marked the spot where Harold is said to have met his death. But Henry VIII did much to cover these tracks. The structure was destroyed at the time of the English Reformation, and now the place where King Harold fell is marked by a plaque on the ground.

## London-by-the-Sea

Upon their victory, William and his warriors traveled the 60 or so miles north to London. Today, many day-trippers make the same journey south from the capital. Around the coast from Hastings, past Normans Bay and Pevensey Bay,

sits Eastbourne. A popular Victorian resort since a railway line connected it with the metropolis, genteel Eastbourne is mostly thought of today as a retirement community.

Moving farther west along the Sussex coastline is another resort, more associated with the 1960s than the 1860s: bold, brash Brighton. Brighton is mentioned as far back as the Domesday Book of 1086, when the Normans who fought at Hastings began to make a record of the kingdom that they had conquered. The town received a great boost when the future King

---

**IN WINCHESTER**

The Great Hall of 1235 boasts the massive **Round Table,** like a giant dartboard in black and white with a red-lipped and curly-bearded King Arthur seated at the top. Legend says that Merlin created it by magic for Arthur's court, but it is, in fact, a resplendent medieval fake.

---

George IV visited in 1783. The ostentatious Royal Pavilion he built there combines Indian design outside with Chinese design inside—"a collection of stone pumpkins and pepper pots," said one contemporary commentator. Another person quipped, "One would think that St. Paul's Cathedral had come to Brighton and pupped."

Reachable in less than an hour by train from the capital's Victoria Station, Brighton—dubbed London-by-the-Sea—has long been a favorite destination for day-trippers. They come for the clubs and restaurants, the amusement arcades along Brighton Pier, and the shingle beach. The Brighton Festival, held in May, is the largest arts festival in Britain after the one in Edinburgh. In the Swinging Sixties, groups of young Londoners flocked here, many ignoring the train in favor of their own motorized forms of transport. Often they belonged to one of two different, and antagonistic, youth movements: the Mods and the Rockers.

The Mods dressed in designer suits under parka jackets and rode Vespa or Lambretta scooters adorned with multiple mirrors. Their iconic rock band

**ROUND TABLE**
Visitors to Winchester hoping for evidence of the elusive Arthur have to settle for this 13th-century table, made as a model of the British king's legendary round table.

was The Who, whose singer Roger Daltrey paid homage to the journey "from Soho down to Brighton" in the song "Pinball Wizard." The Rockers preferred to dress in leather and ride large motorcycles. Their favorite artists included Elvis Presley and Gene Vincent. One holiday weekend in 1964, more than a thousand Mods and Rockers waged running battles on the shingle beach at Brighton. The events of the weekend were dramatized in The Who's rock opera (and later film) *Quadrophenia*.

## [ Coastal Landmarks ]

**1 Beachy Head** One of the high points of England's most striking and iconic landscapes, this series of high chalk cliffs stretches along part of England's southeast coast, culminating in the famous White Cliffs of Dover.

**2 Chesil Beach** One of England's most spectacular coastal features, more than 17 miles long, and consisting of a 100-million-ton, 50-feet-high pebble ridge being driven inland by tides and currents at a rate of 17 feet a year.

**3 The Cobb** Lyme Regis is one of the principal towns on the Jurassic Coast, noted for its fossil-filled beaches and the Cobb, an ancient and iconic harbor defense immortalized in the film of John Fowles's novel *The French Lieutenant's Woman* (1981).

**4 The Jurassic Coast** England's first natural (as opposed to cultural) UNESCO World Heritage site stretches for 95 miles from Exmouth in East Devon to beyond Swanage, Dorset, and embraces 185 million years of geological history, with a wealth of fossils and striking coastal features, such as Lulworth Cover and Durdle Door, a vast 150-million-year-old Portland limestone arch.

**5 Land's End** This dramatic rocky headland in Cornwall is known by name to virtually everyone in England, thanks to the fact that it is considered the westernmost point of the mainland United Kingdom.

**LAND'S END CASTLE**

An ancient carved face (opposite) gazes out to sea at St. Michael's Mount, not far from Land's End in Cornwall. Visits to the castle in the background are organized through the National Trust.

## Battle of Britain

Back during the summer of 1940, a different kind of warfare raged on the south coast of England. In the skies over this part of the country, the fighter pilots of the Royal Air Force fought with the German fighter planes and Luftwaffe bombers who were on their way to pound Britain's cities.

World War II had been under way for almost a year by then. Country after country had fallen to the Nazis on the European mainland, most significantly France in June 1940. Britain now stood alone. With the defeat of the country's main ally on the continent, Prime Minister Winston Churchill addressed the House of Commons: "The Battle of France is over. I expect that the Battle of Britain is about to begin. Upon this battle depends the survival of Christian civilization . . . Let us therefore brace ourselves to our duties, and so bear ourselves, that if the British Empire and its Commonwealth last for a thousand years, men will still say, 'This was their finest hour.'"

The British had good reason to brace themselves for the coming onslaught. Before Hitler could send his armies across the English Channel, though, he had to control the airspace over it by destroying the Royal Air Force (RAF). The Luftwaffe estimated that this could be done in four days. Then its bombers would be able to fly across Britain, taking out military installations and aircraft production facilities at will.

And so the Battle of Britain began with German efforts to wipe out the RAF, either in the air or on the ground. Week after week along the south coast, British fighter pilots scrambled into their Spitfires and Hurricanes to intercept the German formations, inflicting disproportionate damage on the enemy. The British were losing planes, too. But although factories were able to replace the aircraft, the air force could not find enough pilots to fly them. Soon the overwhelming numbers on the German

side would prove decisive. Fortunately, a decision made by Hitler saved the RAF—and perhaps the nation—from eventual defeat.

From the outset, the German leader had forbidden the bombing of British cities, saving it as an absolute last resort. During one raid, though, Luftwaffe bombers (accidentally, it seems) dropped their payload on London. Two days later, RAF bombers retaliated by hitting Berlin. Furious, Hitler ordered the wholesale bombing of the British capital. On September 7, 1940, nearly 400 Luftwaffe bombers escorted by 600 fighter planes began pounding the east end of London around the clock.

In the weeks ahead, the citizens of London, Birmingham, Coventry, Belfast, and other British cities suffered terrible casualties. But in switching his attention to Britain's most populous cities, Hitler had taken his eye off the Royal Air Force and its airfields in southern England. This provided breathing space for the RAF to lick its wounds, build up its strength again, and take to the air to challenge the waves of German warplanes.

On September 15, the British inflicted devastating losses on the enemy during two massive German attacks. Some 60 Luftwaffe aircraft were shot down, while less than half that number of RAF planes were lost. In response, Hitler called off the invasion. His bombers would continue their campaign of terror against Britain's cities, but thanks to the air force's fighter pilots, the threat of a seaborne landing on the south coast of England was gone. As Churchill told the members of the House of Commons, "Never in the field of human conflict was so much owed by so many to so few."

## Great Ports

Having held off the German invasion, Britain began to prepare for the Allied invasion of Nazi-occupied Europe. The south coast of England transformed itself into one huge armed camp. The two great port cities of Portsmouth and Southampton played a pivotal role in the operation. From these points, the convoys of the great D-Day landings set forth in June 1944, skirting around the diamond-shaped Isle of Wight and out toward France.

Hitler had expected the invasion force to make the short Channel crossing to the Pas de Calais. But the Allies surprised him by taking the longer route to

## [ Portsmouth's Historic Ships ]

1 **H.M.S. *Victory*** One of three famous ships in the Portsmouth Historic Dockyard. Flagship of Lord Nelson, Britain's greatest admiral, at the Battle of Trafalgar (1805), in which Nelson defeated the French. Once had a crew of 850 and is the oldest commissioned ship in the Royal Navy, still being the official flagship of the Second Sea Lord.

2 ***Mary Rose*** A 700-ton Tudor warship beloved of Henry VIII, which sank in the English Channel, in mysterious circumstances, in 1545, but which was raised from the seabed in a remarkable piece of marine archaeology in 1982.

3 **H.M.S. *Warrior*** Commissioned in 1860, during the reign of Queen Victoria, and at its launch, the most advanced warship in the world. It looks much as it did 150 years ago, when it marked the transition from wood to iron ships, and from sail to steam power.

**H.M.S. *VICTORY***
Built in the mid-18th century, the *Victory* was Horatio Nelson's flagship at the Battle of Trafalgar. It is the oldest naval ship still in commission, and can be seen in dry dock in Portsmouth's Naval Heritage Area.

Normandy. It was the largest single-day amphibious operation of all time as some 160,000 Allied troops set out for beaches that were code-named Utah, Omaha, Gold, Juno, and Sword.

Portsmouth, in the county of Hampshire, has a long and distinguished maritime record in the service of the nation, and was the Royal Navy's home port during the centuries in which Britannia ruled the waves. Today, Henry VIII's flagship, the *Mary Rose,* bobs at anchor at the historic dockyard. Also here is the restored—and aptly named—H.M.S. *Victory,* aboard which Lord

**HARDY'S COTTAGE**

Visitors to Hardy's Cottage in Dorset find the thatched home and its garden much as they were when the writer lived there.

---

### IN DORSET

The death of Thomas Hardy evoked controversy over the location of his burial. A novel, if grisly, compromise resulted: His heart was removed and buried in his preferred site, **Stinsford Church graveyard,** next to his first wife, Emma. His remaining ashes went to Poets' Corner in Westminster Abbey, for posterity.

---

Horatio Nelson won a great battle over the French at Trafalgar, though at the cost of his own life.

The Battle of Trafalgar was the decisive sea battle of the Napoleonic Wars. Under the command of Nelson, a British force defeated a larger fleet of French and Spanish ships off the coast of Spain. The British sank 22 of the enemies' ships, without a single loss of their own. The victory confirmed the Royal Navy's supremacy in European waters—and the hopelessness of French plans to send an invasion force across the Channel.

## Hardy Country

Moving from Hampshire into Dorset means entering Thomas Hardy country. This area of southwest England is immortalized in Hardy's "Wessex novels": *Under the Greenwood Tree, Far from the Madding Crowd, The Return of the Native,* and *Tess of the d'Urbervilles.*

Just north of the town of Dorchester is Hardy's Cottage, where the author was born in 1840 and lived for the first 34 years of his

life. He wrote *Far from the Madding Crowd* here, and used it as the setting for tranter Dewy's house in *Under the Greenwood Tree*. The thatched cottage was built by Hardy's grandfather, a known smuggler, and the peephole in the porch is said to have been used to watch for the authorities. The main bedroom, where Hardy was born, looks east toward the desolate Egdon Heath. In *The Return of the Native,* the heath symbolizes the dark mood that runs through so much of Hardy's work.

North of Dorset is the county of Wiltshire, home to the most famous collection of standing stones from the ancient world, Stonehenge, on Salisbury Plain. The first of the great stones were maneuvered into place here around 2950 B.C., and there were additions and modifications to the arrangement until approximately 1600 B.C. The effort required to move the stones—some of them from as far away as 200 miles—would have been enormous.

What, precisely, was its purpose? Speculations have abounded over the centuries. Stonehenge has been called a temple to the sun (on Midsummer Day, June 24, when viewed from the central Altar Stone, the sun rises directly over the Heel Stone 256 feet away). It has also been called a symbol of power and status, used for specific ceremonial purposes, and an observatory for seasonal timekeeping. One recent theory is that it was a place of healing, another that it was a place for the ancestral dead.

In *Tess of the d'Urbervilles,* Hardy alludes to another, pagan association with the mysterious standing stones. As the book reaches its climax, the tragic figure of Tess, ever the innocent victim, finds herself at Stonehenge, where she pauses to rest. She lies on the Altar Stone, its surface still warm from the sun. Hardy's heroine, "a pure woman," as the subtitle of the book tells us, is made ready for her final act of sacrifice.

The mystery surrounding the stones is, doubtless, part of their attraction. In the summer of 1688, the diarist Samuel Pepys hired a horse and a guide and set out across the expanse of Salisbury Plain to visit Stonehenge. The stones, he wrote, were "as prodigious as any tales I ever heard of them and worth going this journey to see. God knows what their use was."

## The "English Riviera"

Leaving Dorset and going into Devon, we enter what Basil Fawlty, the hapless innkeeper from the classic BBC comedy series *Fawlty Towers*, would have us believe is the "English Riviera." In it, John Cleese's character runs a hotel in Torquay, and Fawlty likes to impress visitors by talking up the exotic

## STONEHENGE

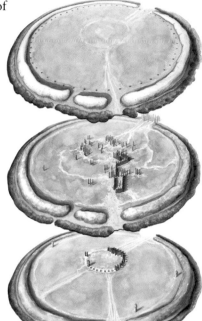

A circular ditch-and-bank monument, approximately 375 feet across, is cut into the Salisbury Plain about 3000 B.C.

In the neolithic period, timber posts are erected in linear patterns. The site is used as a cemetery.

By 2500 B.C. pairs of four-ton bluestones are brought about 250 miles from Wales.

Stonehenge gains its iconic shape with the creation of the 16-foot-high Sarsen Circle—30 worked stones topped by lintels.

Bluestones that had been cast aside are repositioned as a circle and a double ring of pits is dug.

**STONE CIPHER**
The great stone circle of Stonehenge, whose stages of construction are shown above, stands as it has done for millennia on Salisbury Plain. Its exact purpose remains a mystery.

qualities of the English town. He does have a point, for the palm trees and other tropical plants of this part of coastal Britain do testify to the particular warming powers of the Gulf Stream waters. The "warmth" of the welcome extended by the class-obsessed, neurotic Fawlty, however, is another matter.

Agatha Christie, the "Queen of Crime," was born in Torquay and lived much of her life there. She's been called the bestselling author of all time, with only the Bible selling more copies than her books. Christie's classic whodunit, *The Mousetrap*—performed at London's St. Martin's Theatre—is the world's longest running play. Some of her novels were set in her hometown, in quaint English villages, or in London. But Christie's mystery novels also transported her readers to places all around the world, such as in *Murder on the Orient Express* and *Death on the Nile,* starring her famed Belgian detective, Hercule Poirot.

It's said that Christie grew tired of Poirot in the end, much as Sir Arthur Conan Doyle did of Sherlock Holmes. Unlike Conan Doyle, she refused to kill off her diminutive detective while he was still popular with the reading public. But she did not want him to outlive her. An elderly and infirm Poirot eventually dies in *Curtain* (1975), the last of Christie's books to be published during her lifetime. Christie was more fond of her other main protagonist, Miss Marple, who is featured in *The Murder at the Vicarage* and *4.50 from Paddington.* Miss Marple fared better than Poirot in the end, retiring to the charms of the village of St. Mary Mead.

Inland from Torquay is Dartmoor, a wild and desolate place with equally wild legends, which is perhaps where Conan Doyle was tempted to do away with Holmes. For it was here that the great sleuth and Dr. Watson confronted the awful "hound from hell" in *The Hound of the Baskervilles.*

Back on the coast, just before the border with Cornwall, is Plymouth. From here, many sea

**PANCAKE DAY**

A group of young trainee choristers flip pancakes in front of Salisbury Cathedral in celebration of Shrove Tuesday. The day is traditionally one of preparation for the fast of Lent.

captains have sailed out into waters now as much Atlantic as Channel. In November 1577, Sir Francis Drake set out from Plymouth aboard the *Golden Hinde* to circumnavigate the world, and nearly two years later he returned, the first captain to successfully make the voyage (Portugal's Ferdinand Magellan having died on the way home in his attempt).

In 1588, the swashbuckling Drake boldly sailed out to battle the Spanish Armada, which was bent on invading England. And in 1620, the Pilgrim Fathers left Plymouth for the New World. A century later, Captain James Cook departed for his three-year voyage through the Pacific to Australia and New Zealand.

Plymouth continues to send forth great mariners. In 1966, the year England's World Cup–winning soccer team was performing great feats on dry land, Francis Chichester became the first yachtsman to single-handedly sail around the world. A modern-day Drake, he was also knighted as Sir Francis by the current Queen Elizabeth on his return.

## Celtic Cornwall

A traditional tale from the far southwest of England claims that the devil would not dare cross the River Tamar for fear of being turned into a pasty filling. For the River Tamar marks the boundary of Cornwall. And a pasty—pronounced PAS-tee, with a short *a,* as in "cat"—is a traditional Cornish pie filled with diced beef, sliced potato, and onion.

Cornwall, where mainland England ends, is a long peninsula thrusting out toward the Celtic Sea, which also washes the coasts of Wales, Ireland, and Brittany in France. Like Cornwall, these are all Celtic lands. It was to this part of the country that the ancient Celts retreated in the face of the Saxon advance. And it is in this region of England that the legends of the great Saxon foe, King Arthur, are strongest.

In Cornwall, the locals preserved the Celtic language until about 200 years ago, and they held on to the practice of tin mining—one of the reasons the Romans came to Britain in the first place—until 1998. The south coast of the county is all high headlands and sandy bays, curving inexorably toward the forked tip to the wild and seldom-visited Lizard Peninsula and on to Land's End. There, England tapers off in pinnacles and stacks of granite that disappear under the sea, only to resurface for one

## [ Five Ancient Sites ]

**1 Avebury** Overshadowed by the fame of nearby Stonehenge, but in many ways more impressive: With a diameter of 1,142 feet, it is the world's largest stone circle and dates from 2500 to 2200 B.C. The surrounding countryside is scattered with hundreds of other ancient stones and burial mounds.

**2 Cerne Abbas Giant** Ancient figures—often horses—cut into the chalk grassland are common across the hills of southern England, but none are as celebrated as this 180-foot-high nude and famously well-endowed male figure near Dorchester, in Dorset. Its age is unknown. The first historical reference comes in 1654, but it may be Roman, or older.

**3 Maiden Castle** Iron Age earth fortifications adorn many hilltops in southern England. None are as impressive as Maiden Castle, near Dorchester, which dates from around 500 B.C. and covers an area equivalent to 50 soccer fields, making it the largest such fort in Britain.

**4 Silbury Hill** This spectacular manmade hill near Avebury is 4,500 years old and over 120 feet high, making it the largest constructed mound in Europe. The reasons for its creation are unknown, and no artifacts have ever been found.

**5 Stonehenge** Britain's most famous archaeological site is around 5,000 years old, but although there have been many theories, nobody is precisely sure of the function served by the majestic stone circle and its surrounding monuments.

**ANCIENT ARTIFACTS**
Opposite, visitors walk among the standing stones at Avebury, a World Heritage site in Wiltshire. Sometimes archaeologists need to dig a little more carefully to find artifacts of the past, such as the ancient inland brooch above, excavated at a site on the Scilly Isles.

last hurrah in the archipelago known as the Isles of Scilly, some 28 miles off Land's End. A subtropical paradise, the exotic species that thrive on the Scillies might even earn a word of praise from Torquay-proud Basil Fawlty. *Might*.

Rounding to the north side of Cornwall, the coast becomes bleaker and more rugged, an exposed stretch of cliffs and rocky coves dotted with towns like St. Ives (where a branch of the Tate Gallery is located), Padstow, and Tintagel. On the headland at Tintagel, jutting out into the sea, are the ruins of a castle that was a stronghold of the earls of Cornwall from the 12th to the 15th centuries. But the castle is thought to sit on the site of an even earlier fortress dating back to the fifth or the sixth century. It is said that this castle was the birthplace of Arthur—the site of Camelot.

By necessity, phrases like "thought to" and "it is said" frequently accompany any talk of the legendary fifth-century King of the Britons. King Arthur may have been based on a historical figure, as the leader of a group of armed horsemen who resisted the invading Saxons immediately after the Roman withdrawal from Britain. But his story has been greatly enhanced over the centuries, germinating into a collection of ancient tales about the deeds of knights errant who roamed the world in search of adventure.

**CORNISH TREATS**
Cornish pasties are pinched into shape, above. Opposite, Tintagel Castle, a tourist site run by the English Heritage Organization, is the reputed birthplace of King Arthur.

At sea level in Tintagel is a beach and the entrance to Merlin's Cave. According to Alfred Lord Tennyson's *Idylls of the King*, Arthur and Merlin first met here. The magician became Arthur's tutor, and he was by the young king's side when Arthur happened upon the sword "Excalibur" that was embedded in an anvil on top of a stone. On the sword were these prophetic words: "Whoever pulls this sword from this stone and anvil is the rightful-born king." After many others had failed, Arthur pulled out the sword with little effort.

The young king gathered a band of dedicated knights around him, including Galahad, Bors, Perceval, Gareth, and Gawain. Their purpose was to "live pure, speak true, right wrong, follow the King." One of the most famous tales associated with Arthur and his Knights of the Round Table is their quest for the Holy Grail. This was the chalice used by Christ and his disciples at the Last Supper. The story, pieced together from several versions, tells how Pontius Pilate gave the chalice to Joseph of Arimathea, who used it to collect the blood of Christ on the cross. Joseph eventually made his way to southwestern Britain, where he founded Glastonbury Abbey (now the site of the famous Glastonbury Festival). There, he buried the Grail. Merlin is said to have related this story of the Holy Grail to the knights, and Sir Perceval, Sir Galahad, and Sir Bors set off to find it, their quest a Christian allegory for the believer's search for divine grace.

The most famous of the knights, Lancelot, fell in love with Queen Guinevere and ultimately brought about the destruction of the realm. It is said that Arthur died after the traitor Mordred exposed Guinevere's adultery and tried to seize his throne. The king killed Mordred in single combat, but was mortally wounded in the process. His supposed final resting place is not far from Tintagel.

Rising above the Somerset countryside, this scene of Arthur's final battle—Glastonbury Tor—is today topped by a 14th-century church tower. The knoll is thought to be the "pointed rock" of Avalon, where Arthur dies from his wounds. Legend has it that the "once and future king" of the Britons and his faithful knights lie sleeping under Glastonbury Tor, ready to arise and lead their country in its time of greatest peril.

## Roman Bath

Few man-made features of the southwest predate the time of King Arthur. But the Roman remains in the spa town of Bath are one spectacular exception. The Romans arrived here around A.D. 44, and found that the locals were already making use of the hot springs. In addition to constructing baths, they built a temple to Sulis Minerva, a goddess of healing, as well as a number of other fine buildings. The Great Bath is filled with waters from the adjacent springs (the only naturally occurring hot springs in Britain) and is kept at a temperature of 115°F.

After the Romans departed, Bath and its baths sank into disrepair. One 16th-century visitor noted that its waters "rikketh like a seething pot" and found the town "sumwhat decayed." And so it might have remained were it not for Richard "Beau" Nash. A dandy and a ladies' man, Nash set about prettifying the city in the early 18th century, commissioning several grand new public buildings. In an echo of the city's classical beginnings, the three-tiered colonnaded Circus was completed in 1768, modeled after the Colosseum in Rome. The town became England's great showpiece of Georgian architecture.

Jane Austen was a resident of Bath from 1801 to 1806, and the characters she created often promenaded in their Sunday best along the palatial Royal Crescent after attending church. "I really believe I shall always be talking of Bath when I am at home again," says Catherine Morland in Austen's novel *Northanger Abbey*. "I do like it so very much."

## The Thames from Henley to Runnymede

This chapter began on the far side of London, heading east just as Chaucer's intrepid band did on the road to Canterbury into Kent. From there, it swung west along the Channel coast to where the Romans—and then the Angles and Saxons and Normans—came ashore (though not the Nazis or the Napoleonic French).

The chapter continued west, from the Arthurian sites and the mysteries of Stonehenge to the scene of Drake's triumphs and the Armada's defeat, all the way to Land's End in Cornwall, where the Celts could retreat no farther. There, it turned back east, and now it approaches London again.

But first there are a few notable sites along the Thames to visit—though not as far as Wordsworth's Westminster Bridge or the Kinks' "Waterloo Sunset." Moving downstream, the first is Henley, then Windsor, and finally Runnymede.

Henley-on-Thames, its full name, is one of the more pleasant stops along the east-flowing waterway. Indeed, for the English upper classes the town acts as

# Bath Walk

This walk (one and a half miles, half a day) takes you on a tour of the highlights of Bath—from the superbly preserved Roman Baths to the parks, terraces, and squares and the Royal Crescent, the epitome of Georgian elegance.

❶ **The Roman Baths** were built in about A.D. 65–75; in the Baths Museum is a model of the whole bath/temple complex, along with fascinating artifacts excavated here, most striking among them a superb bronze head of Sulis Minerva.

❷ **The Abbey Church** stands outside the Roman Baths; begun by Bishop Oliver King in 1499, it features on its west front a host of angels climbing up and tumbling down ladders.

❸ **The Royal Crescent's** harmonious frontages were built in the 1760s and 1770s, by John Wood the Younger, and speculators ran up the houses behind as they pleased.

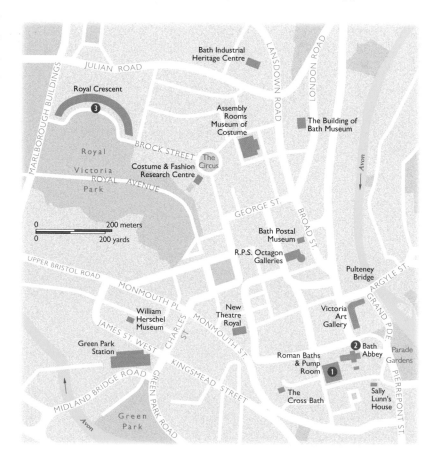

WORTH A VISIT

The English countryside holds many pleasures. Horse and hounds were once a more common sight than they are now. Since the Hunting Act of 2004, fox hunting with dogs has been banned in England and Wales. The issue continues to be an extremely divisive one among the British public.

a setting in which to act out their nostalgia for a bygone era. For one week each July, Henley Week, they get the chance to take out their straw boaters, dust off their blazers, and tie a fancy cravat—all in preparation for the world-renowned Henley Royal Regatta.

The regatta began as a challenge between the boat crews of Oxford and Cambridge Universities in 1829, and a decade later the race became an annual event. And alumni, as well as fans of rowing, all suitably attired, head off for Henley with their champagne picnics in tow. They eventually take their places in the

> ### IN WINDSOR
>
> Few can resist the charm of **Queen Mary's Dolls' House,** despite the inevitable long line to see it. Designed in 1923, it is a 1:12 scale (one inch to the foot) palace with miniature books, pictures, electric lighting, running water, and many exact replicas of Windsor Castle items.

bunting-draped grandstands beside the River Thames to watch the royal boat race.

Downriver from Henley, we arrive at the public school of Eton. It was founded in 1440 as the King's College of Our Lady of Eton beside Windsor, the king in question Henry VI. Doubtless a sizable number of the Oxbridge rowers from the boat race began their school days—and their rowing—at Eton (about a third of Etonians go on to Oxford or Cambridge). On the Fourth of June, crews of Eton schoolboys don naval costumes and ceremonially stand and shake the flowers from their boaters during the Procession of Boats.

Eton is the country's most exclusive school. Called the "chief nurse of England's statesmen," it has educated former British prime ministers, royals, and other famous figures. Premiers include William Gladstone and the Duke of Wellington, who supposedly said, "The Battle of Waterloo was won on the playing fields of Eton." Prince William and Prince Harry are Old Etonians. So were the writer George Orwell and the philosopher Henry More. P. G. Wodehouse's fictional Bertie Wooster was at Eton before he

**ROYAL ROAD**

For nearly a millennium, visitors have been traveling to Windsor Castle, which is the largest inhabited castle in the world. Although parts of it are usually open to the public, the castle may be closed for state visits and other occasions.

was a member of the Drones Club in London, as was Hugh Laurie, the actor who played him in the television adaptations of the books. Ian Fleming's secret agent James Bond also attended Eton.

Across a footbridge over the Thames is Windsor, an easy commute for Princes William and Harry, had that ever become necessary. The castle at Windsor has been a royal residence for 900 years, preferred by the present royals over Buckingham Palace, which is in the center of London. Windsor Castle was built by the Normans and is only a day's march from the Tower of London, built on the far side of the capital by William the Conqueror as his main residence. Despite the damage done by a fire in 1992, Windsor remains the world's largest inhabited fortress.

To the south of Windsor is Royal Ascot, where a four-day race that was begun by horse-loving Queen Anne in 1711 takes place. Gentlemen come in top hats and tails, ladies in the most extravagant headwear they can find. The royal family attends, too, for the running of the Ascot Gold Cup.

Beyond Eton and Windsor, the River Thames reaches Runnymede. When asked, "Where was the Magna Carta signed?" schoolchildren often reply, with a straight face and daring anyone to contradict them, "At the bottom." As a matter of fact, the document was sealed rather than signed. And it was done so here, at this watery meadow, or mead, along the river.

The year was 1215, and King John had been backed into a corner by his increasingly powerful barons. A stone monument at the site declares what happened at Runnymede:

*In these Meads on 15th June 1215 King John at the instance of Deputies from the whole community of the Realm granted the Great Charter the earliest of constitutional documents whereunder ancient and cherished customs were confirmed abuses redressed and the administration of justice facilitated new provisions formulated for the preservation of peace and every individual perpetually secured in the free enjoyment of his life and property.*

Beyond this point, the Thames slides under the M25, the great orbital highway that circles the capital. Downtown London is now just 20 miles distant, and here the chapter must come to an end.

## [ Seven Famous Homes ]

**1  Arundel Castle**  This imposing castle in West Sussex dates from the 11th century and has long been the principal home of the dukes of Norfolk, historically—with the dukes of Northumberland—the most powerful nobles in England.

**2  Bateman's Burwash**  This beautiful 1634 Jacobean house in East Sussex was home to Rudyard Kipling (1865–1936) for 34 years, and the place where he wrote many of his famous works, including the *Just So Stories* and *The Jungle Book*. Everything in the house and lovely gardens remains as the writer left it at his death—even the blotting paper on his desk.

**3  Chartwell**  One of a cluster of famous properties in Kent, 19th-century Chartwell, six miles east of Sevenoaks, was home to Sir Winston Churchill from 1924 until his death in 1965. Full of books, paintings, and personal mementos, the house and its gardens are still much as Churchill left them.

**4  Clouds Hill**  This tiny, charming cottage near Wareham, Dorset, was the home of T. E. Lawrence (1888–1935), better known as Lawrence of Arabia, and still looks much as it did when Lawrence died.

**5  Down House**  Charles Darwin lived in this Kent house from 1842 until his death in 1882. Both the gardens and house look much as they did in Darwin's day, notably the study in which he formulated his theory of evolution by natural selection.

**6  Hever Castle**  Picture-perfect Hever, just south of Sevenoaks, looks like a castle from a Hollywood set. It dates from 1270 and is famous as the childhood home of Anne Boleyn, mistress and then doomed queen of Henry VIII. The American William Waldorf Astor bought and restored the castle in 1903.

**7  Leeds Castle**  One of the most romantic and visited castles in England, Leeds has a 1,000-year history in which it was home to numerous kings and queens, including Catherine of Aragon, Henry VIII's first wife. In the 20th century, under society hostess Lady Baillie, it played host to guests such as Errol Flynn, Douglas Fairbanks, and John F. Kennedy.

**MAD HATTERS**
Two race-goers cheer home their horses during the third day of Royal Ascot, known as Ladies' Day. The occasion is a milliner's dream, with headgear ranging from the tasteful to the truly outrageous.

# Sites and Sights in Southern England

**County Kent** is often overlooked by travelers, but well known by Britons. Called the Garden of England, Kent boasts more than its share of historic great houses, smallish castles, and popular beaches. *www.visitkent.co.uk*

**Penshurst Place** is one of England's oldest and grandest country houses, built in 1341 for a wealthy London merchant. Many of its architectural elements are truly awe inspiring, including a 60 foot chestnut roof and a rare octagonal hearth—still functional—in the center of the great hall. *www.penshurstplace.com*

The stunning **Canterbury Cathedral**, immortalized by Chaucer, continues to beckon pilgrims and travelers to pray at the shrine of St. Thomas á Becket. *www.canterbury-cathedral.org*

Four miles east of Maidstone, **Leeds Castle**—often named the most beautiful castle in England—rises dreamily above its own reflection in a lake under wooded hills. The castle is superbly situated on two islands in a lake formed by the River Len. *www.leeds-castle.com*

At **Chartwell**, Winston Churchill's Victorian country house from 1924 until his death in 1965, the personality of Sir Winston comes to life. The rooms were left as they were in Churchill's lifetime. The garden studio contains his easel and paintbox and several of his paintings. An avid part time bricklayer, Churchill built a brick wall on the grounds. *www.nationaltrust.org.uk*

The dramatic **White Cliffs of Dover**, which overlook the Strait of Dover and France, owe their unusual appearance to pure white calcium carbonate with streaks of black flint.

Brighton has long been a favorite seaside resort. Prince Regent put Brighton on the map when he built his **Royal Pavilion**, an India-inspired palace. Although losing popularity over the last century to Europe's sunnier resorts, Brighton boasts some of the finest examples of Regency architecture and remains a delightful and popular getaway. *www.royalpavilion.org.uk*

Churchill's Art Studio at Chartwell

Don't miss the **Jurassic Coast**, officially called the Dorset and East Devon Coast World Heritage site, for this a geological journey back through time, spanning the Triassic, Jurassic, and Cretaceous periods. *www.jurassiccoast.com*

At 556 feet, **Winchester Cathedral** is the world's longest medieval building, a truly mighty church. The cathedral's 12th-century front is especially beautiful, its black marble carved with scenes from the life of the patron saint of seafarers, St. Nicholas. *www.winchester-cathedral.org.uk*

Legend says that Merlin used magic to create a **Round Table** for Arthur's court, its shape symbolizing equality among all the knights. Some say the massive wood artifact hanging in the Great Hall of Winchester Castle, home to Henry III and Edward I, is that Round Table. Experts date it to the 13th or 14th century, however; it was repainted in the time of Henry VIII. The names of 24 knights including Galahad and Lancelot encircle the table. *www. hants.gov.uk/greathall*

Jane Austen and her mother and sister lived in a simple redbrick house in Chawton for only eight years, but they were extraordinarily prolific ones. Today **Jane Austen's House Museum** is full of mementos, first editions, manuscripts, portraits, and Jane's comb. *www.jane-austens-house-museum.org.uk*

Everyone enjoys visiting **Windsor Castle**, the official residence of the British royal family for more than 900 years. An easy excursion from London, the icon stands on a hill in the Windsor town center, its fairy-tale towers silhouetted against the sky. *www.windsor.gov.uk*

Few can resist the charm of **Queen Mary's Doll House** at Windsor Castle, despite the inevitable long line to see it. Designed in 1923, it is a 1:12 scale (one inch to the foot) palace with miniature books, pictures, electric lighting, and running water and many exact replicas of Windsor Castle items. *www.victorianstation.com/dollent.html*

The evocative **Glastonbury Tor** is visible for miles around and is forever associated with King Arthur as the mystical island of Avalon that rose out of the marshes. Visitors traditionally climb the sides of the Tor (Celtic for "conical hill") in vain search of the Holy Grail. *www.glastonburytor.org.uk*

The diamond shaped **Isle of Wight**, separated from the mainland by the Solent Channel, is a small but distinct world apart. Chief attractions are Carisbrooke Castle and Osborne House, where Queen Victoria and Prince Albert relaxed.
*www.iwight.com/just_visiting*

There is no mistaking **Salisbury Cathedral**; its pale gray spire, at 404 feet the tallest in Britain, dominates the medieval city in its hollow among the hills.
*www.salisburycathedral.org.uk*

**Stonehenge**, near Wiltshire, is 5,000 years old and one of the most famous and iconic prehistoric monuments in the world. Its massive trilithons continue to provoke questions of when, how, and why.
*www.stonehenge.co.uk*

Wiltshire also has lesser known but equally intriguing ancient monuments. A notable group lies around **Avebury**, north of the Salisbury Plain. From the Early Bronze Age stone circle, made up of about 100 sarsen stones, a ceremonial avenue of standing stones leads to Overton Hill.
*www.stonehenge-avebury.net*

**Wells** is England's smallest city, but its Cathedral is one of the most impressive in all of Europe. The imposing west front boasts six tiers of 13th century statues of priests, kings, and saints—300 figures in all.
*www.wellscathedral.org.uk*

**Hardy's Cottage** is quintessentially British, with its cob construction, thatched roof, and beautiful cottage garden. Tours of this tiny home include his bedroom, where he wrote *Under the Greenwood Tree* and *Far from the Madding Crowd*.
*www.hardysociety.org/hardycountry.htm*

The **Stinsford Church graveyard** is the burial site of Hardy's first wife, Emma, and the planned site for Hardy's heart. His remaining ashes went to Poet's Corner in Westminster Abbey, for posterity.

A late medieval model of King Arthur's Round Table, which hangs on the wall of the Great Hall in Winchester Castle

**Corfe Castle** is a village and a parish in Dorset, but it is best known for its namesake, the ruin of the castle that has dominated the landscape here for a thousand years.
*www.corfecastle.net*

**Bath** is England's showpiece of elegant and harmonious Georgian architecture as well as superbly preserved Roman Baths and is an absolute must for any traveler through Britain. This beautiful city is one of the most enjoyable and rewarding in Europe for strolling and exploring.
*www.cityofbath.co.uk*

The **Roman Great Bath**, once covered by a roof, is now exposed to the elements. The **Baths Museum** has a model of the whole bath/temple complex, along with fascinating artifacts excavated here, the most striking among them a superb bronze head of Sulis Minerva and a giant, staring god's head fashioned in stone, with knotted hair and beard.
*www.romanbaths.co.uk*

In the elegant 18th-century **Pump Room** you can take tea to the sound of piano

playing, or dare to drink a glass of the health-giving water—tasting faintly of eggs, soap, and metal.
*www.romanbaths.co.uk/pump_room.aspx*

In Claverton, near Bath, is the lesser known **American Museum in Britain**, which takes you on a journey through American domestic life from colonial days to the end of the 19th century. It features quilting, rug making, Navajo art, and Shaker furniture, and you can snack on Connecticut snickerdoodles.
*www.americanmuseum.org*

The **Exeter Cathedral** is one of Britain's finest. In the cathedral close are a number of fine buildings. The most striking is the late **Tudor Mol's Coffee House**, dated 1596 on its lion-and-dragon coat of arms. Mol's is a handsome timber-framed house with curly gables and a railed gallery high on the third story.
*www.exeter-cathedral.org.uk*

The port of Plymouth has a storied maritime legacy. From this stunning port, Captain Drake sailed in 1588 to challenge and beat the Spanish Armada; in 1620, the Pilgrim Fathers set out for the New World; and in 1772, Captain Cook embarked on his three-year voyage through the South Seas. The **Mayflower Steps**, a simple arch monument, honors the Pilgrims.
*www.visitplymouth.co.uk*

Spinnaker Tower and south coast of Portsmouth, in Hampshire

## 5

The Midlands

When travel books seek to use a more evocative term for this part of the country, they come up with phrases like the "English Heartland" or the "Shires of England," which people in England never use. Sometimes the books divide the area into "Southern Midlands" and "Northern Midlands." But these distinctions don't really address the matter, because the difficulty seems to be with the word "Midlands" itself.

The problem is compounded by the fact that the English seem to have their reservations about the term, too. No one describes him- or herself as a Midlander, not in the way that others might call themselves Northerners or Southerners—or even Yorkshire men or women.

In fact, the term "Midlands" appears to be little more than a way to describe the land between the south and north—the bit that's left over. It has Wales, with all of its distinctiveness, bordering its west side, the North Sea completing the border on the east.

**GETTING YOUR BEARINGS**

Central England is a study in contrasts, from the Black Country in the west to the Fens in the east. It includes industrial cities like Birmingham, Coventry, and Wolverhampton, the great centers of learning Oxford and Cambridge, and the flat farmland of East Anglia.

# MIDLANDS AND EAST ANGLIA

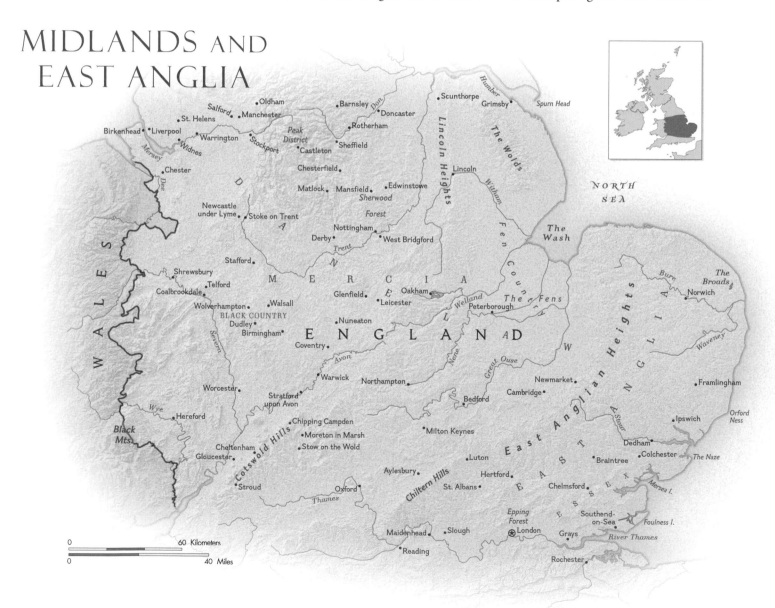

Perhaps a "city identity" is a possibility for residents of the Midlands. After all, those living in the capital call themselves Londoners, someone from Liverpool is a Liverpudlian, from Newcastle a Geordie, from Glasgow a Glaswegian, from Dublin a Dubliner. But what is the name for someone from Birmingham, which is, after all, England's second biggest city? Or Nottingham? Or Stoke? Or Leicester, Wolverhampton, or Derby?

As a matter of fact, there is a name for someone from Birmingham: a Brummie. The name sounds strange to outsiders, as does the accent that goes with it. Indeed, there are strong local loyalties and defining characteristics throughout the Midlands. And as we'll see, the limitations of "South Midlands" and "North Midlands" notwithstanding, there are real and striking differences throughout this central belt of the country.

The Anglo-Saxons had a name for the region that resonates a little better. To them, it was Mercia, one of the kingdoms set up by the Germanic invaders. The name comes from the Old English word *mierce*, or "border people," and was given to those who lived on the edges of the Celts in Wales.

**ANGLO-SAXON ARTIFACT**
The "Great Buckle" is part of the seventh-century Sutton Hoo treasure. Found in Suffolk at one of Britain's most important archaeological sites, the gold buckle with intricate interlacing design is on display at the British Museum. *Previous pages:* Chocolate-box cottages in Castle Combe, Wiltshire.

Bede—the Father of English History—indicates that Kent was the most powerful of these Anglo-Saxon kingdoms by the end of the fifth century. But Mercia was on the rise. The so-called Mercian Supremacy took place during the eighth century, when that kingdom spread across what is now the entire Midlands and beyond. It included today's East Anglia, the land of the east Angles, where the famous Sutton Hoo treasure was discovered in the late 1930s—a burial site from around the early seventh century with a treasure trove of Anglo-Saxon artifacts. Today, the term "Mercia" survives in the names of two regiments in the British army, an appropriate reminder, perhaps, of the region's warlike forbears.

## Dreaming Spires

If the word "evocative" is used to depict the Midlands, then there are surely few places in England that meet that description more completely than Oxford, Matthew Arnold's "sweet city with her dreaming spires." A host of literary greats have lived in the shadows of these spires, including Dorothy L. Sayers, Percy Bysshe Shelley, and Lewis Carroll. Oxford professors C. S. Lewis and J. R. R. Tolkien, as members of a group known as the Inklings, met in the Rabbit Room of the Eagle and Child pub—known locally as the Bird and the Baby—to discuss their various writing projects. "My happiest hours," recalled Lewis, "are spent with three or four old friends in old clothes tramping together and putting up in small pubs." Oxford resident Colin Dexter set his Inspector Morse mysteries here as well.

The country's oldest seat of learning, Oxford first appears in the written record in the year 912, in the *Anglo-Saxon Chronicle*. The first settlements were those of monastic orders, and by the time the English students who were expelled from the University of Paris settled here in 1167, Oxford was already a center of education. The monastic influence could be seen in the layout of colleges, with a chapel and a refectory, or dining hall, forming part of a quadrangle and the senior students' rooms gathered around it like monastic cells. The students were often rowdy and far from

**IN OXFORD**

Several scenes from the Harry Potter movies were shot at Oxford University. The staircase leading to **Christ Church's Great Hall** and the hall itself—a massive 550-person dining room with dark, vaulted ceilings and some of the longest tables in the world—were replicated in Hogwarts School of Witchcraft and Wizardry.

monastic, however, and "town and gown" relations could be fractious, at times resulting in bloodshed.

Oxford is ranked as the number one university in Britain in a number of subjects including politics, English, fine art, business studies, music, and philosophy. However, the university is actually a federation of around 40 self-governing colleges. Every student is a member of the university as well as of his or her particular college, each of which offers a broad range of subjects. There is a fierce rivalry between the colleges, both in academics and athletics.

Oxford is a place of superlatives. University College is the oldest, established in 1249—but even New College dates back to 1379, when it was founded to train new priests to replace those who had died during the Black Death. Christ Church College is the university's largest and wealthiest, Corpus Christi the smallest. Lady Margaret Hall, founded in 1878, was the first Oxford college established for women. Oriel was the last of the colleges to admit women,

**MEETING OF THE MINDS**
Two university students converse within the cloistered confines of one of Oxford's colleges. Visitors are welcome, and some of the colleges organize group tours.

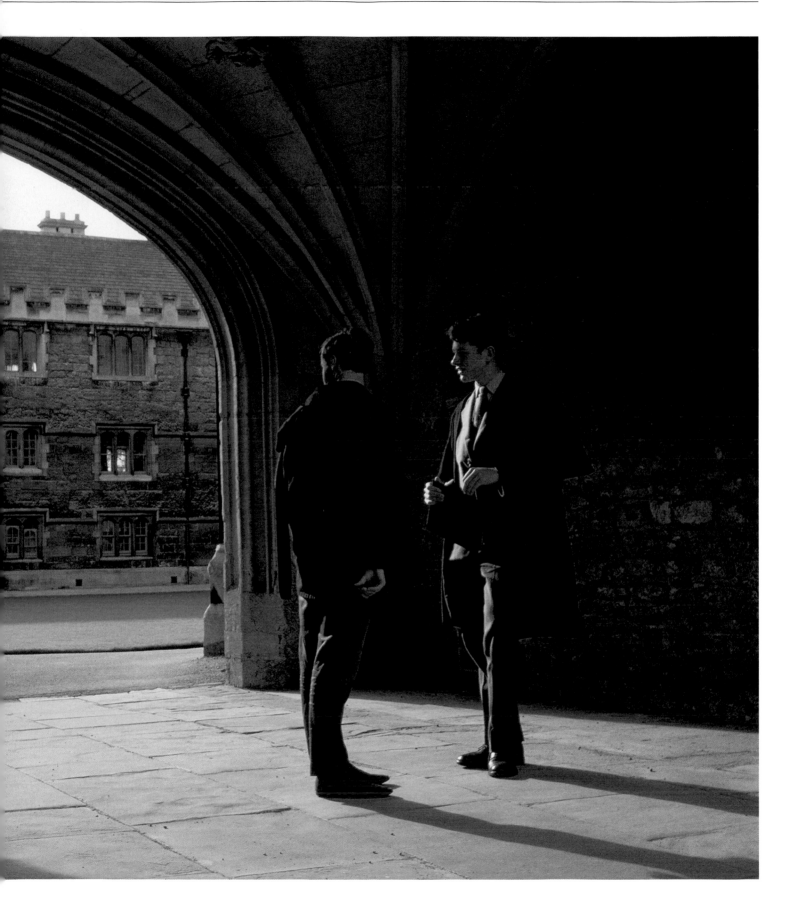

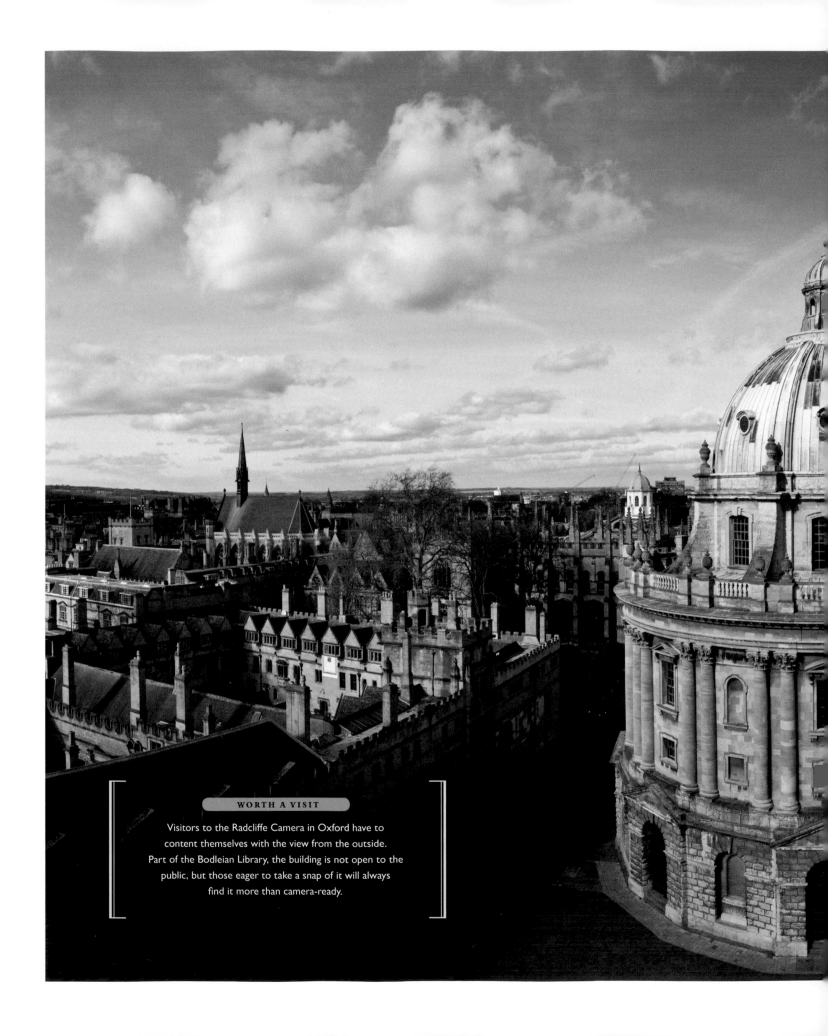

**WORTH A VISIT**

Visitors to the Radcliffe Camera in Oxford have to
content themselves with the view from the outside.
Part of the Bodleian Library, the building is not open to the
public, but those eager to take a snap of it will always
find it more than camera-ready.

only doing so in 1984. Oriel also has the longest name, officially, "The Provost and Scholars of the House of the Blessed Mary the Virgin in Oxford, commonly called Oriel College, the foundation of Edward the Second of famous memory, sometime King of England." The Queen's College was the last to give up brewing its own beer, which it did in the mid-20th century.

Oxford's roster of alumni, called "Oxonians," is a distinguished one. It includes more than two dozen prime ministers, from William Gladstone to Margaret Thatcher and Tony Blair. Among the international statesmen educated at Oxford were Indian prime minister Indira Gandhi, Burmese democracy activist Aung San Suu Kyi, and Bill Clinton, the first U.S. president to have attended Oxford as a Rhodes Scholar.

Literary Oxonians include Graham Greene, Oscar Wilde, John Fowles, W. H. Auden, and John Donne. Scientist and author Stephen Hawking attended, as did Monty Python members Michael Palin and Terry Jones, and the current Archbishop of Canterbury, Rowan Williams.

SCOTSMAN JOHN BALLIOL founded Balliol College in the 13th century as a penance for insulting the Bishop of Durham. But between Balliol and the Ashmolean Museum—Britain's oldest—is a monument that reminds us that even bishops encountered persecution. Amid the bustle and traffic of the city, the graceful Martyrs' Memorial bears silent testimony to the religious strife that often characterized Reformation England. The three figures depicted on the 1843 memorial are the Oxford Martyrs: Archbishop Thomas Cranmer, and Bishops Nicholas Ridley and Hugh Latimer.

Cranmer had been the Archbishop of Canterbury during the reign of Henry VIII. He supported the king's efforts to obtain a divorce from Catherine of Aragon, which led to the separation of the Church of England from the Church of Rome. After Henry's death in 1547, his son with Jane Seymour, the boy-king Edward, ascended the throne. Cranmer continued to head the new church, incorporating Lutheran teachings from the continent into its practices and doctrines. His *Book of Common Prayer* would become an enduring gift to English-speaking believers throughout the centuries. Edward VI's reign was a short one, though, and he died, perhaps of tuberculosis, after just six years as king.

During that time, Cranmer had transformed England into a Protestant nation. So when Edward's half-sister, Mary—the Catholic daughter of Henry's first wife,

## Oxford Walk

In all of Europe there is nothing comparable to the riches of Oxford's concentration of religio-academic architecture. This walk (two and a half miles, six hours) lets you taste the cream of it. Highlights include:

❶ **The University Botanic Gardens**, founded in 1621, was the first garden in Britain dedicated to the scientific study of plants, and is always beautiful, with herbaceous borders, Jacobean formal flower beds, and big greenhouses.

❷ **The Sheldonian Theatre** was built by Sir Christopher Wren in 1669, his first design; the painted ceiling shows Art and Science banishing Ignorance and Jealousy, two chubby miscreants looking suitably downcast.

❸ **The Ashmolean Museum** is the UK's oldest museum and art gallery (founded in 1683), its eclectic contents from the collection of John Tradescant (1570–circa 1638).

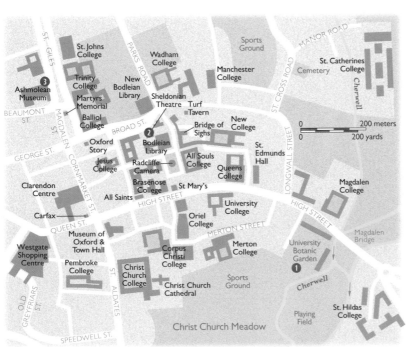

Catherine of Aragon—was crowned, the flames of religious conflict began to flare, literally. Mary was determined to restore Catholicism to England. "Bloody Mary" had nearly 300 Protestants burned at the stake, and one of her early targets was Archbishop Cranmer.

At Mary's orders, Cranmer was summoned before the Star Chamber and sent to the Tower of London to join Nicholas Ridley, the Protestant Bishop of London, and Hugh Latimer, the Protestant Bishop of Worcester. All three were tried and found guilty of treason and heresy, then sentenced to death.

The sentences were carried out in Oxford, near the site where the Victorian memorial to the martyrs stands today. Ridley and Latimer were burned first, with Cranmer forced to watch their final moments. At this time, the archbishop wrote several statements recanting his Protestant faith, which should have saved his life. But Mary wanted him dead. He was taken to the same place where the other bishops had died and there he, too, was tied to the stake. As the flames began to rise around him, Cranmer deliberately stretched the hand that had written the recantations

**TABLE MANNERS**
A formal dinner is held in the Great Hall of Christ Church College. Scenes from the Harry Potter movies were filmed here.

into the hottest part of the fire. "Lord Jesus, receive my spirit," those nearest heard him say right at the end. "I see the heavens open and Jesus standing at the right hand of God."

Just north of Oxford stands Blenheim Palace, designed to rival the Versailles Palace of Louis XIV itself. The land on which it stands was granted to John Churchill, the first Duke of Marlborough, by a grateful nation after his defeat of the armies of the Sun King at the Battle of Blenheim in 1704. Parliament also voted the duke monies to build a huge baroque palace there—the only non-royal palace in the country—complete with 2,700 acres of landscaped parks. It includes a formal Italian garden; a water terrace garden with sinuous ponds, fountains, and statues; a river dammed to create a lake; a Temple of Diana; a Victory Column topped by the duke dressed as a Roman general; and a 100-foot-wide Grand Bridge. The task took 17 years to complete, by which time the warlike duke had died.

British prime minister Winston Churchill is a descendant of the Duke of Marlborough. "At Blenheim I took two very important decisions: to be born and to marry," he once said. Although he never lived there, Churchill frequently visited the ancestral home. His body is buried in the grounds of the vast park.

## The Other Half of Oxbridge

About 80 miles northeast of Oxford is its great rival, the city often mentioned in the same breath—Cambridge. Just as students exiled from Paris helped to develop Oxford University, so those forced to leave Oxford helped to develop Cambridge as a center of learning. Once again, the students (who must have been a troublesome lot) would have found a monastic center of learning along the banks of the Cam when they got here. Like those at Oxford, the colleges at Cambridge were developed along a monastic pattern: chapel, refectory, and accommodations around an open square.

At Trinity College, the enclosed square, or court, is said to be the largest in Europe. It is also the scene of the Great Court Run, a footrace in which undergraduates sprint around its perimeter while the clock is striking noon. The race is re-created in the 1981 Academy Award–winning film *Chariots of Fire,* which tells the true story of two

## [ Oxford's 5 Oldest Colleges ]

**1 University College (1249*)** Alfred the Great is often said—erroneously—to have founded this college, which, until the 16th century, only admitted students of theology. Famous alumni include the Romantic poet Percy Bysshe Shelley (1792–1822)—who reportedly attended just one lecture—President Bill Clinton, and Professor Stephen Hawking.

**2 Balliol (1263*)** Students here have a reputation for scholarly achievement (five alumni would become Nobel laureates, the most of any Oxford college) and (often left-wing) politics. Alumni include three British prime ministers and the political economist Adam Smith.

**3 Merton (1264*)** First to adopt the collegiate system, with tutors and students brought together in a planned community with on-site lodgings. J. R. R. Tolkien is said to have spent much time in the college's medieval library writing *The Lord of the Rings*.

**4 Exeter (1314*)** Began life with just 12 students, and remains one of the smaller and more close-knit colleges. Exeter took its name from founder Walter de Stapledon, Bishop of Exeter and Treasurer of England under Edward II.

**5 Oriel (1326*)** The oldest royal foundation in Oxford, founded with the patronage of Edward II. It has four old halls, one of which is Tackley's Inn, the oldest medieval hall in the city.

* Date of foundation, though the precise order and dates of foundation, except those of Oriel, are disputed.

**A PINT IN THE PUB**
Book at the ready, an Oxford man lights up his pipe in one of the city's pubs. Among the most famous of Oxford watering holes is the Eagle and Child, where C. S. Lewis and J. R. R. Tolkien often met.

# Cambridge Walk

This walk (two miles) around the compact center of Cambridge can easily be done in a day; it can also be split into north and south Cambridge, with a day allotted to each to allow thorough exploration of one of the finest assemblies of medieval buildings in all of Europe.

❶ **Trinity College** was founded in 1546; witness the famous statue of Henry VIII over the gateway.

❷ **King's College Chapel** is one of the best known churches in the world, thanks to its annual radio and television broadcast of the Christmas service of Nine Lessons and Carols.

❸ **Queen's College** is among Cambridge's most beautiful colleges, with wonderful Tudor courts and the half-timbered President's Lodge.

❹ **The Fitzwilliam Museum** includes a ceramics collection and numerous illuminated medieval manuscripts.

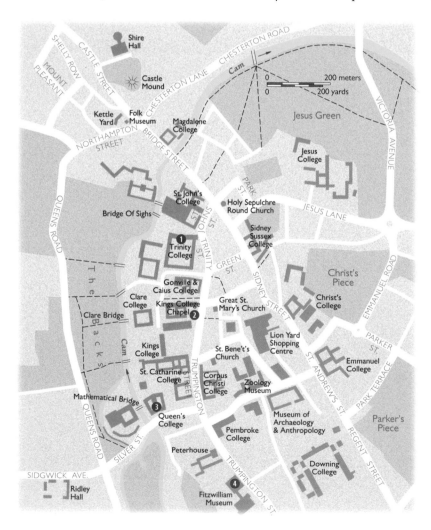

British athletes who competed during the 1924 Olympics in Paris. One is Englishman Harold Abrahams, who struggles with the anti-Semitism of the college authorities, the other Eric Liddell, the "Flying Scotsman," who eventually heeds the call of the mission field in China.

Liddell and Abrahams were both 100-meter runners. This was Liddell's best event, and he had already beaten Abrahams over that distance. But when he learned that the 100-meter race was to be held on a Sunday, the Christian Sabbath, Liddell decided not to take part. Abrahams went on to win the gold medal in the event. Liddell instead entered the 400-meter race, which he won, setting a new world record in the process.

Liddell remains extremely popular in his native Scotland. At the 1980 Moscow Olympics, fellow Scot Allan Wells won gold in the 100 meters, the first Briton to do so since Paris in 1924. When asked if he had won it for Harold Abrahams, Wells's answer was immediate: "No, this one was for Eric Liddell."

A year after the Paris Olympics, Liddell was in China, serving as a missionary. He would spend the rest of his life there. He died in 1943, in a World War II Japanese internment camp. Today, at the site of the former camp, a memorial headstone of Scottish granite carries one of Liddell's favorite scriptures, taken from the Book of Isaiah: "They shall mount up with wings as eagles; they shall run and not be weary."

LIKE OXFORD, CAMBRIDGE is a collegiate university, comprising 31 different colleges, each with its own distinctions and traditions. Trinity has the most students of any college at Cambridge or Oxford, and is considered the most aristocratic—the college of choice for the British royal family. Christ's College has educated more British prime ministers than any other, at 13.

Peterhouse is the oldest Cambridge college, established in 1284, and Robinson the newest (1977). Emmanuel claims to be the only Cambridge college to offer a free laundry service. Girton, established in 1869, was the first residential women's college in Britain. Pembroke is home to the first chapel designed by Sir Christopher Wren. Sidney Sussex College claims to have the cheapest (student-run) bar in Cambridge, and Wolfson College, with

**MESSING ABOUT IN BOATS**

A student punts past the houseboat, or "barge," belonging to Corpus Christi College. Punting on the Isis, as the Thames is called here, is one of the classic Oxford activities.

students from more than 70 countries, professes to be Cambridge's most cosmopolitan. Magdalene (pronounced MAWD-lin) has the most lavish May Ball, held at the end of the academic year, and insists on a white-tie dress code.

## East Anglia and Constable Country

England's two ancient centers of learning are both flanked by great rural expanses. To the west of Oxford are the Cotswolds, and to the east of Cambridge the much larger East Anglia.

East Anglia is an uncrowded, mostly flat region, a land of long horizons. It contains some of the most fertile soil in the country. Parts of the region are reclaimed marshland and rich fenland that was drained of its water in the 17th century by Dutch engineers who had accomplished similar feats in their own homeland. Two hundred years later, the writer Charles Kingsley declared:

> *They have a beauty of their own, these great fens, even now, when they are dyked and drained, tilled and fenced—a beauty as of the sea, of boundless expanse and freedom.*

As its name implies, East Anglia was at one time the kingdom of the East Angles, who came from across the North Sea. Other, later arrivals from the continent,

weavers from Flanders, helped to develop textile production here, which made East Anglia the wealthiest and one of the most populous parts of England by the 13th century.

The low-lying agricultural region is more of a backwater today. As a glance at the map on page 124 shows, East Anglia is somewhat set apart from the rest of England, a bit off the beaten track. An agricultural revolution took place here in the 18th century, when experiments in crop rotation and the growing of fodder crops eliminated the need for a fallow year. But when the *indus-*

> ### IN THE COTSWOLDS
>
> The **Cotswold Hills,** with their gently rounded pastures and hanging beech and oak woods, their secret little valleys, and above all, their beloved small towns and villages, churches, and limestone field walls, are quintessential rural England, the classic southern English landscape.

*trial* revolution began in England, it did so in the Midlands, the north, and elsewhere. East Anglia was left generally untouched. And so it remains for the most part today.

Here visitors will find "Constable Country" along the banks of the River Stour through the Dedham Vale. The tranquil landscapes that inspired John Constable, that most English of painters, remain remarkably unchanged since he captured them in such meticulous detail more than 150 years ago. "I associate my 'careless boyhood' with all that lies on the banks of the Stour," Constable once wrote. "Those scenes made me a painter, and I am grateful; that is, I had often thought of pictures of them before I ever touched a pencil."

During World War II, East Anglia's proximity to the continent and its level terrain made the region a favored location for constructing military airfields. Down their runways thundered heavy bombers on the way to pound targets in Nazi-occupied Europe— the United States Army Air Force by day, the Royal Air Force by night.

Today, the thunder of horse hooves is a more enduring sound in

**EAST ANGLIAN IDYLL**
A country church overlooks cultivated fields in East Anglia. A little off the beaten track, this part of England offers much to visitors eager to take the road less traveled.

this part of the country. East of Cambridge sits the town of Newmarket, which has long been at the heart of British horse racing and has the largest training center in Britain. The Jockey Club was established here in the mid-18th century to regulate this Sport of Kings, which over time had acquired a less than respectable reputation.

## [ Constable Picturesque ]

**1 Dedham Vale** The pretty countryside around the River Stour, between the villages of Manningham and Bures, is at the heart of so-called Constable Country. "Dedham Vale" (1802), now in London's Victoria & Albert Museum, is one of the artist's most celebrated works.

**2 Hadleigh Castle** Constable painted at least ten preparatory oil sketches of this 13th-century castle, already ruined in the painter's day, which overlooks the River Thames in Essex, south of the village of Hadleigh. One sketch is in the Tate Gallery, London, while the main painting (1829) is in the Yale Center for British Art in New Haven, in the United States.

**3 Flatford Mill** This surviving watermill in Flatford, Suffolk, dates from 1733, and was owned by Constable's father. It features in several works by the artist, but is more famous as the point from which Constable painted his most famous work, "The Hay Wain" (1821), now in London's National Gallery.

**4 The River Stour** Constable painted many scenes depicting the beautiful pastoral scenery and the working life of this river, including "Stratford Mill" (1820; the National Gallery, London), "The White Horse" (1819; the Frick Collection, New York), and "The Lock" (1824; Thyssen-Bornemisza Museum, Madrid).

**5 Willy Lott's Cottage** The actual 16th-century cottage depicted in "The Hay Wain" can still be seen at Flatford, East Bergholt, the village of Constable's birth. Another surviving cottage nearby, Bridge Cottage, is also depicted in several works by the artist.

Newmarket has been a favorite location for racing enthusiasts since the time of King James I, who is said to have introduced the sport to England and early on saw the advantages of the deep silt loam of New-market Heath. In 1622, the first recorded horse race took place. James's son, Charles I, an accomplished horseman, frequently participated in the races.

Under James's grandson, Charles II, Newmarket became one of the most fashionable places in the kingdom. Every spring and summer, the king would relocate the whole court to a new royal palace there, which can still be seen. Charles II was an avid rider, and he once risked life and limb by taking part in—and winning—the four-mile Newmarket Town Plate Race.

The Merry Monarch, as he was known, had other reasons to frequent Newmarket, too, not the least of which was to rendezvous with "pretty, witty Nell," his royal mistress. Today, the Nell Gwyn Stakes is run each spring at Newmarket's Rowley Mile, named after the king's favorite horse, Old Rowley.

## Cotswolds to Stratford

The Cotswolds are archetypal English countryside, stretching west of Oxford toward the Welsh borders. If any place can carry off the vaunted title "Heart of England," it might be the Cotswolds.

Tourists, at least, seem prepared to go along with this description, and they come here in the hundreds of thousands to take in the beauty of villages built with silvery or creamy limestone and set harmoniously in the gently rolling landscape. Their names—Chipping Camden, Moreton-in-Marsh, Stow-on-the-Wold—evoke images of cozy little collections of houses, which are huddled near stands of beech and oak.

North of the Cotswolds is another great tourist draw—in fact, England's premier cultural destination outside London—Stratford-upon-Avon. William Shakespeare, the man who would become the world's most celebrated playwright, was born in the

Tudor town in 1564. The reconstructed family home, a rambling half-timbered building on Henley Street, housed Shakespeare's descendants until the early 19th century. Among the literati who have made the pilgrimage here are Charles Dickens, John Keats, and Sir Walter Scott. Along the banks of the River Avon stands the redbrick Royal Shakespeare Theatre, where many of the Bard's plays are performed.

The date of Shakespeare's birth is not known for sure. His birthday is celebrated on April 26, 1564, the date of his baptism. He was married to Anne Hathaway, who lived in a tiny village about a mile distant, in 1582 at the age of 18. Some time between 1585 and 1592, he made his way to London, drawn by the opportunities offered by the capital like countless other artists and performers since. There, Shakespeare wrote some 37 plays in all, as well as poems and sonnets. In the process, he paved the way for English—a fusion of the language of the Anglo-Saxon invaders with that of the Celts and the Normans—to become the language of the world.

By 1610, Shakespeare returned to the town that is ever associated with his name. He died on April 23, 1616, St. George's Day, the feast day of England's patron saint.

**UNPACKING THE BARD**

Members of the Shakespeare Birthplace Trust take possession of a recently discovered portrait of the Bard on April 17, 2009. Dating from around 1610, the painting shows Shakespeare in his mid-forties and is thought to be the only authentic image of him made during his lifetime.

**ALL THE WORLD'S A STAGE**
The cast takes a curtain call after a performance at the Royal Shakespeare Theatre in Stratford-upon-Avon. Other attractions in town include Shakespeare's birthplace, Anne Hathaway's Cottage, and Holy Trinity Church.

The Bard is buried in Stratford's Holy Trinity Church. The words inscribed over his grave are said to be his own, the last written by a man who did so much for the English language:

*Good friend for Jesus sake forbeare,*
*To dig the dust encloased heare.*
*Bleste be ye man yt spares the stones,*
*And curst be he yt moves my bones.*

## Civil War

Shakespeare's bones had been unmoved for a quarter century when England was wracked by civil war. Since early in his reign, King Charles I had been at odds with Parliament. Many members of Parliament (MPs) had strong puritan sympathies, and they not only suspected that Charles had his sights on absolute power (noting his insistence on "the divine right of kings"), but they also were leery of his Catholic sympathies.

After years of squabbling, the battle lines between Parliament and the king were drawn: By 1642, Parliament controlled London, East Anglia, and the southeast; and the Royalists commanded the north of England, Wales, and the southwest. The Midlands they divided, and it was here that many decisive battles took place.

The first pitched battle of the war erupted at Edgehill, a dozen miles southeast of Stratford. Both sides claimed victory. After further fighting, King Charles withdrew to Oxford, which became his headquarters for the rest of the conflict. While in Oxford, Charles lived at Christ Church College. His French-born queen, Henrietta Maria, stayed at nearby Merton College. It is said that a private passage was made between the two colleges so that the king could visit the queen. Today, their time in Oxford is commemorated with statues of the king and queen that stand at the west and the east ends in the quad of St. John's College.

The Royalists won many of the early encounters in the war. But in its second year, a new leader came to the fore for the "Roundheads," as the parliamentary soldiers were known because of their distinctive haircuts. He was the member of Parliament for Cambridge and would go on to become the leader of the parliamentary army, a regicide, and Lord Protector. But first Oliver Cromwell would establish himself as a ruthless—and winning—military commander.

Cromwell, a committed puritan, began the war in charge of a lowly troop of cavalry that fought at Edgehill. He soon increased his command to a full regiment and gained valuable experience in fighting throughout East Anglia. In 1644, Cromwell's troops helped win the battle at Marston Moor in the north of England.

The following year, Cromwell was second in command of Parliament's New Model Army. That summer at Naseby, right in the center of England, Cromwell's army smashed the Royalist forces. It was the decisive battle of the civil war—indeed, after the Battle of Hastings and the Battle of Britain, perhaps the most significant in English history. Within a year, Oliver Cromwell had accepted the Royalist surrender at Oxford and Charles I was a prisoner of Parliament. Today, a memorial looks out over the site of the battle.

The king now had one option left. Taking advantage of the country's uncertainty over what to do about him, Charles managed to escape custody. But instead of fleeing to France, as some urged him to do, he enlisted the support of the Scots and launched a second civil war. Risings in support of the king, however—in Essex, Kent, Cumberland, and Wales—soon petered out. At the Battle of Preston in Lancashire, Cromwell defeated the Scottish army and its English Royalist supporters. The king was captured again.

Now regarded as "the man of blood," Charles stood trial for treason and "other high crimes." He was found guilty and condemned to death. On the day of his execution, January 30, 1649, the king wore two shirts against the bitter weather, lest any in the assembled crowd mistake his shivers for fear. Placing his head on the block, he uttered his last words: "I shall go from a corruptible to an incorruptible crown, where no disturbance can be."

A masked executioner stepped forward and raised his ax. The man's identity is not known for sure. The usual London executioner had refused the task, and a replacement had to be found. With the skill of an experienced headsman, he severed the king's head with a single stroke.

In the aftermath of the king's death, Cromwell moved swiftly to subdue Ireland, where the Royalists had forged an alliance with the island's Catholics, and then Scotland, which refused to accept Parliament's victory. After that,

## [ Three Historic East Anglia Wool Towns ]

**1** **Hadleigh** Now a quiet country town, but in its day, one of East Anglia's largest and most prosperous wool towns. Monuments to its past glory include the medieval St. Mary's Church and the three-story, 15th-century Guildhall.

**2** **Long Melford** At more than two miles, Long Melford's High Street is supposedly England's longest and is lined with exquisite medieval, Georgian, and Victorian buildings, a legacy of a time in the 16th century when the surrounding region produced more cloth than anywhere else in Britain.

**3** **Lavenham** East Anglia's most beautiful town is an almost unchanged 15th-century gem, with 300 medieval half-timbered houses, ancient inns, and thatched cottages, many painted in "Suffolk pink," a traditional finish of whitewash stained with red ocher.

the man who had done so much to dictate events during the war retained a firm hold during the peace, as Lord Protector of the Commonwealth of England.

The puritan republic that he forged did not long outlast him. When Cromwell died in 1658, his son, Richard Cromwell, succeeded him as Lord Protector. But Richard had none of his father's leadership abilities, and by 1660 Parliament had restored Charles I's eldest son to the throne as King Charles II. The interregnum was over.

The younger Charles had fled England after the final battle of the civil war. To escape capture by parliamentary troops, he had famously hid in an oak tree before making it safely to France. The king's escape is celebrated every year on Garland Day in Castleton, Derbyshire. Each May 29, a horseman who is dressed as a Stuart king parades through the village, enveloped in a three-foot-tall garland of wildflowers and leaves that symbolizes Charles's hiding place. Followed by his "queen" in

**INSPIRING SUFFOLK**

St. Mary's Church in the small Suffolk town of Hadleigh boasts a big church with a wood-and-lead spire that dates from the 14th century. The redbrick Deanery to the left was added in 1495.

similar period attire, a procession of villagers, and a band, the king visits each of the pubs in the village. Then he is relieved of his garland, which is hoisted to the tower of the local church and left to wither there. The ceremony ends with dancing around the maypole, an ancient fertility rite that the puritans had outlawed as a pagan practice.

When Charles II returned, he restored such revels. It was not the only change he made during the Restoration. The new king moved against those who had supported the republican regime during the interregnum. One was the great John Milton. Prior to the civil war, the poet had written tracts against episcopacy within the Church of England and in favor of the puritan and parliamentary cause. He later wrote pamphlets in support of regicide.

After the Restoration, Milton was for a time imprisoned, his writings burned. In 1667, he finally released his masterpiece *Paradise Lost*. By this time the great man was blind. He had composed the epic entirely in his head and dictated it to his secretary.

Those who had signed the death warrant of the king in 1649 fared worse than Milton. Tried for regicide, some were imprisoned for life, others hanged, drawn, and quartered.

Special retribution was reserved for the Lord Protector himself. Oliver Cromwell's body was exhumed, hanged in chains, and thrown into a pit.

Today, a statue of Cromwell, sword in one hand, Bible in the other, stands outside the Houses of Parliament in London. He is shown with his head slightly bowed, as if in thought. Some have suggested that his eyes might be lowered to avoid the condemning gaze of Charles I, whose bust adorns the exterior of St. Margaret's Church directly across the street.

## Industrial Heartland

Cromwell's Cambridge. Shakespeare's Stratford. James I's Newmarket. Charles I's Oxford. All lie a short distance from that other English "heartland," the industrial Midlands. This is where the industrial revolution began in Britain, and its factories made the area the workshop of the world.

The exact place where it began is said to be Coalbrookdale. It was here, just west of Birmingham, that Abraham Darby became the first person to use coke in iron smelting, thereby laying the foundations of the modern iron industry. In the 1770s, Darby's grandson, Abraham Darby III, proceeded to construct the world's first iron bridge. A permanent monument to his achievements, the span still reaches across the narrow gorge of the River Severn.

Birmingham—valued at 20 shillings by the conquering Normans in the Domesday Book—is part of the great conurbation in the West Midlands, along with cities like Coventry and Wolverhampton. Birmingham was the great crucible of the industrial revolution. Here, James Watt began experimenting with the steam engines that would free factories from the need to be located next to fast-running water. Watt is buried at St. Mary's Church in Birmingham, and his statue today stands outside the city's Central Library in Chamberlain Square.

The West Midlands also includes the grim-sounding Black Country, one of the most heavily industrialized areas in Britain. Located just north of Birmingham, it was named by an American who visited in the 1800s and could think of no other name for a place that had so many forges and furnaces spewing smoke and fumes into the air.

In Charles Dickens's *Old Curiosity Shop,* Little Nell also makes her way through this dismal landscape. Dickens writes:

## [ Museums of the Industrial Revolution ]

1 **Cadbury World, Birmingham** England's industrial revolution wasn't all about iron, coal, and textiles: In 1824 the Cadbury family founded a chocolate empire that still produces (in Cadbury's Dairy Milk) the most popular candy in Britain. Cadbury World explores the history and manufacture of the company's products.

2 **Coalbrookdale Museum of Iron, Shropshire** One of several museums at Ironbridge, cradle of the industrial revolution, where the Darby family first smelted iron with coke, produced single beams of iron, and built the world's first (and still surviving) iron bridge.

3 **National Waterways Museum, Gloucester** Before the railroads, canals played a vital role in England's early industrial revolution, a role explored in this museum, which is housed in a restored warehouse in Gloucester Docks, once Britain's largest inland port.

4 **Masson Mills, Matlock** Built in 1783 as a state-of-the-art textile mill for the innovative industrialist Sir Richard Arkwright, and today a working museum that forms part of Derwent Valley Mills, a UNESCO World Heritage site devoted to 200 years of textile production.

5 **Museum of Industry & History, Derby** Housed in a former silk mill, often described as England's first "factory," this museum explores Derby's pivotal role in England's industrial rise, with a special emphasis on its railroad heritage and on the story of the city's Rolls-Royce company.

*On every side, and as far as the eye could see into the heavy distance, tall chimneys, crowding on each other and presenting that endless repetition of the same dull, ugly form, which is the horror of oppressive dreams, poured out their plague of smoke, obscured the light, and made foul the melancholy air. On mounds of ashes by the wayside, sheltered only by a few rough boards, or rotten pent-house roofs, strange engines spun and writhed like tortured creatures; clanking their iron chains, shrieking in their rapid whirl from time to time as though in torment unendurable, and making the ground tremble with their agonies.*

### IN WARWICKSHIRE

If one were to choose the English castle most like the fortresses of childhood fantasy, **Warwick Castle** would be it. Massive and foreboding to approach, it has everything a castle should have: elegant staterooms, a great hall, an armory, a torture chamber, dungeons, a rampart walk, and even a ghost tower.

Farther north, the city of Stoke-on-Trent is the home of the English pottery industry. The Romans made pottery from the Stoke area's red clay, as did craftsmen in the Middle Ages. But the rough mugs and dishes fired in medieval kilns could not be compared to the elegant earthenware that the region eventually began to produce.

The stimulus was tea. In the mid-1600s, the English started to develop their insatiable taste for the brew, which was first brought to Europe from the Far East by Portuguese and Dutch traders. The demand for fancy cups and saucers in which to serve it rose accordingly. World-famous pottery brands were produced here, including Royal Doulton, Spode, Minton, and, most important, Wedgwood.

Perhaps no one came closer to the ideal of marrying manufacture and art than Josiah Wedgwood, the "Vase Maker General to the Universe." The 13th child of a poor potter, Josiah Wedgwood fired more than 10,000 pieces before he perfected jasper. "Everything yields to experiment," he declared. Impressed

**STRONGPOINT**

Perched at a bend of the River Avon, Warwick Castle dominates the surrounding countryside and helped safeguard the Midlands from rebellion against the Normans. The castle ranks as one of Britain's top historic attractions.

by his wares, Catherine the Great ordered a set of cream-colored Queensware with 1,244 hand-painted scenes of England. A keen supporter of the American Revolution, Wedgwood made medallions of George Washington, Benjamin Franklin, and naval hero John Paul Jones as well.

But Josiah Wedgwood was ever seeking ways to harness industrial methods of production. He used an early steam engine designed by James Watt to drive his clay mixers with stone grinders. He also helped complete the nearly 100-mile-long Trent and Mersey Canal in 1777. This gave an outlet to the ports of Liverpool on the Irish Sea and Hull on the North Sea, enabling Wedgwood to speedily export his wares around the world. For good reason, this area became known as the Potteries.

## The Winter of Discontent

The Midlands are traditionally the heart of Britain's automobile and engineering industries. During the recession that swept Britain during the late 1970s, these industries were particularly hard hit. To combat the economic slowdown, the Labour Party limited all public sector raises to no more than 5 percent per annum in order to reduce galloping inflation. The government policy was intended to encourage businesses in the private sector to stick to similar pay restrictions. In the winter of 1978–79, however, public sector labor unions responded by launching a series of strikes. And when the management of Ford Motor Company attempted to impose the government's 5 percent cap, its workers came out on strike, too. Truck drivers joined the strike, as did railroad workers. Ambulance drivers reduced their coverage to a skeleton service. Flying pickets shut down facilities all across the country, including oil refineries. Most infamously, gravediggers went on strike, as did refuse collectors. Soldiers stood by, ready to be called into action should the government announce a state of emergency.

It was, declared the *Evening Standard* newspaper, Britain's "winter of discontent," borrowing the opening line from Shakespeare's play *Richard III*. In the polls, the opposition Conservative Party went from strength to strength. In November 1978, it had trailed the Labour Party by 5 percent. But by February 1979, it established a lead of some 20 percent. In the May general elections, the Conservatives swept to power, and the party's leader, Margaret Thatcher, became Britain's first female prime minister.

Thatcher had been an MP since 1959 and had long aroused strong feelings. In 1971, as Britain's Secretary of Education during a previous Conservative administration, "Maggie Thatcher, Milk Snatcher" had stopped the practice of providing free milk in schools for children over the age of seven. Now Thatcher would hold the premiership

**SHERWOOD STALWARTS**
Taking aim, this modern statue of Robin Hood stands in what was once the moat of Nottingham Castle. At left, one of the largest maiden oaks in Sherwood Forest, where the legendary outlaw once resided.

**151**

until 1990, the longest term of any British prime minister since Lord Liverpool's 25-year run in the early 1800s.

## Dark Satanic Mills

Birmingham and Stratford-upon-Avon are only 20 miles apart. And in between the two cities, indeed throughout the Midlands, are beautiful stretches of countryside. This juxtaposition of the rural and urban, industrial towns dropped into quiet green landscapes, is a feature of the novels of D. H. Lawrence. The author of *Sons and Lovers* and *Women in Love* was himself born in a coal-mining village in this part of the country, near Nottingham.

Nottingham is a city with a distinct medieval past that it has done little to preserve. At this strategically important crossing of the River Trent, William the Conqueror built a fortress in 1068, which became the key to controlling the Midlands. Nottingham became famous as a center of lace-making, and is also where the most violent Luddite riots of the early 19th century took place, in which starving weavers destroyed the machines they held responsible for their misery.

The Luddites were named after a worker named Ned Ludd, who made stockings on his employer's frames. When he had to endure a whipping one day for laziness, Ludd responded by smashing his employer's equipment. Inspired by his show of rebellion, masked Luddites roamed throughout the Midlands, venting their rage on the hated machines. Nottingham's Luddites wrecked factories and homes, and even burned the 13th-century Norman castle.

Today, outside the castle gatehouse stands a modern statue of the man who is most associated with Nottingham: Robin Hood. It was here, at the castle, that the outlaw is said to have won an archery contest against Nottingham's sheriff (a word derived from "shire reeve," the royal overseer of the county). According to the tales, this is the castle in which the Sheriff of Nottingham had Robin Hood imprisoned—and the place from which he kept escaping.

Over the centuries, Robin Hood has been portrayed in many ways: as a yeoman officer, an impoverished nobleman, an Anglo-Saxon rebel fighting Norman rule, and today as the romantic bandit who stole from the rich and gave to the poor. Historical

## [ Great Stately Homes ]

**1** **Burghley House, near Stamford** A glorious 16th-century palace built to impress by William Cecil, advisor to Elizabeth I. Filled with artistic masterpieces by Gainsborough, Brueghel, and others, and used as a setting for movies such as *The Da Vinci Code* and *Elizabeth: The Golden Age*.

**2** **Chatsworth, near Bakewell** One of the greatest of England's stately homes, begun in 1551, and home to the dukes of Devonshire. Filled with room after room of antiques and precious works of art, along with 25 square miles of gardens and extensive parkland. Mary Queen of Scots was imprisoned here between 1570 and 1581 on the orders of Elizabeth I.

**3** **Haddon Hall, near Bakewell** Where nearby Chatsworth dates mostly from the 18th century, Haddon Hall was begun in the 12th century, and retains an almost entirely medieval appearance, notably in the banqueting hall, virtually unchanged since the days of Henry VIII.

**4** **Hardwick Hall, near Chesterfield** Bess of Hardwick was the second-most powerful Englishwoman of the 16th century after Elizabeth I, largely because of the wealth accumulated by marrying upwards four times. Hardwick was built using the inheritance from her fourth husband in 1590 and is one of England's finest Elizabethan-era houses.

**5** **Kedleston Hall, near Derby** The Curzon family has lived here since the 12th century, though the present stately home dates from 1758, when Sir Nanthaniel Curzon tore down the existing hall and insisted the peasants of Kedleston Village move their homes a mile down the road as their dwellings spoiled his view.

**ROYAL BOUDOIR**

Guests can pay a visit but just not spend the night—at Queen Elizabeth's Bedroom in Burghley House near Stamford, Cambridgeshire. The room was built between 1565 and 1587 by the queen's lord chancellor, William Cecil.

accounts of an outlaw named Robin Hood date back to the late 13th century. But his true identity remains as elusive as the fugitive who hid in Sherwood Forest.

That forest lies north of town. The former royal hunting ground once spread across a huge tract of the east Midlands. At the time when Robin and his band of Merry Men may actually have lived there, the 12th century, Sherwood Forest stretched for nearly 30 miles north of Nottingham. Since then, foresting, coal mining, agriculture, and urbanization have cut the forest back.

Twenty miles north of Nottingham sits Edwinstone, one of the more untouched parts of the forest. It is here that Robin is said to have married Maid Marian in St. Mary's Church. A nearby oak tree, known as the Major Oak, was supposedly a gathering place for Robin's band, who hailed from the surrounding area. According to the tales, Robin met Friar Tuck in Fountain Dale, and Little John came from the nearby village of Wentbridge. Evil Sir Guy was from Gisborne.

The landscape of the Midlands, from the pastoral to the industrial, is markedly different. Urban, built-up areas often end abruptly and give way to fields of wheat and meadows with grazing cattle. Even Birmingham's "Spaghetti Junction," where highway

after highway intersects, provides a speedy escape to the countryside. This duality was a theme of the poet William Blake, who spoke of England's "green and pleasant land" as well as its "dark, satanic mills."

These words come from Blake's short poem "Jerusalem" (1804), which was later set to music as a popular hymn. A favorite patriotic song, it has become for England an alternative national anthem. The poem is based on the tale that Jesus had once traveled to England and, briefly, created a New Jerusalem here to

---

**IN OXFORDSHIRE**

**Blenheim Palace** is a "must-see," even leaving aside the spectacular palace. The view of the grounds and palace upon arrival is unforgettable. A narrow-gauge railway leads to the Pleasure Gardens, called the finest in Britain, which include a rose garden, butterfly house, secret garden, and one of the world's largest mazes.

---

"shine forth upon our clouded hills," one that contrasts with the industrial England of Blake's day.

Blake's England continues to be transformed. Today, the cities of the Midlands have been revitalized by the ethnic communities who have settled here. Many immigrants from the Indian subcontinent have made this part of England home. Near the center of Birmingham, for example, is the so-called Balti Triangle, named because of its concentration of restaurants specializing in balti curry. This form of one-pot curry, typically eaten with naan, first appeared there in the late 1970s, and is extremely popular among all sections of the population.

Another curry dish, a mild curry known as chicken tikka masala, is said to be more popular nationwide than the traditional English fish and chips. Although its exact origins are obscure, chicken tikka masala was developed specifically for the British palate and is not a subcontinental import. One former British foreign secretary even went so far as to declare that it was "Britain's true national dish." A transformative Britain indeed.

**SUNBATHED BLENHEIM**
A short trip north of Oxford—and past the grazing sheep—brings visitors to Blenheim Palace and its spectacular grounds, the site of the grave of Winston Churchill.

# Sites and Sights in the Midlands

Matthew Arnold called **Oxford** the "sweet city with her dreaming spires," referring to the many spires of Oxford University. Many literary greats have lived in the shadows of these spires, including Percy Bysshe Shelley, Lewis Carroll, C. S. Lewis, and many others.

Still a popular Oxford pub and restaurant, **the Eagle and the Child Pub**, nicknamed the Bird and the Baby, is best known as the meeting place in the 1940s and '50s of a group of writers known as the Inklings that included C. S. Lewis, J. R. R. Tolkien, Charles Williams, and Owen Barfield.

Several scenes from Harry Potter movies were shot at Oxford University. The staircase leading to the **Christ Church's Great Hall** and the hall itself—a massive 550-person dining room with dark, vaulted ceilings and some of the longest tables in the world—was replicated for use as the Hogwart's Dining Hall.

Oxford has its own **Bridge of Sighs**, a beautiful 20th-century replica of Venice's famous bridge, which serves as a stunning backdrop on the processional route for Hertford College's graduation ceremonies.

**Cambridge**, like its sister city Oxford, is all about ambience: a mellow, beautiful mixture of medieval architecture, church spires rising above ancient centers of learning, neat lawns and gardens surrounded by arcaded or gabled quadrangles, and always in the background the sight or sound of a river. Cambridge is less built up and urbanized and has a more relaxed feel.

A statue of Henry VIII presides over the gateway of the famous **Trinity College**. Trinity's two courts—Cambridge's equivalent of Oxford's quad—are also famous. **Great Court** is the scene of a well-known annual race in which undergraduates try to run around its perimeter while the clock is striking 12.

In **Nevile's Court**, Isaac Newton calculated the speed of sound by stamping and timing the echo.
*www.trin.cam.ac.uk*

Cambridge's **King's College Chapel** is one of the best known churches in the world, thanks to its annual radio and television broadcast of the Christmas service of Nine Lessons and Carols.
*www.kings.cam.ac.uk*

**Blenheim Palace**, Churchill's country estate, is a "must-see," even leaving aside the spectacular palace. The view of the grounds and palace upon arrival is unforgettable. A narrow gauge railway leads to the Pleasure Gardens, called the finest in Britain, which include a rose garden, a butterfly house, a secret garden, and one of the world's largest mazes.
*www.blenheimpalace.com*

The **Cotswold Hills**, with their gently rounded pastures and hanging beech and oak woods, their secret little valleys, and above all, their beloved small towns and villages, churches, and limestone field walls, are quintessential rural England, the classic Southern English landscape.

**Cheltenham**, in the Cotswold Hills, has been a spa town since the early 18th century and contains some of Britain's best Regency architecture. From

the green-roofed Rotunda and the extravagantly curlicued wrought-iron trellises and balconies of Montpellier, descend to the town's broad central Promenade, lined with flower beds, trees, a splendid Neptune fountain, and a parade of exclusive stores.
*www.visitcheltenham.com/site/index.php*

Three cathedral cities and county capitals of **Gloucester**, **Hereford** and **Worcester** form a triangle in the southwest Midlands. This is cattle-grazing and fruit-growing country of red earth and green meadows, well provided with orchards of apples for eating and cider making.

**Gloucester Cathedral** is one of the most glorious in Britain, marked by its beautiful 225-foot tower. The beautiful vaulted 14th-century Great Cloister provided a suitably Gothic setting for the Hogwarts School in the Harry Potter films.
*www.gloucestercathedral.org.uk*

**Hereford Cathedral** is a marvelous Romanesque building of pink-gray sandstone, full of memorably decorated tombs such as those of St. Thomas of Hereford with his guard-of-honor of sorrowing Knights Templar.
*www.herefordcathedral.org*

**Worcester Cathedral** occupies a splendid position, with its great east window overlooking the county cricket ground and the looping River Severn. Its 14th-century tower is a notable landmark, though much of the cathedral is, in fact, a Victorian restoration.
*www.worcestercathedral.co.uk*

Statue of William Herbert, third Earl of Pembroke, Oxford

Just southwest of Worcester are the **Malvern Hills**, a nine-mile succession of ridges and peaks of ancient granite with a high-level footpath running their length. You can see seven counties and the three cathedrals from the 1,394-foot summit of **Worcestershire Beacon.**
*www.malverntrail.co.uk/walkingmalvern.htm*

**Stratford-upon-Avon**, on the River Avon, is England's premier cultural visitor destination outside London, thanks to the genius of the world's most celebrated playwright/poet, William Shakespeare.
*www.shakespeare.org.uk*

At the bottom of Old Town is the golden gray **Holy Trinity Church**, above the River Avon. Inside the altar rail lies the body of Shakespeare, flanked by his wife, daughter, and son-in-law. Visitors can obtain a copy of the parish register entries of his birth and death and admire the 19th-century stained glass window, donated by U.S. enthusiasts, which depicts the seven ages of man from *As You Like It.*

From the church, a riverside footbath leads to the red bulk of the **Royal Shakespeare Theatre**, opened in 1932, where the Royal Shakespeare Company performs the Bard's plays.
*www.rsc.org.uk*

**Shakespeare's Birthplace**, the Tudor half-timbered building where the Bard was born, was once a pub called the Swan and Maidenhead before it was bought for the nation and reconstructed and refurbished for posterity.

**Anne Hathaway's Cottage**, in the hamlet of Shottery on the northern outskirts of town, is a thatched farmhouse of some size, timber-framed and brick-built, with Tudor furniture. The lovely garden outside is planted with a representation of each species of tree mentioned in the works of Shakespeare.
*www.shakespeare.org.uk/content/view/50/50*

Birmingham, once one of the powerhouses of Midlands industry, is loud, energetic, brazen, and enormous fun. The superb **Birmingham**

**Museum and Art Gallery** on Chamberlain Square is rich in pre-Raphaelite art.
*www.bmag.org.uk*

East of Birmingham is **Coventry**, which was horrifically bombed in 1940. **Coventry Cathedral** has a rich history that spans nearly 1,000 years. The shell of the medieval cathedral, burned out in the raid, stands next to its modern replacement, Britain's most remarkable postwar church building.
*www.coventrycathedral.org.uk*

Front entrance, Gloucester Cathedral

**Warwick Castle**, near Stratford-upon-Avon, is the quintessential British castle, complete with every imaginable element of fantasy, including elegant staterooms, a great hall, an armory, a torture chamber, dungeons, a rampart walk, and even a ghost tower. It now offers themed dining experiences with live entertainment.
*www.warwick-castle.co.uk*

**Nottingham Castle**, in the North Midlands, has a history packed with drama. It stands on a high rock honeycombed with caves and passages. The restored Norman castle was twice destroyed and rebuilt during the 12th-century civil war. Today it houses the **Nottingham Castle Museum and Art Gallery**, with some fine Pre-Raphaelite and modern paintings and a display of late medieval alabaster sculpture.
*www.nottinghamcity.gov.uk/index*
*.aspx?articleid=1036*

The intriguing **Castle Caves Tour** allows visitors to walk the underground passages in the Castle Rock that were allegedly the paths of sneaky royal escapes.

**Sherwood Forest**, the ancient royal hunting forest where Robin Hood and his Merry Men had their hideout, once covered a vast area. Today all that remains near the ancient Major Oak, with its 33-foot girth, is Sherwood Forest Country Park in Edwinstowe, whose footpaths lead off among the oaks and bracken.
*www.sherwoodforest.org.uk*

The coal-mining village of **Eastwood**, north of Nottingham, was the birthplace of the novelist D. H. Lawrence (*Sons and Lovers*). Fourth son of a miner, he was born in a "two-up, two-down" row house, now the **D. H. Lawrence Birthplace Museum**. A heritage center depicts the origins of Eastwood itself and its links with Lawrence.
*www.lawrenceeastwood.co.uk*

Crossing the wild moorland and rolling limestone dales of Britain's first national park, **Peak National Park**, this drive passes through the charming Georgian towns of Buxton, Ashbourne, and Matlock, and visits two of the Peak's great country houses, medieval Haddon Hill and stately Chatsworth House.
*www.peakdistrict.gov.uk*

**Chatsworth House** has one of Britain's most regal approaches to a historic house with a carefully planned message of grandeur. Chatsworth is a country palace, a baroque mansion with a harmonious Palladian facade, built from 1687 to 1707 for the immensely rich first Duke of Devonshire.
*www.chatsworth.org*

The Peak District spills over into Cheshire, a broad county of plains and low hills. Its ancient capital city of **Chester**, full of medieval, Tudor, and Stuart buildings, lies on the eastern border near the wide Dee Estuary. Founded more than 2,000 years ago by the Romans, Chester has the most complete Roman city walls in Britain.
*www.chester.com/visitchester/aboutchester*

## 6

Northern England

When you cross the River Humber, you know you are in the north. More exactly, you know you are in Yorkshire, the biggest county in England. Yorkshire men and women have a particular pride in their region. They will take great pains to make clear the differences between this part of the country and that of the "soft southerners." In Yorkshire especially, those differences abound.

In ancient times, this was the heartland of the Brigantes, the largest of the Celtic tribes of Britain. According to the northward-marching Romans, the Brigantes were also the most militant. By the third century, the north of England had become part of the Roman province of Britannia Inferior.

Offensive as this may seem at first to proud northerners, "inferior" merely indicates that it was known as Lower Britain, as defined by the region's relative proximity to the imperial capital of Rome. The capital of Britannia Superior was Londinium, and the capital of Britannia Inferior was Eboracum, or as it is known today, York.

York is a jewel of a city. Small and compact, it is still enclosed by magnificently preserved defensive walls. Today, these walls—reconstructed and fortified with Norman permanence—contain just remnants of the original Roman walls designed to protect Eboracum. The moat that ran around the perimeter also no longer exists, but four fortified gateways still lead through the walls. Below these walls spreads a tangle of narrow, medieval streets and alleys. Rising majestically above it all are the twin towers of York Minster. Construction of the great church began in 1220, but it was some 250 years in the making. York Minster is the seat of the Archbishop of York.

**NOT QUITE CRICKET**
"Ball tampering" to alter the state of a cricket ball during a match is strictly prohibited. *Previous pages:* The Dent Head Viaduct above the Cumbria moors.

The young man that history would remember as Constantine the Great traveled all the way to the Roman military base at Eboracum. He came with his father, the emperor Constantius, to help fight against the Picts of Caledonia, as the Romans referred to Scotland. But in A.D. 306, Constantine's sickly father died.

Constantine went on to become the first Roman emperor to convert to Christianity. He moved the imperial capital out of Rome to the shores of the Bosporus, where he built a new Christian capital at Byzantium, which was later renamed Constantinople (and now Istanbul). Back in York, a bronze statue of Constantine now stands outside the Minster near the spot where his father, right before dying, proclaimed him emperor.

In 2005, York Minster became the home to a man who had begun his journey from even farther away than Rome. That year, Ugandan-born John Sentamu was enthroned as Archbishop of York,

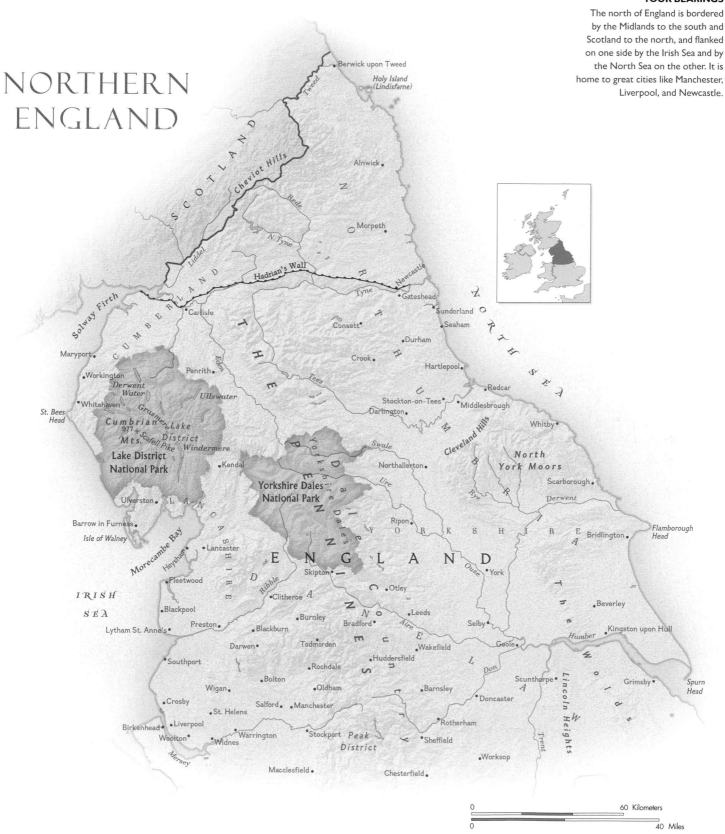

# NORTHERN ENGLAND

**GETTING
YOUR BEARINGS**
The north of England is bordered
by the Midlands to the south and
Scotland to the north, and flanked
on one side by the Irish Sea and by
the North Sea on the other. It is
home to great cities like Manchester,
Liverpool, and Newcastle.

SCOTLAND

Berwick upon Tweed

Tweed

Holy Island
(Lindisfarne)

Cheviot Hills

Alnwick

Rede

N O R T H

Morpeth

N. Tyne

Liddel

Hadrian's Wall

Newcastle

Tyne

Gateshead

CUMBERLAND

Carlisle

Sunderland

NORTH SEA

Solway Firth

Consett

Seaham

THE

Durham

Maryport

Eden

Crook

Workington

Penrith

Hartlepool

Derwent
Water

Ullswater

Tees

Redcar

St. Bees
Head

Whitehaven

Grasmere Lake
District

Stockton-on-Tees

Middlesbrough

Cumbrian
977 +Scafell Pike
Mts.

Windermere

Darlington

Cleveland Hills

Whitby

Lake District
National Park

Kendal

Swale

North
York Moors

Yorkshire Dales

Northallerton

Scarborough

Ulverston

Ure

Rye

Derwent

LANCASHIRE

Yorkshire Dales
National Park

Y O R K S H I R E

Barrow in Furness

Ripon

Flamborough
Head

Isle of Walney

Morecambe Bay

Bridlington

Heysham

Lancaster

Skipton

Ouse

York

Fleetwood

Ribble

Otley

IRISH

Clitheroe

Leeds

Beverley

SEA

Blackpool

Burnley

Bradford

Aire

Selby

Kingston upon Hull

Preston

Blackburn

Humber

Lytham St. Anne's

Darwen

Todmorden

Wakefield

Goole

Spurn
Head

Southport

Huddersfield

Don

Scunthorpe

Grimsby

Rochdale

The Wolds

Wigan

Bolton

Oldham

Barnsley

Lincoln Heights

Crosby

Salford

Manchester

Doncaster

St. Helens

Rotherham

Birkenhead

Liverpool

Stockport

Peak
District

Sheffield

Woolton

Warrington

Widnes

Worksop

Mersey

Macclesfield

Chesterfield

Trent

ENGLAND

0      60 Kilometers

0      40 Miles

the second most senior cleric in the Church of England, after the Archbishop of Canterbury.

## The County of York

All around York unfolds the great county of Yorkshire. To the west, the land rises as it approaches the Yorkshire Dales. To the east, the hill country runs all the way to the coast. And to the southwest and south are the manufacturing cities that grew exponentially during the years of the industrial revolution. Bradford

**SHAMBLES OF A CITY**
Step back in time in the Shambles, a maze of narrow streets in York that still retains its medieval air.

> **IN YORK**
>
> Unlike the mostly eroded walls of other medieval cities, York has an almost complete ring of about three miles of tall and sturdy walls. The tangle of **medieval alleyways** and streets (here called "gates") connect fine museums, shops, and churches, including the massive York Minster.

was an important mill town then and now has a thriving South Asian population, with one of the highest proportions of Muslim residents in the country. Leeds, Yorkshire's main commercial hub, was once dependent on the nearby coalfields but is today one of Britain's leading financial centers. And Sheffield was the heart of British steelmaking, with a worldwide reputation.

The city of Sheffield is also home to the first association football (soccer) club in the world, Sheffield F.C., which was founded in 1857. Today, Sheffield F.C. is a minor club, overshadowed by two other city giants, Sheffield United and Sheffield Wednesday. These two larger clubs have played the keenly contested Steel City Derby game since 1893.

All three soccer clubs were formed by cricketers eager to play another sport when cricket's summer season ended. Cricket has a long history in Yorkshire. The county's first recorded match was in 1751, between two Sheffield teams. Cricket matches can take one day or up to five full days. Players stop the game for lunch and tea, as do the fans.

Cricket quickly became the national sport of England. And as the British Empire expanded, so did cricket, to countries all around the world. By the mid-1800s the first international matches were being played, and currently the top national teams—in addition to England—are Australia, India, Pakistan, and South Africa. Today, cricket is the second most popular spectator sport in the world after soccer, a consequence of it being so passionately followed in the Indian subcontinent. For the same reason, field hockey ranks as number three, with, like cricket, more than two billion fans.

One particularly intense cricket rivalry is between England and Australia. Every two years, the two nations play against each other for a trophy called the Ashes, whose origins date back to an 1882 match at the Oval Cricket Ground in London. That year, after England's first defeat at the hands of Australia on its own home soil, an obituary appeared in the *Sporting Times*, announcing the death of English cricket:

*In Affectionate Remembrance of English Cricket, which died at the Oval on 29th August, 1882,*
*deeply lamented by a large circle of sorrowing friends and acquaintances.*
*R.I.P.*
*N.B.—The body will be cremated and the ashes taken to Australia.*

## York Walk

Unlike many other British cities whose medieval walls survive only in half-eroded bits and pieces, York has an almost complete ring of about 3 miles of sturdy wall—15 or 20 feet high in most places. Highlights of the walk (3 miles, two hours) include:

❶ **Clifford's Tower** was completed in 1313 to replace a wooden keep in which 150 Jews killed themselves during a pogrom in 1190 rather than fall into the hands of the rioting mob outside.

❷ **The Museum Gardens** are beside the ruins of St. Mary's Abbey and the Roman masonry of the big Multangular Tower.

❸ **York Minster** looms close above the city walls, dwarfing the trees, flowers, and vegetable patches in the Deanery gardens below.

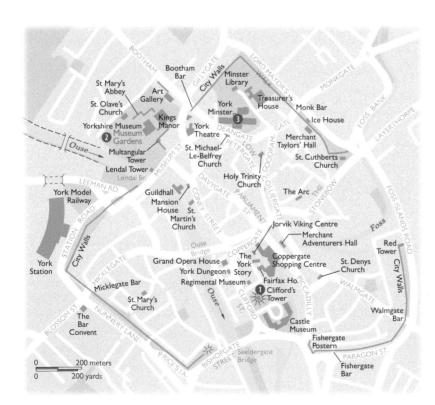

**IN THE DETAILS**

The red devil opposite used to get the blame for any typos that were made in the nearby printing shop.

The next time England traveled to the antipodes to play its great rivals, it was dubbed a quest to "regain the Ashes." The Australians entered into the spirit of things with gusto: After England's victory in Melbourne, a group of local women presented the team captain with a small terra-cotta urn said to contain the remains of part of a cricket wicket. Ever since, matches between the countries are to either retain or take back the prized Ashes.

In England, major league cricket is organized on a county basis. For years, the highly successful Yorkshire County Cricket Club insisted that its players had to be born within the county's historic borders. Such county pride may have made sense at one time, and with only Yorkshire men playing, the team would have been cohesive and motivated. But in the 1970s and 1980s, the sport was developing fast in England, attracting to its ranks players from India, Pakistan, Australia, the West Indies, and elsewhere. By insisting on selecting only native-born Yorkshire men, the county was not only depriving itself of top players from Lancashire, Somerset, and Kent, but it was also excluding the top overseas players, who were signing up for rival counties. The YCC finally dropped its nativist rule in 1992.

**EPISCOPAL SPLENDOR**

Seen above by twilight and opposite in cutaway, York Minister is the largest Gothic cathedral in northern Europe and a huge draw for tourists. In addition to religious services, the cathedral offers guided tours, tea rooms, concerts, exhibitions, and lectures.

## Nonconformism

The Yorkshire Dales comprise a great stretch of heathery upland moors, broad green valleys, and shallow, rushing rivers. Edged with drystone walls, the pastureland is some of the most lush in Britain. Just to the south of the Yorkshire Dales National Park is the West Riding of Yorkshire. This is Brontë Country. The literary sisters lived and wrote here, and it is the setting for Emily Brontë's masterpiece, *Wuthering Heights,* which, said Charlotte, "was hewn in a wild workshop."

The Yorkshire Dales were a place of tragedy for Charlotte. Here, her brother, Branwell, then her sisters, Emily and Anne, died of tuberculosis. "I am free to walk on the moors," she wrote. "But when I go out there alone, everything reminds me of the times when others were with me, and then the moors seem a wilderness, featureless, solitary, saddening." Charlotte went on to write such novels as *Shirley* and *Villette.* Her most famous book is *Jane Eyre.*

This part of the country was also particularly fertile ground for the work of John Wesley and the teachings of nonconformism—which, by the mid-1700s, was the latest major development in the history of the Church of England. Henry VIII had established the Anglican Church of England in the 16th century, but his Catholic daughter, Mary, had plunged the country back into religious conflict and dispute. Ecclesiastical equilibrium was restored under Good Queen Bess (Elizabeth I). Dismissing many of the religious contentions and controversies of her day, she declared: "There is only one Christ, Jesus, one faith. All else is a dispute over trifles."

However, mounting tensions shattered that equilibrium in the years after Elizabeth's death. With Parliament's victory in the civil war, the Puritans had the upper hand in the Church of England. It wasn't until King Charles II was restored to the throne that there was a return to the middle ground, or *via media*, of the established church.

Such tolerance set the stage for the 18th-century preacher John Wesley and his hymn-writing brother, Charles. Together, they sought to revitalize Anglicanism, launching a new evangelical movement within the church that promoted the importance of a personal relationship with Jesus Christ over the ritualistic performance of religious rites. The new movement, which was based on open-air preaching by itinerant lay ministers, quickly spread throughout the British Isles and across the Atlantic Ocean to the colonies in America.

Although he remained within the established Church of England, John Wesley formed "Methodist" societies to organize the work of evangelism. These societies built the small chapels that have become characteristic of Yorkshire, Wales, and several other parts of Britain. Wesley's followers would preach in Anglican churches when invited and in open fields when not, to congregations in their Sunday best or to assemblies of miners in their work clothes.

Like his followers, Wesley would preach anywhere, even on occasion using his father's tombstone as a pulpit to address an audience. He constantly traveled on horseback, preaching two or three times a day. Some claim that during his lifetime, Wesley rode 250,000 miles and preached more than 40,000 sermons on either side of the Atlantic. Wesley rose at four every morning to begin his day's tasks. A simple, "methodical" man, he was often criticized by the clergy of the established church.

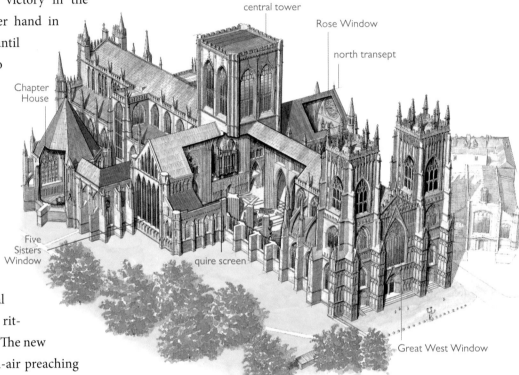

## INSIDE YORK CATHEDRAL

central tower

Rose Window

north transept

Chapter House

Five Sisters Window

quire screen

Great West Window

**MAGNIFICENT MINSTER**
Begun in 1220 and finished in 1472, York Minster is the largest medieval church in northern Europe and a great storehouse of fine artistic treasures. Its official title is the Cathedral and Metropolitan Church of St. Peter in York.

# [ The Brontë Trail ]

**1 Haworth Church** A venerable-looking church built on the site of the church the Brontës would have known well—their father, Patrick Brontë, was the vicar there. The original was demolished in 1879.

**2 Oakwell Hall, Birstall** This Elizabethan manor, built in 1583, and 100-acre park (both open to the public), were the inspiration for Fieldhead in Charlotte Brontë's novel *Shirley* (1849).

**3 The Brontë Parsonage** Home to the Brontës between 1820 and 1861, including Patrick, who outlived all of his children. Now it is a museum with much Brontë memorabilia and rooms furnished just as they were in the Brontës' day.

**4 Red House, Gomersal** This Georgian country house, with its lovely 1830s gardens (both open to the public), was owned by the Taylor family, prosperous cloth merchants and great friends of Charlotte Brontë. It featured as Briarmains in her novel *Shirley*.

**5 Rose & Co. Apothecary** This historic, beautifully restored chemist shop (pharmacy) at 84 Main Street, Haworth, was much frequented by Branwell Brontë, a failed painter and the brother of Charlotte, Emily, and Anne. It was here that he purchased the laudanum (opium tincture) to which he became addicted.

**6 Thornton Bradford** This surviving house on Market Street in Thornton Village was home to the Brontë family from 1815 to 1820 and the birthplace of Charlotte, Emily, Anne, and Branwell.

**7 Top Withens** A ruined farm on the bleak, brooding moorland 6.5 miles' walk from Haworth, it is often considered to have been the inspiration for Emily Brontë's *Wuthering Heights* (1847).

**BRONTË PARSONAGE**
Seen here from the adjacent graveyard, the Brontë Parsonage in Haworth, West Yorkshire, has been converted into a museum run by the Brontë Society. Its collection includes manuscripts, letters, drawings, household items, and other personal possessions.

The Methodist movement became a new and dynamic force within Christendom. But it was also a force for good in the secular world, its members dedicated prison reformers and abolitionists who adhered to the Bible's teaching that in Christ "there is neither Jew nor Gentile, slave nor free."

One of the last letters John Wesley wrote before he died in 1791 were words of encouragement for one of his ministry's recent converts: William Wilberforce, a member of Parliament for Yorkshire. "O be not weary of well doing!" Wesley wrote the young abolitionist.

Sixteen years after Wesley's death, Wilberforce finally persuaded Parliament to outlaw the slave trade in Britain and its overseas colonies, events that were dramatized for the big screen in the 2006 film *Amazing Grace*.

## The Northeast Coast

From the Humber estuary to the Scottish border, the towns and cities of northeast England are strung along the coast like beads on a chain. The Yorkshire resort of Scarborough has long been a popular destination for locals. Farther north is the fishing port of Whitby, where representatives from the Celtic and the Roman branches of Christianity famously met for their synod in 664. The synod took place in Whitby Abbey. Still on the site are the ruins of a later, 13th-century Norman abbey, destroyed by Henry VIII during the Dissolution of the Monasteries.

In 1890, Bram Stoker arrived in Whitby, conducting research for his upcoming gothic horror novel *Dracula*. The mist-shrouded port provided a dramatic backdrop for the book:

*Masses of sea fog came drifting inland . . . so dank and damp and cold that it needed but little effort of imagination to think that the spirits of those lost at sea were touching their living brethren with the clammy hands of death.*

Townsfolk told Stoker how a few years earlier a ship called the *Demetrius* had foundered at night off Whitby's coast, discharging into the waters its cargo of occupied coffins. The next morning, the locals had found the coffins scattered along the

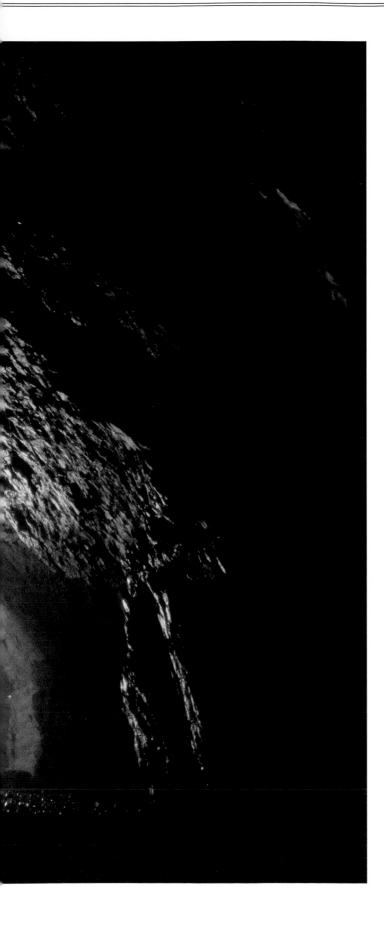

beach, and were horrified to find within them bodies at various stages of decomposition. The story gave Stoker an idea to incorporate into his novel. In it, Count Dracula arrives in England after the ship he is traveling in, the Russian schooner *Demeter,* is shipwrecked near Whitby. In the guise of a great dog, Dracula then comes ashore and bounds up the 199 steps leading to St. Mary's Church. The church's ancient graveyard is filled with crumbling tombstones, and there, Dracula claims his first victim in England, Lucy Westenra, before disappearing into the night.

Farther up that "dank and damp" coast are industrial Middleborough, Sunderland, and Newcastle. The natives of Newcastle-upon-Tyne, once an important shipbuilding center, are fiercely loyal to their hometown, and known for their quick wit and distinctive "Geordie" accent. Local attractions include the 66-foot-tall "Angel of the North" sculpture, the 1928 Tyne Bridge, and the nearby rotating "Blinking Eye" bridge, built in 2000 to celebrate the end of the second millennium.

Impressive as they are, these modern engineering feats pale in comparison to what the Romans built here 2,000 years prior—Hadrian's Wall. West of Newcastle, the wall runs 73 miles all the way across the narrow neck of England to the Solway Firth on the Irish Sea.

In A.D. 120, the emperor Hadrian ordered the wall built to keep out the barbarians from the north. It was eight feet thick and 15 feet high, with six-foot-tall battlements on top. At every Roman mile there stood a castle, garrisoned by troops, and every five miles a fort. Much of the wall, particularly the middle section, can still be seen today.

## The Norsemen

The coast of Northumbria stretches some 70 miles from where the Tyne flows into the North Sea at Newcastle to the Scottish border—a succession of low rock cliffs and sandy bays. Before reaching the border, however, travelers can stop at the holy island of Lindisfarne.

Around A.D. 635, the Irish monk St. Aidan and his followers founded a monastery on Lindisfarne, now in ruins. He had come from Iona off the west coast of Scotland to evangelize

**SIGHTSEEING UNDERGROUND**

Potholers explore the giant cavern of Gaping Gill in North Yorkshire. A number of pothole clubs organize rides to the bottom for visitors.

the north of England. It was here that the famous illuminated manuscript known
as the Lindisfarne Gospels was produced early in the next century. Today, the gospels are housed in the British Library in London, despite a campaign to have them
returned to a suitable place in the northeast of England, such as Durham Cathedral,
where a modern facsimile of the gospels is on display.

Other visitors arrived at the island before the century was out. These newcomers
ushered in a new era in England's history. On June 8, 793, sails appeared off the coast of
Lindisfarne. The Norsemen were here—the Viking age had begun.

The raiders destroyed the abbey on the island and looted its treasures. A monk of
the period described them:

*Never before has such terror appeared in Britain as we have now suffered from a pagan race.
. . . The heathens poured out the blood of saints around the altar, and trampled on the bodies
of saints in the temple of God, like dung in the streets.*

This marked the beginning of waves of assaults by the Danes on the coastlines
of the British Isles. The great Christian champion in the fight against the pagan

Danes was Alfred the Great, incidentally the only English monarch to be given that epithet.

Popular legend tells how after one defeat, Alfred fled for his life. Seeking shelter, he found refuge in the home of a peasant woman who did not know the identity of her guest. She put him to work watching cakes cook on the fire. But the king, his mind elsewhere, let the cakes burn. Just as the woman began to berate Alfred about his carelessness, her husband returned home. He recognized the king immediately. Falling to his knees, the man begged Alfred's forgiveness, as did his wife. But the humble warrior quickly reassured them, insisting that he was the one who should apologize.

Despite Alfred's efforts, the Danes managed to defeat all the other independent English kingdoms. By this time, Saxon fortunes had reached their lowest ebb. Only Alfred and his followers were left to defend Wessex, the English culture, and, significantly, the new English language. Alfred took on the Viking invaders, driving them back. In the process, he began to style himself "King of the Anglo-Saxons," the first ruler to do so.

Eventually, Saxon and Dane reached a compromise. By this time, more and more settlers were arriving from Denmark, following in the footsteps of the first warriors. They were coming in such numbers that Alfred saw the need to establish treaties defining boundaries between the rival kingdoms and creating peaceful relations between them.

The new Norse realm was known as *Danelov*—the Danelaw. The Danelaw extended along much of northern and eastern England, effectively making it a province of Denmark. In the years ahead, the Danelaw would come under attack by other Viking raiders. Further conflict with the Saxons would also sap its strength. Eventually, the Danelaw agreed to merge back with its Saxon neighbors, submitting to the rule of Edward the Elder in an enlarged kingdom of England.

The north of England has hundreds of place-names with the suffixes *by* or *thorpe*, which come from Old Norse. Place-names that end with *by*, such as Whitby, were often settlements the Vikings established first. Places with *thorpe*, like Newthorpe, were likely secondary settlements, on poor land. Yorkshire has about 150 such place-names.

## Brave Little Berwick

The most northerly town in England is Berwick-upon-Tweed. Here, the border with Scotland is just two and a half miles away, and throughout history, this has left the small town in both a strategic and a precarious position.

Since 1018, when the Scots defeated the Northumbrians and won control of Berwick, the city has changed hands over and

over again. During one 35-year-period in the 12th century, it switched between Scotland and England no fewer than 13 times. Today, Berwick is in the English county of Northumbria (not to be confused with the county of Berwickshire in Scotland). As if still making up their minds, however, Berwick's soccer and rugby teams play not in English but in Scottish leagues.

Berwick-upon-Tweed's fluctuating allegiances have resulted in some strange happenings over the years. But none is more bizarre than the town's "international relations" with Russia. Because of

> **IN NORTHERN ENGLAND**
>
> Though abandoned by the early fifth century and tumbledown and obliterated in places, **Hadrian's Wall** remains a stunning sight— particularly where it rides the rim of the great dolerite cliffs of the Whin Sill like the crest of an enormous, breaking wave.

its ever changing status, Berwick often had to be specially accommodated in official proclamations, resulting in references to "England, Scotland, and Berwick-upon-Tweed." Such is said to have been the case in 1853 when Queen Victoria signed a declaration of war against Russia.

The Crimean War pitted Britain and France against an expansionist Russian Empire. At stake, as the Western powers saw it, was growing Russian influence in the Black Sea and in the territories of an Ottoman Empire in terminal decline. Much of the fighting occurred on the Crimean Peninsula. Most people know little about the causes, events, or outcomes of what was in many ways a calamitous and badly organized war. But they do know about the nurse Florence Nightingale, whose image once adorned the reverse side of a British ten-pound note.

After the outbreak of the Crimean War, reports reached Britain about the awful conditions in which the wounded were being treated. Florence Nightingale organized a group of 38 other volunteer nurses and

**WALKING THE WALL**
A hiker makes his way along a section of Hadrian's Wall, which undulates for more than 70 miles across the north of England. Experienced walkers can cover the entire length in six days, which allows time for visiting various Roman sites along the way.

headed for the front. There, she found that ten times more British soldiers were dying from typhus, typhoid, dysentery, and cholera than from battle wounds. Nightingale and her team immediately set about improving conditions at the field hospitals, proving the link between sanitation and the health of the wounded.

The Sanitary Commission later arrived from Britain, and hospital sewers were flushed out and ventilation improved. Death rates dropped dramatically as the wounded began to receive adequate hygiene, diet, and attention. Florence Nightingale returned to Britain, having become the most famous Victorian after the queen herself. She later helped establish a Royal Commission on the Health of the Army, which revolutionized medical care in the British military.

The period during the Crimean War saw many other developments: It was the first war that made significant use of the telegraph. It also saw the first "live" war reporting, by the *Times,* and was the first European conflict to be photographed. After one report by the London newspaper described Nightingale as a "ministering angel," making her way among the sick by night, she became known affectionately as the Lady with the Lamp.

The *Times* coined another term during the war's Battle of Balaclava. In the course of the fighting, the overwhelming Russian forces seemed poised to break through to the vulnerable British rear camp at the Black Sea port. All that stood between the Russians and victory was a thin line of Scottish foot soldiers from the 93rd Sutherland Highlanders.

On the morning of October 25, 1854, the Russian cavalry launched an attack against the red-coated infantrymen. The Scottish commander warned his troops that there could be no retreat; they would have to die where they stood. Meanwhile, the Russians came on. From a nearby hill, the *Times'* war correspondent watched events unfold as this "thin red streak tipped with a line of steel" repulsed the attack. The idea of the "thin red line" came to symbolize the British army's coolness under fire in battle.

Momentum in the battle began to swing. The Russians went on the defensive, lining up their artillery around the sides of a valley through which British light cavalry were preparing to attack. What followed, however, was one of the most

## [ Northern Specialties ]

1 **Black pudding** A dark sausage made with pig's blood, fat, herbs, spices, and other ingredients, often served fried for breakfast.

2 **Butty** A sandwich often called, as in Liverpool, a "chip butty"—buttered white bread layered with chips (fries) and tomato sauce.

3 **Cumberland sauce** A sauce made with red-currant jelly and usually served cold with gammon, game, and other meats. It is not, however, served with Cumberland sausage—a long, thin sausage made in a distinctive coil.

4 **Cheshire cheese** A hard, white, slightly crumbly cheese, and, according to the British Cheese Board, the third most popular cheese in Britain after Cheddar and Stilton. Another hard white cheese, Wensleydale, from the Yorkshire Dales region, is Britain's fourth favorite cheese.

5 **Eccles cake** A flat, round cake made with flaky (shortcrust) pastry and filled with currants; named after the town of Eccles in Lancashire. Chorley cake, another Lancashire invention, is similar. Both are often eaten with a slice of Lancashire cheese.

6 **Faggots** Also known as "ducks," these large meatballs are traditionally made from offal or meat off-cuts, notably pig's heart, liver, pork belly, or bacon, with herbs and, sometimes, bread crumbs. Traditionally wrapped in caul fat, the membrane from a pig's abdomen.

7 **Pan haggerty** A traditional Northumberland dish of layered potatoes, onions, and cheese slow-cooked in a pan until crispy.

**BEST OF BRITISH**
A deli in York offers local meats, beers, and cheeses as well as imported fare.

## WORTH A VISIT

The English Lake District has drawn visitors for centuries.
Those inclined to take to the water don't have to just head
out in rowboats, picturesque as they are. Also available
are everything from 19th-century steamers to luxury
motor yachts to solar electric passenger boats.

ill-fated moves in Britain's long military history—the Charge of the Light Brigade, immortalized by Alfred, Lord Tennyson:

*Half a league, half a league,*
*Half a league onward,*
*All in the valley of Death*
*Rode the six hundred.*
*"Forward the Light Brigade!*
*Charge for the guns!" he said.*
*Into the valley of Death*
*Rode the six hundred.*

### IN THE LAKE DISTRICT

The 900-square mile **Lake District National Park,** created in 1951, includes 16 natural lakes, several reservoirs, and 180 fells over 2,000 feet high. This is England's best loved, most jealously guarded, and most frequented piece of landscape—too well loved, many would say. The vast majority of visitors stick to the main roads, but the fells out on the fringes of the district are still remarkably uncrowded.

The charge of the British Light Brigade at Balaclava was an act of magnificent but reckless—and ultimately futile—bravery. About one-third of the more than 600 cavalrymen fell to the heavy Russian gunfire. *"C'est magnifique, mais ce n'est pas la guerre"* ("it is magnificent, but it is not war"), commented a watching French officer. In February 1856, the war ended, with the British and French confident they had checked Russian power in the Black Sea region and protected the territorial integrity of the Ottoman Empire. The peace was formalized by the Treaty of Paris, which brings us back to the question of Berwick-upon-Tweed. Although the city had been mentioned in the declaration of war by Queen Victoria, it was omitted from the peace treaty. Strictly speaking, the story goes, Berwick was still at war with the Russian Empire.

In 1966, a Soviet official visited Berwick. He came to meet with the mayor and to sign a formal treaty between the small English town and the largest country in the world.

**LONELY AS A CLOUD**
A solitary spectator watches sun, shadow, mountain, and water combine from the vantage point of Sphinx Rock in the Lake District National Park.

"Please tell the Russian people that they can sleep peacefully in their beds," the mayor presumably assured his guest from Moscow.

## The English Lake District

The border between England and Scotland, legally established since the 13th century, is one of the oldest extant in the world. Along the border run the high Cheviot Hills, but otherwise, the frontier is unremarkable. Today, travelers pay it as little attention as invading Scottish armies did over the centuries.

Turning south at the far side of the border, where northwest England bulges out into the Irish Sea, we reach a region much prized by the English, past and present: the Lake District. The highest peak in England rises here, to a height of 3,210 feet. Around Scafell Pike are 900 square miles of magnificent fells (hills), lakes, moors, and fertile valley bottoms. Even the names of the lakes themselves are evocative: Windermere, Derwent Water, Ullswater, Grasmere.

The most famous resident of the Lake District was the Romantic poet William Wordsworth, who was born in the small market town of Cockermouth in 1770 and spent much of his life writing about this part of England.

Wordsworth could be awed by the sight of London from Westminster Bridge, and for several years he lived in the south of England. But he was irresistibly drawn back to the Lake District. It was here, amid the lakes and fells of his childhood, that Wordsworth was at home, his adult years filled with "plain living, but high thinking."

Other writers came to this "English Switzerland," like Samuel Taylor Coleridge and Sir Walter Scott. Painters gathered here, too, such as Thomas Gainsborough, John Constable, and J. M. W. Turner. But no one has captured the essence of the place as evocatively as Wordsworth, whose name is ever associated with the Lake District.

Wordsworth's poem "I Wandered Lonely as a Cloud" is one of his best loved, revealing—as many of his poems did—his sense of joy and elation at the beauty of nature. The poet, who is said to have walked some 175,000 miles during the course of his life, wrote as he rambled throughout the region. One can imagine him as he strolled across the flower-filled landscape, writing:

## [ On the Lakes ]

**1 Coniston Water** Famous as the site of world-record speed attempts by Sir Malcolm Campbell and his son, Donald, in the 1930s and 1960s, and as the inspiration for Arthur Ransome's children's classic, *Swallows and Amazons* (1930). Visitors can board the solar-powered Coniston Launch or the historic steam-yacht *Gondola*—built in 1859 and restored and owned by the National Trust—for scenic rides that include Brantwood, home of the celebrated Victorian critic, John Ruskin.

**2 Derwent Water** The small, elegant boats of the Keswick Launch Company visit seven points on Derwent Water, widely considered the most idyllic of the region's smaller lakes.

**3 Ullswater** Second only to Windermere in terms of beauty and stature, and dominated by Helvellyn, one of the region's finest mountains. Historic ferries such as *Lady of the Lake* (1887) and *Raven* (1889) have been operating from Pooley Bridge for over a century.

**4 Windermere** This is the most celebrated of the lakes, with a ferry service that started around 1845. Today, Windermere Lake Cruises offers scenic services between most points of the 10.5-mile-long lake. More than a million people a year use the service.

*I wandered lonely as a cloud*
*That floats on high o'er vales and hills,*
*When all at once I saw a crowd,*
*A host, of golden daffodils;*
*Beside the lake, beneath the trees,*
*Fluttering and dancing in the breeze.*

William Wordsworth is buried in the churchyard in Grasmere, the place he referred to as "the loveliest spot that man hath ever found." He never forgot his first glimpse of the village from the brow of a nearby hill, writing, "And, if I thought of dying, if a thought of mortal separation could intrude with paradise before him, here to die!"

Millions of visitors from Britain and all over the world make their way to Wordsworth's Lake District every year. A favorite for many is Hill Top, the home of children's author Beatrix Potter, who set many of her Peter Rabbit books in the area. The Lake District National Park was established in 1951 to protect the landscape and prevent unwanted development.

## Lancashire, Past and Present

In the second half of the 15th century, a civil war erupted in the north of England. This struggle was not between Parliament and king, like the war between puritans and royalists in the 17th century. It was a dynastic fight for the throne of England between two rival houses from two rival counties: the House of Lancaster and the House of York. The heraldic badge of Lancaster was the red rose; the white rose stood for York. The conflict was known as the Wars of the Roses.

> ### IN NORTH ENGLAND
>
> **The Pennine Hills**, or Pennies, run from the north Midlands through the great industrial conglomeration around Manchester and northward to Scotland. These are high, bleak uplands with huge swaths of high grassland—exhilarating walking country, under skies that can deliver rain, hail, mist, and sunshine within the space of an hour.

Both houses could claim descent from King Edward III. But the ruling monarch, Henry VI, a Lancastrian, was feeble and suffered from mental illness. He had also surrounded himself with unpopular nobles. Civil unrest broke out across much of the land.

The wars—a series of clashes—went on for 30 years. At the Battle of Bosworth in 1485, Henry Tudor of Lancaster was finally victorious in the quest for the crown. As a symbolic act of reunification, Henry married a Yorkist princess. The Tudor era had begun.

Below the Lake District is Lancashire. Here, the county transitions from a mostly rural and agricultural north to an industrial and urban south. The towns are tightly packed in these parts and include Burnley, Blackburn, Rochdale, Bolton, Salford, Wigan—and most importantly, Manchester and Liverpool.

Manchester in the 19th century was the greatest textile town in the world, earning the nickname of Cottonopolis. Today, it is most famous for its Manchester United soccer team. Across the Pennines, which divide it from Manchester,

**CROSS-TRAINING**
Cyclists carry their bikes up a hill and over a stone wall during an annual cross-country bike race near Horton in the Yorkshire Dales National Park.

**BEATLES FOREVER**

The location that inspired the famous Beatles' song drew more visitors than ever in 2008, when Liverpool celebrated its status as European Capital of Culture. Strawberry Field is one stop along the way for the organized Beatles tours around the city.

Yorkshire might claim to be home to the first association soccer (football) club in the world: Sheffield F.C. But Lancashire's "Man United" can brag of being best, biggest, and most popular (although Real Madrid can probably make an equally strong case).

Traditionally, Manchester United has had a number of particularly fierce rivals, including cross-town Manchester City and Leeds United in Yorkshire. Currently, its biggest rival is Liverpool Football Club, approximately 35 miles down the Trent and Mersey Canal, which provided such an important link between Manchester, Liverpool, and the Irish Sea during the industrial revolution.

During the 18th century, Liverpool grew into a major port city thanks to trade with North America, the West Indies, and mainland Europe. By the beginning of the next century, the city's docks were handling some 40 percent of the world's trade. In 2007, Liverpool was honored as the European Capital of Culture, an annual honor awarded by the European Union. For many, however, Liverpool's greatest cultural contribution to the world will always be the Beatles.

Visitors to Liverpool can embark on their very own Magical Mystery Tour of Beatles sites and reference points: For instance, Matthew Street was home to the Cavern

Club, where the Silver Beatles, as they were known before 1962, were discovered by Brian Epstein. Stanley Street has a statue of a seated Eleanor Rigby. The suburb of Woolton, close to where Paul McCartney and John Lennon lived, provided the inspiration for the Beatles's double-A-side single featuring "Strawberry Fields Forever" and "Penny Lane." And it was at a St. Peter's Church dance in Woolton that the songwriting team first met.

Like many large port cities, Liverpool has a diverse population. It is home to the United Kingdom's oldest black community and Europe's oldest Chinese community. Since the Irish potato famine, the city has also had a large Irish population, with more than 20 percent of its inhabitants hailing from Ireland by 1851. And the city has such strong links to Wales that it is sometimes called "the capital of North Wales."

## Isle of Man

Before visiting the principality of Wales, however, we'll take a short detour to the Isle of Man. This great humpbacked island, 30 miles long and 10 miles wide, is set in the middle of the Irish Sea, right at the geographical center of the British Isles, a three-and-a-half-hour ferry ride from Heysham on the Lancashire coast.

Technically, the Isle of Man is not a part of the United Kingdom, but an internally self-governing jurisdiction. The island has its own parliament, the Tynwald, a Norse name that reflects early Viking settlement here. The Tynwald dates from around A.D. 979 and claims to be the oldest continuously existing parliament in the world.

The Isle of Man may have gotten its name from Manannán mac Lir, a Celtic sea god who was said to have drawn his cloak around the island to protect it from invaders. Today, its only invaders are tourists who come from the surrounding countries—England and Wales, Scotland, and northern and southern Ireland.

Indeed, the Irish have their own tradition about how the island was formed. According to Irish tales, one of their legendary giants, Finn McCool, scooped up a chunk of earth and threw it at a Scottish rival while in the middle of an argument. His throw fell short, though, and landed in the sea, creating the Isle of Man. And the place where he scooped up the earth became the site of a lake, Lough Neagh, the biggest in the British Isles.

## [ Beatles Liverpool Landmarks ]

1 **Arnold Grove, Wavertree** George Harrison was born on this street at No. 12.

2 **Forthlin Road** Paul McCartney grew up on this street of terraced houses at No. 20. Today, a heritage body, the National Trust, owns the house.

3 **Quarry Bank Grammar School, Harthill Road** The school attended by John Lennon and the place where he formed his first band, the Quarry Men.

4 **Jacaranda, 23 Slater Street** The Beatles played many concerts at the "Jac," which is still a popular nightclub.

5 **Lewis's, Ranelagh Street** A well-known department store where Paul McCartney once worked, and where the band played at several staff parties.

6 **Penny Lane, off Smithdown Road, Allerton** A tiny street in southeast Liverpool, which still boasts the bank, fish and chips shop, and barber shop featured in the eponymous song.

7 **St. Peter's Church, Woolton** This is where the Quarry Men played their first concert and where Paul McCartney and John Lennon first met.

8 **Strawberry Field, Beaconsfield Road** A Salvation Army children's home on the outskirts of Liverpool where John Lennon played as a child, and which lent its name—slightly altered—to the song "Strawberry Fields Forever."

9 **The Cavern, 10 Mathew Street** A former Victorian warehouse that became a popular basement club at which the Beatles performed more than 300 times. The original has gone, but a club of the same name exists on the site.

# Sites and Sights in Northern England

**York** is the finest small city in the north of England. Other places have ancient town walls, narrow old streets, good museums, and fine big churches, but none has them in quite such a concentration of excellence as does York. Unlike the mostly eroded walls of other medieval cities, York has an almost complete ring of about three miles of tall and sturdy walls. The tangle of medieval alleyways and streets (here called "gates") connect fine museums, shops, and churches, including the massive York Minster.

Begun in 1220 and finished in 1472, **York Minster** is the largest medieval church in northern Europe, a great storehouse of fine artistic treasures—chief among them the 120-odd stained glass windows. Its official title is the Cathedral and Metropolitan Church of St. Peter in York.
*www.yorkminster.org*

The **York Dungeon** serves up a spine-chilling tour around the plague-infested streets of 14th-century York. You can follow Dick Turpin to the gallows and be introduced to ghostly reincarnations of Roman legionaries.
*www.yorkdungeonguide.com*

The **Yorkshire Dales National Park**, north of Keighley and west of Harrogate, has hundreds of square miles of wild upland moors, grasslands, and hills, cut by broad valleys with shallow rushing rivers where some of the lushest pasture in Britain makes everything green. Dales folk are extremely proud of their small, neat villages; cozy little pubs; green fields seamed with drystone walls; and far-ranging views.
*www.yorkshiredales.org.uk*

The Brontë sisters lived and wrote in the hilltop village of **Haworth** amid the wild, brooding landscape that seems full of their spirit. Here in the spare and sober dining room of the

sandstone Georgian house now known as the **Brontë Parsonage Museum**, the sisters wrote their astonishing novels.
*www.bronte.org.uk*

**Fountains Abbey**, set in a lovely wooded valley, was founded by Benedictines in 1132 and taken over by Cistercians three years later. Within a generation it was the richest abbey in Britain through wool, lead, quarrying, and agricultural interests. In 1720, the remaining ruins and land were transformed into Studley Royal water garden and 1,800 acres of landscaped grounds with grottoes, cascades, temples, lakes, bowers, deer parks, woods, and wide-open spaces—a World Heritage site and a treat not to be missed.
*www.fountainsabbey.org.uk*

Durham Cathedral

**Scarborough** is a popular British resort town, but perhaps it is best known worldwide for Scarborough Fair, made famous by Simon and Garfunkel's song of the same name. The ancient song, said to be sung by wandering bards during the Middle Ages, has many versions and lyrics not included in the recent version.
*www.scarborough-online.co.uk*

**Whitby** is charm encapsulated, with its 13th-century abbey ruins on the cliff

overlooking **Robin Hoods Bay**. At the top of the 199 Church Stairs stands the Norman Church of St. Mary, its interior woodwork reputedly the creation of ships' carpenters. Part of Dracula was set in the graveyard.
*http://www.robin-hoods-bay.co.uk/*

**Durham**'s compact and hilly town center with its steep and winding alleys, known as vennels, is one of the best townscapes in Britain and a treasure trove to explore. While here, walk across the 14th-century bridge **Framwellgate Bridge** for a wonderful view of the castle walls and cathedral towers rising up from the town.

**Durham Castle**—together with nearby Durham Cathedral now a World Heritage site—is a masterpiece of Norman architecture. Begun in 1072, it retains some older features, notably a Tudor chapel with some beautiful misericords and a 15th-century kitchen. Most of it, though, is an 18th-century Gothic rebuild for the bishops of Durham, who remained in residence until 1836 when the castle was given to Durham University.
*www.dur.ac.uk/university.college*

**Durham Cathedral** is often called the finest and most spectacularly sited Norman castle in Britain. Adjacent to the castle, it has imposing twin towers that loom over Jesus Mill on the bank of the River Wear.
*www.durhamcathedral.co.uk*

Northumbrian Coast stretches 70 miles from Newcastle to the Scottish border. **Newcastle-upon-Tyne**, the former capital city of England's northernmost county of Northumberland, is a vibrant, lively place. It has seen its shipbuilding and heavy engineering fade away, but the Geordies (Newcastle natives) have not lost their strong, distinctive local accent.
*www.visitnorthumberland.com*

The **Blinking Eye Bridge**, officially the Gateshead Millennium Bridge, built in 2000 to celebrate the Millennium, is also called the "tilting bridge." An aesthetic and engineering marvel, it has a pedestrian deck and a "cycleway" a foot apart, allowing safety and clear views of the River Tyne while crossing it.
*www.gateshead.gov.uk/Leisure%20and%20Culture/attractions/bridge/Home.aspx*

**Berwick-upon-Tweed** is an ancient border town that has long been bloodily disputed between England and Scotland.
*www.exploreberwick.co.uk*

No site in England is more of an icon for Harry Potter fans than **Alnwick Castle**, Hogwarts School of Witchcraft and Wizardry in the first two films—unforgettable as the site of the quiddich match. It is inhabited by the Duke and Duchess of Northumberland and their family, as it has been for 700 years.
*www.alnwickcastle.com*

A short drive over the causeway from Beal leads to a delightful adventure—a compact, picturesque village with a church and priory founded A.D. 635, a castle, and the seabirds of St. Cuthbert's **Holy Island of Lindisfarne**.

**Hadrian's Wall** is far and away the most important relic of Roman rule in Britain. Its sheer size (73 miles in length) and unbroken westward run give it a coherence and solidity that helps bring the 400 years of Roman occupation alive across two millennia.
*www.hadrians-wall.org*

**The Hadrian's Wall Path National Trail** runs for 84 miles from Newcastle to Bowness-on-Solway, passing through outstanding scenery along the way and taking in all the forts, museums, and existing sections of the wall.
*www.nationaltrail.co.uk/hadrianswall*

**Liverpool** was once the British Empire's second most important port after London, but it is now best known as the home of the Beatles. No visit here is complete without wandering around Liverpool to see the National Trust-owned childhood homes of John Lennon and Paul McCartney and seeing The Beatles Story, a museum extravaganza that explores the lives of the Fab Four.
*www.beatlesstory.com*

From the *Lindisfarne Gospels*

Down on the waterfront the **Mersey Ferries** embark passengers for Birkenhead across the water and run several excellent themed cruises. These are enjoyable rides and worth taking for the view back to **Liverpool**'s grand Merseyside threesome: the domed **Port of Liverpool Building**, the great bulk of the **Cunard Building**, and the soaring clock towers of the **Royal Liver Building**.
*www.merseyferries.co.uk*

Manchester's **Albert Square** is dominated by the giant Gothic **Town Hall** with its 280-foot clock tower. The first-floor Great Hall has Pre-Raphaelite murals by Ford Madox Brown.

The **Museum of Science and Industry in Manchester** celebrates the city's industrial past with hot oil and hissing engines in the Power Hall, ramshackle early gliders, and huge reconnaissance planes in the Air and Space Gallery.
*www.mosi.org.uk*

The 900-square-mile **Lake District National Park**, established in 1951, includes 16 natural lakes, several reservoirs, and 180 fells more than 2,000 feet high. This is England's best loved, most jealously guarded, and most frequented piece of landscape—too well loved, many would say. The vast majority of visitors stick to the main roads, but the fells out on the fringes of the district are still remarkably uncrowded.
*www.lakedistrict.gov.uk*

**Grasmere** is the prime attraction for Wordsworth fans. Here is **Dove Cottage**, William and Dorothy's home from 1799 to 1808, prolific years in which he wrote some of his best known poetry. Household items belonging to the Wordsworths, such as furniture, portraits, and family possessions, are displayed here.
*www.wordsworth.org.uk*

It takes about two to three hours by ferry to reach the **Isle of Man**. The humpbacked island in the Irish Sea is 30 miles long and 10 wide. It possesses its own parliament, customs, and special atmosphere. The best way to see the island is to walk the 25-mile **Millennium Way footpath**, which runs from Ramsay to Castletown down the hilly spine of Man.
*www.gov.im*

**The Pennines** run from the north Midlands through the great industrial conglomeration around Manchester and northward to Scotland. These are high, bleak uplands with huge swaths of high grassland—exhilarating walking country, under skies that can deliver rain, hail, mist, and sunshine within the space of an hour. The 259-mile **Pennine Way National Trail**, one of Britain's longest and toughest long-distance paths, takes about three weeks to complete at a reasonable pace.
*www.nationaltrail.co.uk/PennineWay*

The ruined drum towers and curtain walls of the Norman-era **Barnard Castle** stand dramatically on their wooded crag above the River Tees in Teesdale. Charles Dickens stayed here in 1838 at the King's Head Hotel while researching his setting for Dotheboys Hall in Nicholas Nickleby.
*www.barnardcastlelife.co.uk*

Wales juts out from mainland Britain as if unsure whether it belongs to Anglo-Saxon England or to Celtic Ireland just across the Irish Sea. Like sentries standing guard, three large English cities stake out its borders: Liverpool in the northeast corner, Bristol in the southeast, and in the middle, some distance back, England's second city of Birmingham, but with forward pickets in Shrewsbury and Hereford.

However, visitors who cross the Severn Bridge into Wales at Bristol are immediately aware that this is not just another region of England. Here, the road signs are in Welsh as well as English. And as we journey around the country, we will find that the differences become more and more apparent with every twist and turn of the dramatic Welsh coastline.

**LAND MEETS SEA**
Waves process into a rocky cove along the rugged Pembrokeshire coast in southwest Wales.
*Previous pages:* Sheep, shepherds, and dogs in Snowdonia National Park.

Cardiff, the capital of Wales and the country's largest city, can be accessed by way of the Severn Estuary. In the first half of the 20th century, Cardiff was the busiest coal port in the world, but today it is no longer the port it once was. North of the capital, the mines in the Rhonnda, Ebbw, and Sirhowy Valleys once poured tons of coal down to the docks of Cardiff. But these mines are now silent, too.

As these industries have disappeared, so has a way of life that was once distinctively Welsh. The changing face of Wales was captured beautifully in the 1939 novel by Richard Llewellyn, *How Green Was My Valley,* and in the 1941 film of the same name directed by John Ford. It tells the story of a Welsh mining village at the turn of the 20th century as it is transformed from an unspoiled, rural valley community to an industrialized region bound to the black gold beneath its green pastures.

Disaster struck one of those valleys in 1966, in the small village of Aberfan. For more than half a century, the debris from a local mine had been piled up on the side of a mountain overlooking the village. On the morning of October 21, after several days of rain, the loose rock and mining slag began to slide downhill, crashing on the village like a huge avalanche.

It was a Friday, and thus a school day at Pantglas Junior School. The students were attending assembly when the slide began, singing "All Things Bright and Beautiful." By 9:15 a.m. they were back in their classrooms when the debris smashed into the school.

Parents and emergency service workers rushed to the scene and began digging with their bare hands. They managed to pull a few children out alive, but no survivors were found after 11 a.m. In all, 144 people perished in Aberfan, 116 of them children. Most died from asphyxia or were crushed to death.

# WALES

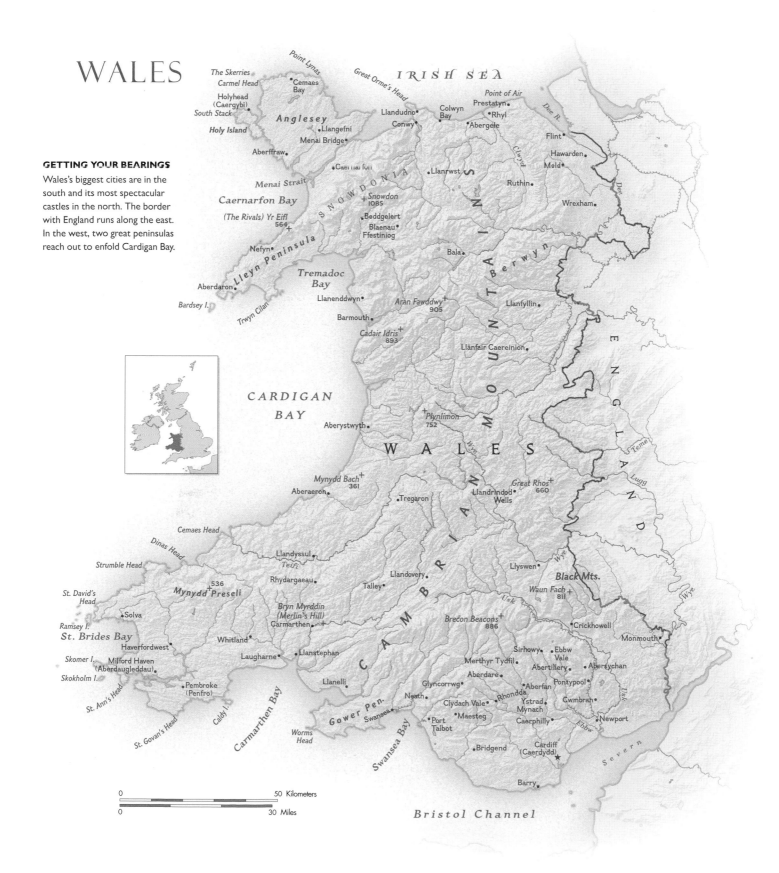

**GETTING YOUR BEARINGS**

Wales's biggest cities are in the south and its most spectacular castles in the north. The border with England runs along the east. In the west, two great peninsulas reach out to enfold Cardigan Bay.

*IRISH SEA*

Point Lynas
The Skerries
Carmel Head
Cemaes Bay
Great Orme's Head
Point of Air
Prestatyn
Holyhead (Caergybi)
South Stack
Holy Island
*Anglesey*
Llandudno
Colwyn Bay
Rhyl
Abergele
Conwy
Langefni
Aberffraw
Menai Bridge
Caernarfon
Llanrwst
Ruthin
Flint
Hawarden
Mold
Wrexham
*Menai Strait*
*Caernarfon Bay*
*SNOWDONIA*
Snowdon 1085
+Snowdon
1085
(The Rivals) Yr Eifl 564
Beddgelert
Blaenau Ffestiniog
Nefyn
*Lleyn Peninsula*
Bala
*Berwyn*
Aberdaron
*Tremadoc Bay*
Llanenddwyn
Aran Fawddwy 905
Llanfyllin
Bardsey I.
Barmouth
Trwyn Cilan
Cadair Idris 893
Llanfair Caereinion

*CARDIGAN BAY*
Plynlimon 752
*MOUNTAINS*
Aberystwyth
*W A L E S*
*E N G L A N D*

Mynydd Bach 361
Aberaeron
Great Rhos 660
Llandrindod Wells
Tregaron

Cemaes Head
Dinas Head
Llandyssul
*Teifi*
Llyswen
Strumble Head
Rhydargaeau
*CAMBRIAN*
Llandovery
Talley
*Black Mts.*
St. David's Head
Mynydd Preseli 536
Waun Fach 811
Ramsey I.
Solva
Bryn Myrddin (Merlin's Hill)
Carmarthen
Brecon Beacons 886
Crickhowell
*St. Brides Bay*
Whitland
Monmouth
Haverfordwest
Skomer I.
Milford Haven (Aberdaugleddau)
Laugharne
Llanstephan
Sirhowy
Ebbw Vale
Abersychan
Skokholm I.
Merthyr Tydfil
Abertillery
St. Ann's Head
Pembroke (Penfro)
Llanelli
Aberdare
Aberfan
Pontypool
Cwmbran
Caldy I.
Glyncorrwg
Rhondda
St. Govan's Head
*Gower Pen.*
Neath
Clydach Vale
Ystrad Mynach
*Carmarthen Bay*
Swansea
Maesteg
Caerphilly
Newport
Worms Head
Port Talbot
*Swansea Bay*
Bridgend
Cardiff (Caerdydd)
*Severn*
Barry

*Bristol Channel*

0        50 Kilometers
0        30 Miles

## A Country Looking Forward, a Country Looking Back

Now, more than 50 years after the Aberfan disaster, the coal seams have been mined to exhaustion, and production is at an end. Much about Wales is now modern and forward-looking: Cardiff is a fashionable city, cosmopolitan and devoted to the arts—the biggest media center in the United Kingdom after London. But the recent resurgence of the Welsh language and culture suggests the country is also looking back to its ancient and Celtic past.

**IN LAUGHARNE**

The lyrical **Welsh language** is enjoying a revival, being taught in the public schools and appearing widely in regional newspapers and magazines. Place names like Betwys y Coed look as if they must contain a typographical error, but the spellings are actually logical and phonetic and the words fairly simple to pronounce (sounds like bet-is-i-COID).

It was during the reign of Henry VIII that the Welsh language was almost stamped out in its own land. At his orders, government officials were forced to speak only English, which was also the language used in the courts of law. That Welsh survived in the early 1700s was largely thanks to its usage in the pulpits of the country's nonconformist and Methodist chapels, which were and continue to be an integral part of the Welsh culture. Preachers spoke in Welsh, congregations sang in Welsh, and today, schoolchildren are taught in Welsh as well as in English.

Moving around the rugged coastline, we pass Swansea, a manufacturing center and the second city of Wales, and the spectacular cliffs and beaches of the Gower Peninsula. Just beyond it is a river estuary that leads up to Carmarthen, said to be Wales's oldest town. This is the supposed birthplace of Merlin, the wizard of Arthurian lore. According to local legend, he was the son of a Welsh princess and a spirit who lived between the moon and the earth.

**CARDIFF CASTLE**
The ruined stone keep of Cardiff's Norman castle stands on the motte of an earlier stronghold. Located near the city center, the castle is today more welcoming of outsiders, offering traditional Welsh banquets and music, mead tasting, lectures on art and architecture, medieval jousting, and even a venue for weddings.

Carmarthen is also supposedly the place where Merlin remains. As an old man, he was living in a cave on what is now Merlin's Hill, overlooking the town, when he fell in love with a beautiful young maiden named Vivien. Eventually, she talked him into revealing his magical secrets in return for her unending love. But when he acquiesced, Vivien used what she had learned to cast a spell on Merlin, sending him into a slumber. Now he lies sleeping in this cave for all eternity, only to come forth if and when King Arthur and his knights awaken.

Legend also claims that Merlin made a prophecy that tied the fate of Carmarthen to the well-being of an ancient local oak tree. It bore this inscription:

*When Merlin's Tree shall tumble down,*
*Then shall fall Carmarthen Town.*

The locals shuddered when the tree had to be removed to make way for a road. They are still awaiting disaster.

## A Poet in a Land of Poets

Back down the river estuary sits the small coastal town of Laugharne. For the great Welsh poet Dylan Thomas, it made for a good stopping point, the place where Thomas "got off the bus and forgot to get back on."

Dylan Thomas lived the last years of his short life in Laugharne. Here, he wrote his famous "play for voices," *Under Milk Wood,* an earthy comedy that eavesdrops on the innermost thoughts of the residents of a fictional Welsh village. Broadcast on BBC Radio in 1954, the play opens in the dead of night:

*To begin at the beginning: It is spring, moonless night in the small town, starless and bible-black, the cobblestreets silent and the hunched, courters-and-rabbits wood limping invisible down to the sloeblack, slow, black, crowblack, fishingboat-bobbing sea. The houses are blind as moles (though moles see fine tonight in the snouting, velvet dingles) or blind as Captain Cat there in the muffled middle by the pump and the town clock, the shops in mourning, the Welfare Hall in widows' weeds. And all the people of the lulled and dumbfound town are sleeping now.*

The first radio production of *Under Milk Wood* featured the voices of the Welsh-born Hollywood star Richard Burton and a cast of lesser-known Welsh actors. Their names capture the unique cadence of the Welsh language: Dafydd Harvard, Sybil Williams, Dylis Davies, Gwenllian Owen, Gwenyth Petty, John Huw Jones, Ieuan Rhys Williams, Olwen Brookes, Dillwyn Owen, John Glyn-Jones.

The BBC production aired a year after Thomas died, at the age of 39. A flawed genius, Thomas drank himself to death. As the play's

**WRITER'S CHAIR**
This bronze statue of Dylan Thomas sits, literally, outside the Dylan Thomas Theatre in Swansea. Opposite, the "writing shed" at the boathouse in Laugharne is where the great poet actually sat to write.

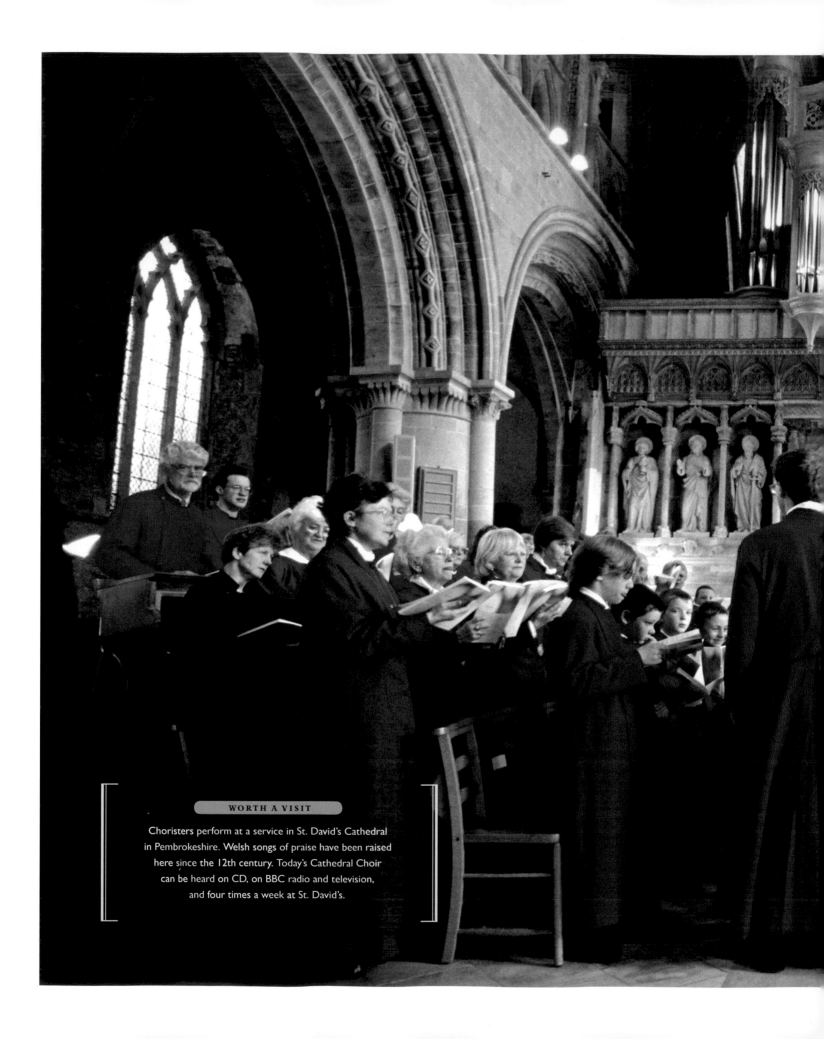

Choristers perform at a service in St. David's Cathedral
in Pembrokeshire. Welsh songs of praise have been raised
here since the 12th century. Today's Cathedral Choir
can be heard on CD, on BBC radio and television,
and four times a week at St. David's.

Reverend Eli Jenkins might say, he was, like the characters he created, "not wholly bad or good, who live our lives under Milk Wood." His grave is in St. Martin's churchyard in Laugharne, marked by a plain white wooden cross.

Two years before his own passing, Thomas composed a poem for his dying father. Its words remain as haunting and raw as ever:

*And you, my father, there on that sad height,*
*Curse, bless, me now with your fierce tears, I pray.*
*Do not go gentle into that good night.*
*Rage, rage against the dying of the light.*

## David, Saint of the Little Things

West of Laugharne is the wild and windswept Pembrokeshire coast. Sculpted by the elements, the land here tapers to a peninsula that seems as intent on reaching far out into the Celtic Sea as Cornwall does below it. St. David's, the smallest cathedral city in the United Kingdom, is located on an isolated headland on the peninsula. The cathedral was built in the late 12th century on the site of a monastery founded by the saint himself, around A.D. 550.

David is the least known of all the patron saints in the British Isles. Patrick, the patron saint of Ireland, is the most famous, celebrated on March 17. England's George is renowned for his dragon-fighting exploits, although the Roman-born saint does have to be shared with Russia, Georgia, Ethiopia, Portugal, and a number of other countries that likewise claim him. And many are familiar with St. Andrew of Scotland, the early follower of Christ who, deeming himself unworthy to die as his master had, requested to be crucified on an X-shaped cross instead. Few, however, have heard of David.

To add insult to Welsh injury, the crosses of Saints Patrick, George, and Andrew are all represented in the Union Flag of the United Kingdom, but the flag of St. David is nowhere to be found. Wales has to rely on its own flag, although it is a striking one at that: a red dragon on a field of green and white.

When it comes to the emblematic plants and flowers of the four countries, the Welsh might also have cause to feel shortchanged. The shamrock is the defining emblem of Ireland and one of the strongest of national "brands," used both officially by government and tourism agencies and informally by sports teams and pubs. And many people know that the rose is the emblem of England—and that in Scotland it is the thistle, or the Scottish bluebell. What of Wales? The country's emblems are the daffodil or the leek, but most people are not aware of that.

Let's return, however, to saints. In David's defense, he was at least born in Wales, the country of which he is the patron saint. In his final sermon, David told his followers, "Be joyful, and keep your faith and your creed. Do the little things that you

---

**IN SOUTHWEST WALES**

Although no one really knows why or how the massive bluestones of Stonehenge got there, they surely came from the **Preseli Mountains** in southwest Wales. Eighty stones, some as tall as 10 feet and weighing up to 5 tons, traveled 180 miles by land and sea to Salisbury Plain.

---

**ITALY ON CARDIGAN BAY**

Portmeirion is a picturesque Italianate resort town on the Welsh coast. It is run as a private resort, open to day-visitors as well as those who choose to stay in its hotels or self-catering cottages.

have seen me do and heard about. I will walk the path that our fathers have trod before us."

Do the little things in life—*gwnewch y pethau bychain mewn bywyd*. Today, those words have passed into Welsh consciousness, a well-known and oft-repeated phrase that is frequently, in this officially bilingual country, spoken in Welsh as well as in English.

---

**IN MID-WALES**

The Victorian seaside town of **Aberystwyth,** often dubbed "Aber," is quintessentially Welsh and widely regarded as the cultural capital of Wales. Here, small wooden railway carriages rise slowly up a 380-foot cliff for a bird's eye view of this lively village and superb surrounding landscape.

---

St. David supposedly lived to be older than 100, dying on March 1, 589. This date is now commemorated as St. David's Day. His relics were enshrined at St. David's Cathedral, in the most westerly part of Wales, drawing many pilgrims there during the Middle Ages.

A few miles inland from St. David's Cathedral rise the slopes of the Preseli Mountains, where the ancients quarried the huge blue-stones used at Stonehenge some five millennia ago. More than 80 of the stones—weighing up to eight tons each—were transported all the way to Salisbury Plain. (Though a more fanciful tale credits Merlin with spiriting the stones from a site in Ireland, where giants had set them up.)

From here, rounding St. David's Head, the coast of Wales seems to reconsider its dramatic lunge to the west, sweeping back in toward the east in the grand curve of Cardigan Bay. Midway up that bay is the seaside resort town of Aberystwyth, which is also home to Aberystwyth University and a hub of Welsh culture.

**CHAPEL ON THE COAST**
Saint Govan's Chapel hugs the coast of southern Pembrokeshire. The tiny, 13th-century chapel can only be accessed by climbing down 52 steps from the cliff top.

Farther up the coast and then inland looms the 2,927-foot peak of Cader Idris, which is a favorite spot for climbers. Local legend holds that anyone who accomplishes the feat of sleeping at the top of the mountain will awaken the next morning as either a madman or a poet.

Located in the southern part of the Snowdonia region, Cader Idris gives a foretaste of the greater peak to come. Farther north, Snowdon rises to 3,500 feet, the highest spot in Wales. Its name in Welsh is *Yr Wyddfa*, or "tomb," which is a reference to the burial site of the giant Rhita Gawr, who wore a cloak that was woven from the beards of the kings he had killed. One king managed to elude him, however: Arthur. The great King of the Britons killed the giant on Snowdon's peak.

Standing at the top of Snowdon's scree slopes, Arthur would have seen what other visitors who make it to the top on a clear day can see—the neighboring countries of England, Scotland, and Ireland. It was in this remote part of Wales that the Celts made their mountain strongholds, which neither the Romans nor Saxons ever succeeded in penetrating.

According to legend, it was to Snowdonia that the British king Vortigern fled from the pursuing Saxons after the Romans' departure. There, on a hill at the foot of the great mountain, he decided to build a fortress. But every time the walls were constructed, they tumbled to the ground. Vortigern's advisers told him that this was the work of an evil spirit that could only be appeased by sacrificing a child who had no father and then sprinkling the child's blood on the foundations.

Royal messengers were dispatched throughout the land to find such a child. Finally, they found young, fatherless Merlin and brought him before the king. But the boy challenged this story, telling Vortigern that the cause of his troubles was actually a pair of dragons—one white, one red—that lived in a subterranean pool under the hill. Each time they fought, said Merlin, the walls came tumbling down. Only by releasing the dragons would the king be able to build his walls.

At Merlin's word, Vortigern dug deep down and found the dragons, one white, representing the Saxons, the other red, representing the Celtic Britons. The youngster assured him that although the white dragon was winning the fight, the eventual victor would be the red dragon, the one found on the Welsh flag today. Merlin then prophesied that while Vortigern would be slain, another leader would arise, Arthur, who would drive the Saxons out.

## [ Five Welsh Castles ]

**1 Chepstow, 1067** Situated on a loop of the River Wye, the castle was built by the Normans one year after the Conquest to guard a key route from England to Wales. Thus it is one of the oldest Welsh castles and one of the first in Britain built from stone.

**2 Carreg Cennen, 1248** On a majestic outcrop in the countryside near Llandeilo, it is the most romantic and impressively situated castle in Wales. Legend describes an earlier castle on the site built by Sir Urien, one of King Arthur's knights.

**3 Caerphilly, 1268** Close to Cardiff, this majestic castle is one of the most visited attractions in Wales, famous for its three moats, six portcullises, great hall (1317), and a leaning tower, said to have been caused by an explosion during the civil war.

**4 Harlech, 1289** For all its grandeur, Harlech, built by Edward I, and now a UNESCO World Heritage site, is often known as the "Castle of Lost Causes," as it fell so often—to Owain Glyndwr in 1404, to Henry V four years later, to the Yorkists in 1468, and to Cromwell in 1647.

**5 Raglan, 1435** There are bigger Welsh castles but few as well preserved. Built on the site of a Norman motte, it is one of several great castles—including Monmouth, Skenfrith, White, and Grosmont—in this often fought-over corner of south Wales.

**NATIONAL HEARTSTRINGS**

A harpist performs outside Harlech Castle in north Wales. Popular in the Celtic world, the harp is considered the national instrument of Wales, used both as an accompaniment to folksinging and, as shown here, as a solo instrument.

## On to the North Coast

"There is no corner of Europe that I know," wrote the novelist and historian Hilaire Belloc, "which so moves me with awe and majesty of great things as does this mass of the northern Welsh mountains."

It is in the fabled north that most of the Welsh-speakers still live—and where traditional Welsh music and verse have been celebrated since 1176 at the Eisteddfod. This annual gathering of minstrels and poets, now called the National Eisteddfod, continues to be the country's largest festival of poetry and music, all conducted in Welsh. Today, the event is held in a different location each year, generally alternating between the country's north and south.

The language of the Welsh people seems to be laced with poetry. Indeed, their powers of oratory can be traced back to the chanting of their bards. In modern times, their facility with the spoken word can be seen in the political radicalism and labor movements that flourished in the mining villages of south Wales.

Politics has long been an area in which the Welsh thrived. The prime minister who led Britain into World War I, David Lloyd George, was an enchanting orator (even in English, his second language) and a savvy political operator. Known as "the man who won the war," Lloyd George faced a particularly difficult challenge during the peace negotiations at Versailles. There the Welsh Wizard had to steer a delicate middle course between the idealistic president of the United States, Woodrow Wilson, and the punitively inclined president of France, Georges Clemenceau. Asked if he believed he had succeeded in his task, Lloyd George famously replied: "I think I did as well as might be expected—seated as I was between Jesus Christ and Napoleon Bonaparte."

Heading back through Snowdon to Cardigan Bay, we come to Harlech Castle, which anchors the base

**SHEPHERDS IN TRAINING**
Young farmers stand with their prize-winning sheep at the Anglesey County Show. Remote, agricultural Anglesey is in the far northwest of Wales. The boat train to Ireland crosses the island on its way to the port of Holyhead.

of the Lleyn Peninsula. As a schoolboy, World War I poet Robert Graves spent holidays in Harlech before the war began in 1914. He found the hills around the town full of enchantment, writing:

*Time has never journeyed to this lost land,*
*Crakeberry and heather bloom out of date,*
*The rocks jut, the streams flow singing on either hand,*
*Careless if the seasons be early or late,*
*The skies wander overhead, now blue, now slate.*

Graves was in Harlech when the war broke out. He immediately enlisted with the Royal Welsh Fusiliers, recording his experiences in the memoir *Good-bye to All That*. Sometime after the war, he moved to the Spanish island of Majorca, where the scenery reminded him of Harlech.

## [ Historic Mines and Underground Tours ]

**1** **Coal, Blaenavon** The former heart of the South Wales mining industry achieved UNESCO World Heritage status in 2000. Visitors can descend 300 feet into an old shaft with a former miner as a guide at the Big Pit National Coal Museum, which operated from 1880 to 1990. Its Heritage Centre provides an overview of the area's rich industrial past.

**2** **Slate, Blaenau Ffestiniog** Welsh slate is the finest in the world, and it dominated world production in 19th-century north Wales, and the Snowdonia area in particular, answering the vast demand for roofing tiles. The Llechwedd Slate Caverns offers a deep-mine tour and insight into this quintessentially Welsh industry.

**3** **Gold, Dolaucothi** The wedding rings of British monarchs are famously made from Welsh gold, much of it taken from this mine near Llandovery. As the only place in Britain where it is known the Romans worked for gold, the mine was exploited until 1938, but visitors can tour it today.

The castle in Harlech was one in a series of "Iron Ring" fortresses built in north Wales by England's Edward I, each a day's march from the next. For years, the Welsh had been challenging English rule. Prince Llewelyn the Great (one of two Welsh monarchs with that epithet) was one such ruler. He had allied himself with the barons who forced King John's hand at Runnymede in 1215, and in the aftermath, he had established himself as the effective ruler of Wales.

In one famous tale, Llewelyn left his dog Gelert to guard his baby son. Upon returning, he found the cradle overturned, the baby gone, and Gelert covered in blood. In a fit of rage, Llewelyn slew the hound, believing that it had killed his son. Only later, when he discovered the baby alive and well, along with the body of a dead wolf, did he realize that the faithful Gelert had saved his son's life. With great sorrow, he buried the animal at Beddgelert (Gelert's grave), north of Harlech, near Snowdon.

After Llewelyn the Great died, struggles with the English crown resumed. His grandson, Llewelyn the Last, also took up the fight. But he was the final true Welshman to be Prince of Wales. It was his campaign to reestablish local Welsh control that spurred Edward I to build his ring of fortresses and to stamp out all remaining resistance in the mountainous north.

Above Harlech Castle, the Lleyn Peninsula makes another bold reach to the west. The underside of the peninsula is flanked by cliffs that alternate with sandy bays all the way to Hell's Mouth, a three-mile-wide stretch favored

by surfers today but dreaded by the mariners of the past. Beyond Hell's Mouth, the coast begins to turn back to the east, punctuated by more of King Edward's English fortresses. Caernarfon is the mightiest of them, with huge octagonal towers and crenellated walls that left the surrounding population in no doubt who was in charge.

Begun in 1283, Caernarfon was the strongest link in the Iron Ring and the site of many key events in Welsh history. After defeating (and beheading) Llewelyn the Last, Edward I sought to install an English Prince of Wales in order to help secure the land. According to one story, he announced that the person who held that office must have two qualifications: He had to be born in Wales and he had to speak no English. The Welsh agreed to accept the king's decision. Too late they realized that the person Edward I had in mind was none other than his own son, Edward II, who had just been born in Caernarfon Castle.

In the early 1400s the Welsh rebelled again, this time under the leadership of the celebrated Owain Glyndwr. Twice Glyndwr attacked Caernarfon, that great symbol

**THE WELSH WEATHER**
As elsewhere in the British Isles, the weather in Wales is changeable and often wet. Above, a hardy young soul braves the elements to climb a pile of uncut roofing slates at Blaenau Ffestiniog in north Wales.

of English rule in north Wales, and twice he failed. The strength of the fortress was so great that a garrison of just 28 were able to hold his troops off. All dreams of Welsh independence finally ended when Henry VIII united the two countries.

The next of the Iron Ring fortresses along the coast is the huge Conwy Castle, which sits inside a small town still surrounded by medieval walls that were built against a once hostile population.

Across the treacherous waters of the Menai Strait, Edward built the last of his castles at Beaumaris. Not far from the castle is the town said to have the longest place-name in the world: *Llanfairpwllgwyngyllgogerychwyrndrobwyllllantysiliogogogoch.* In English, it means, "The church of St. Mary in the hollow of white hazel trees near the rapid whirlpool by St. Tysilio's of the red cave." Thankfully, it is generally shortened to "Llanfair P. G."

This part of Wales across the Menai Strait is Anglesey, the predominantly Welsh-speaking island just off the northwest coast (about 275 yards at the closest point). Mostly a low-lying region, it was dubbed *Mam Cymru,* the "Mother of Wales," by the medieval chronicler Giraldus Cambrensis for its supposed ability to produce enough food to feed the whole country.

Anglesey is dotted with megalithic reminders of its ancient and mystical past. The farthest refuge from invasion, it was here that the druids sheltered in sacred groves before they were massacred at the hands of the Romans. Indeed, this island of the druids has been under siege since written records began. After the Romans came pirates from Ireland, who set up a colony here. Viking invaders arrived next, then the Saxons, and then the Normans. And in the 13th century the island fell to Edward I of England.

The Isle of Anglesey rolls west to the smaller Holy Island. From Holy Island's port at Holyhead the ferry crosses the Irish Sea to Dun Laoghaire, the port of Dublin. Back on the Welsh mainland, though, the coast continues to wend its way east. Finally, it reaches Merseyside and the English county of Cheshire, completing a great circular loop that began in the far southeast with the crossing of the Severn Estuary.

**A RURAL LAND**

Despite industrialization and urbanization, nowhere in Wales is far from the countryside. At left, a horse grazes in a mist-shrouded pasture at sunset near Swansea.

## A Growing Sense of Welsh Identity

The 20th century was one of growing Welsh nationalism and identity, and in 1925 the political party Plaid Cymru ("the Party of Wales") was formed to fight for greater independence and autonomy. A 1979 referendum on the creation of a National Assembly for Wales, however, was roundly defeated.

In 1997, the Welsh people narrowly cast their ballots in favor. The second referendum did not create an independent Welsh nation state, but it did establish an assembly with powers to determine certain legislative matters, such as the manner of UK-government spending in Wales.

For generations, the Welsh have found other ways to maintain their distinctive culture and traditions. With international singers ranging from Tom Jones to Charlotte Church, it is not surprising to learn that Wales is not only known as a land of poets but also as a land of song. Singing is a national passion. And the Welsh are particularly proud of their Male Voice Choirs.

Such choirs first became popular around the end of the 19th century in the coal mining communities of south Wales. Though the mines have closed, the tradition of singing—which once rang out in the shafts deep underground—has continued. Male Voice Choirs have become as iconically Welsh as that other great national passion, rugby football.

Most people in Wales play or watch soccer. But if cricket is the national sport of England, rugby is the national sport of Wales. Rugby is played in England, Scotland, and Ireland, too. In those countries, though, it is something of an elitist sport, played by a privileged few. As the saying goes, "[Soccer] is a gentleman's game played by ruffians, and rugby is a ruffian's game played by gentlemen." In Wales, however, rugby has always been very much the people's sport, played by village teams made up of coal miners and factory workers who participate on their days off work.

The English claim that the game was invented at Rugby School, one of their oldest and most prestigious boarding schools. But the Welsh, who take particular delight in beating the English—or anyone—at rugby, know better. Since medieval times, they have been playing a rugby-like game called *criapan*, particularly in the western counties of Pembrokeshire and Cardiganshire. The Cornish, East Anglians, Irish, and others can point to their own early versions of the game, too.

Its origins notwithstanding, few nations are as passionate about rugby football as the Welsh. Even fewer play it with such panache. Up until 1999, when the new Millennium Stadium opened in Cardiff, the Welsh national rugby team played its home games at Cardiff Arms Park.

For the Welsh, international fixtures at the Arms Park were momentous occasions. The stadium had its own Cardiff Arms Park Male Choir, but most rousing of all was the singing, in near-perfect unison, of its 60,000 fans before the match. Sport, song, and spirituality merged seamlessly as the voices roared out "Cwm Rhondda," commonly known as the "Welsh Rugby Hymn."

The words were also sung in English at the 1997 funeral service of Diana, Princess of Wales: "Guide me, O thou great Redeemer, / Pilgrim through this barren land. / I am weak, but Thou art mighty, / Hold me with Thy powerful hand. / Bread of Heaven, Bread of Heaven, / Feed me til I want no more."

## [ Best Welsh Steam Railways ]

**1 Festiniog** The Welsh have a particular love affair with old steam engines, and the country has long been celebrated for its restored heritage railroads (15 at last count). The 13-mile Festiniog line, built in 1836 to carry slate, is arguably the prettiest.

**2 Llangollen** This former slate-carrying railway opened in 1865 and runs for 10 miles along the Dee valley. It superseded the nearby Llangollen Canal, which was designed by Thomas Telford, and was one of Britain's premier feats of 19th-century canal engineering.

**3 Talyllyn** The world's first volunteer-run restored railway opened in 1951, taking over a line used for carrying slate since 1866. It runs for seven miles through lovely countryside and was the inspiration for the popular "Thomas the Tank Engine" series of children's books.

**4 Vale of Rheidol** Opened in 1902 to serve local lead mines, this narrow-gauge steam line near Aberystwyth runs for 12 miles, often on narrow cliff ledges, and climbs 600 feet in the process.

**5 Welshpool & Llanfair** This narrow-gauge steam line originally closed in 1931 after less than 30 years of operation, but now runs for eight miles through the scenic Banwy and Sylfaen Valleys.

Note: Visit greatlittletrainsofwales.co.uk for further information on nine of the country's best-known heritage railroads.

# Sites and Sights in Wales

Wales is strikingly attractive, with dramatic mountains in the north; a hilly interior; a coastline of fishing villages among long stretches of cliffs and sandy beaches; and rolling hills and valleys punctuated with castles. The country looks with pride on its artistic heritage of legend, song, and poetry, and on its contribution to British society in the lives of so many politicians, thinkers, orators, and social activists. A good general website to visit is *www.touristwales.co.uk/index.html*. Those with a particular interest in sites such as castles should be sure to visit the Castles of Wales website (*www.castlewales.com*), which features an extensive database.

For visitors crossing the Severn Estuary from Bristol, the **Wye Valley** is their first glimpse of Wales. This heavily wooded, deeply cut valley, with England on its eastern bank and Wales on its west, makes a beautiful introduction to the principality.

The dramatic and enchanting ruins of **Tintern Abbey**—among the most spectacular in the world—inspired William Wordsworth's famous poem of revisitation. These tall gray, stone walls, as delicate as lacework, stand on leveled ground by the river and are surrounded by virtually uninterrupted green, rolling hills. Here Cistercian monks followed the austere Rule of St. Benedict from the 12th century to the 16th.
*www.castlewales.com/tintern*

**Cardiff**, now the capital city of Wales, was a modest coastal town until the Marquess of Bute developed its docks at the dawn of the railway era in the 1830s. Within 100 years it had become the busiest coal port in the world, a conduit for the mighty flood of coal pouring out of the mines in the valleys just to the north.

**Cardiff Castle** is an extravagant fantasy of a romantic castle, assembled from 1867 to 1875 by the third Marquess of Bute around the nucleus of a Norman keep. Heavily carved foliage smothered in gold leaf is one of the Moorish-influenced motifs that form the heavy decorative interior.
*www.cardiffcastle.com*

Also worth seeing in the city is the magnificent **Cardiff City Hall** in Cathays Park, with a dragon perched atop its 200-foot dome. **The National Museum and Gallery** has a superbly displayed prehistoric collection and surprisingly comprehensive coverage of Impressionist art. **The Museum of Welsh Life**, on the outskirts of the city at St. Fagans, highlights old customs and lifestyles of Welsh people.
*www.museumwales.ac.uk*

Pistyll Rhaeadr Waterfall

The **Pembrokeshire Coast National Park** in southwest Wales comprises the wild and storm-sculptured tip of Wales's extreme southwest. The massive bluestones of Stonehenge surely came from the **Preseli Mountains** in Pembrokeshire, although no one really knows why or how. Eighty stones, some as tall as 10 feet and weighing up to five tons, traveled 180 miles by land and sea to the Salisbury Plain.
*www.pcnpa.org.uk*

Out at the westernmost point of Pembrokeshire's rough and rugged peninsula sits **St. David's**, the smallest city in the UK and one of the most appealing. Its pride and glory is the great **St. David's Cathedral**, begun in 1180 on the site of a monastery founded by the saint himself and a beacon to pilgrims since the Middle Ages.
*www.stdavidscathedral.org.uk*

Next to the cathedral stands the grand ruin of the **Bishop's Palace**, with its superb Great Hall rose window and the private chapel of the Bishops of St. David's.
*www.castlewales.com/sdbishop*

Of the many glorious coastal walks in Pembrokeshire, the four-mile round-trip from Whitesands Bay around **St. David's Head** is one of the best. It takes in Iron Age hut circles, Stone Age burial chambers, and the beach from which St. Patrick set off early in the fifth century to convert the Irish.

**Dylan Thomas's Boathouse** is perched on a cliff overlooking the Taf Estuary at Laugharne. Thomas wrote and recited his work, including *Under Milk Wood,* in the adjacent writing shed, working intensively on "fiercely belaboured lines" every day from 2 p.m. until 7 p.m., "prompt as clockwork," according to his wife, Caitlin.

Some of the most unspoiled and beautiful scenery in South Wales is found on the **Gower Peninsula**, just 18 miles long by 5 miles wide. Its beaches and cliffs are considered to be among the finest and most picturesque in Britain.
*www.welcometogower.co.uk*

The high hill ranges of the central highlands of Wales form the heart of the **Brecon Beacons National Park**. They are crisscrossed with horseback-riding routes and paths leading to and around the two main summits of Pen-y-Fan and nearby Corn Du. These sandstone peaks look north over impressive sheer cliffs.
www.breconbeacons.org

**Hay-on-Wye**, on the England and Wales border, is a book lover's mecca, now world famous for its many fine secondhand and antiquarian bookstores. Try to plan to be there for the incomparable Thursday Market in Memorial Square to truly experience the culture and cuisine of the region.
www.hay-on-wye.co.uk

The Victorian seaside town of **Aberystwyth**, often dubbed Aber, is quintessentially Welsh and widely regarded as the cultural capital of Wales. The **Great Aberystwyth Camera Obscura** offers a good overview of this lively, self-possessed town and superb surrounding landscape. It can be reached by the little wooden carriages of the **Aberystwyth Electric Cliff Railway**, which rise slowly up the bushy face of a 380-foot cliff. From here a path runs for six steep and exhilarating miles north to Borth, from which you can journey back to Aberystwyth by train.

Twelve miles inland, half an hour's ride on the **Vale of Rheidol Steam Railway, is Devil's Bridge**, a spectacular spot where the Afon Mynach (Monk's River) leaps 300 feet downward beneath a triple bridge.

North of Aberystwyth rises **Cader Idris**, one of Wales's most satisfying mountains to climb. The steepish path, starting near Dolgellau, is clear all the way to the stony cairn at the top. Sleep here, legend claims, and you will awaken either a poet or a madman.

Plenty of Welsh is spoken on the streets of **Dolgellau**, for the northwest corner of Wales is the heartland of the national language.
www.discoverdolgellaucomogerychwyrn

drobwyllllantysiliogogogoch, the longest place-name in Britain, is generally shortened to Llanfair P.G. The name means "The church of St. Mary in the hollow of white hazel trees near the rapid whirlpool by St. Tysilio's the ofred cave."

**Conwy** is a truly delightful small town still ringed by its medieval walls. The huge **Conwy Castle** is one of Edward I's iron ring, a loop of eight castles placed around the perimeter of the northern half of Wales and forming a defensive chain, each castle a day's march from the next.
www.conwy.com

Cardiff City Hall

**Caernarfon Castle** is the most famous and impressive castle in Wales, though by no means the most beautiful or picturesquely sited. Dourly glowering over the water, it conveys today exactly the message of formidable strength that Edward I intended the Welsh to read in its massive walls and towers. Caernarfon was begun in 1283 as the strongest link in Edward I's iron ring.
www.caernarfon-castle.co.uk

**Snowdonia National Park** covers nearly 840 square miles of northwest Wales and includes some of the most impressive mountains and moorlands in Britain. This is climbers' and outdoor enthusiasts' country, a genuine mountain landscape that tops out on Snowdon, the highest mountain in Wales.
www.snowdoniaguide.com

The jewel in the crown is 3,560-foot **Snowdon**, Yr Wddfa to the Welsh, meaning "tomb." This is the burial place of the giant Rhita Gawr, who wore a cloak woven of the beards of kings he had killed. This monster was killed here by the hero King Arthur himself.

From the **Snowden summit**, in clear weather one can see Wales, England, Scotland, and Ireland in a 250-mile circle. To ascend the mountain it takes five to six hours of steep climbing, an eight-mile circuit. Taking the Snowdon Mountain Railway from Llanberis (closed in the winter and in bad weather) is another delightful option.

**Betwys-y-Coed**, at the confluence of the Conway River and its three tributaries, is one of the most popular and beloved villages in Snowdonia. A well-worn network of paths into the surrounding mountains and dense woodland begins here.
www.betws-y-coed.com

The narrow 30-mile-long **Lleyn Peninsula** droops southwest from Snowdonia, beginning with Portmeirion and including the three seaside resorts of Criccieth, Pwllheli, and Abersoch.

The fantasy "village" of **Portmeirion**, set on a private peninsula, is a must for any visitor to North Wales. This bizarre confection, a theatrical and exuberantly overblown Italianate village, was assembled here between 1925 and 1972 by Welsh architect Sir Clough Williams-Ellis, who collected endangered statues and pieces of buildings from all over the world. Entering through the Triumphal Arch, you find buildings scattered around a central piazza, and on the surrounding slopes and shores a castle, a lighthouse, an Indian hotel bar, and a town hall with a 17th-century fresco of Hercules on its ceiling.

The **Berwyn Mountains** offer pleasant walking and hiking, particularly at Tan-y-Pistyll, where **Pistyll Rhaeadr Waterfall**, the highest in England and Wales, plunges 240 feet in two mighty leaps.

Scotland

# SCOTLAND

**GETTING YOUR BEARINGS**

Scotland stretches north from the English border on one side and Northern Ireland, just a dozen miles distant, on the other. The Southern Uplands give way to the Central Lowlands and then to the highlands and islands beyond.

SHETLAND ISLANDS
Unst
Yell
Fetlar
Muckle Roe
Whalsay
Mainland
Lerwick
Foula
The Deeps
Mousa

Fair Isle

Papa Westray
The North Sound
North Ronaldsay
Westray
Westray Firth
Rousay
Sanday
Eday
Stronsay
Mainland
Kirkwall
Scapa Flow
ORKNEY ISLANDS
Hoy
South Ronaldsay
Pentland Firth

ATLANTIC OCEAN

NORTH SEA

Butt of Lewis
Cape Wrath
Kyle of Durness
Loch Eriboll
Kyle of Tongue
Duncansby Head
Sinclair's Bay
Noss Head
Rhiconich
Loch Loyal
Isle of Lewis
Stornoway
Park
THE MINCH
Loch Broom
Loch Shin
Oykel
Helmsdale
Lybster

St. Kilda
Harris
Sd. of Harris
Loch Ewe
Loch Maree
Dornoch Firth
Tarbat Ness
Cromarty Firth
Moray Firth
Kinnairds Head

Outer Hebrides
Sound of Monach
North Uist
The Little Minch
Lair
Black Isle
Inverness
Elgin
Banff
Forres
Peterhead
Buchan Ness

Benbecula
South Uist
Dunvegan
Raasay
Island of Skye
Glen Mor
Loch Ness
Nairn
Spey
Deveron
Don
Aberdeen

Barra
Sd. of Sleat
HIGHLANDS
Findhorn
Aviemore
Dee

SEA OF THE HEBRIDES
Rum
Sound of Rhum
Eigg
Glenfinnan
CALEDONIAN CANAL
Loch Lochy
Ben Nevis
1344
L. Ericht
Linn of Dee
Grampian Mountains
N. Esk
S. Esk

Coll
Tiree
Morvern
Fort William
L. Shiel
Loch Linnhe
Garry
Loch Rannoch
Lyon
Dunkeld
Strathmore
Forfar
Scurdie Ness

Ulva
Iona
Island of Mull
L. Etive
Lismore
Loch Tay
Dundee
Arbroath
Firth of Tay

SCOTLAND
Loch Awe
Comrie
Perth
St. Andrews
Isle of May

Colonsay
Jura
L. Lomond
Garrick
Earn
Glenrothes

CRINAN CANAL
Stirling
Alloa
Firth of Forth
Kirkintilloch
Dunfermline
Dumbarton
Falkirk
Linlithgow
Haddington

Islay
Lochgilphead
L. Fyne
Greenock
Paisley
Antonine Wall
Glasgow
Edinburgh
Dalkeith

Rinns Point
Gigha I.
Kilbrannan Sd.
I. of Bute
Hamilton
Motherwell
Clyde

Island of Arran
Kilmarnock
Kintyre
Firth of Clyde
Irvine
Ayr
Ayr
Alloway
Southern Uplands
Newtown St. Boswells
Teviot
Tweed

Mull of Kintyre
L. Doon
Nith
Annan
Cheviot Hills

N. IRELAND
North Channel
Corsewall Pt.
The Moors
Stranraer
Dumfries
Gretna Green
ENGLAND

Luce Bay
Dee
Wigtown Bay
Solway Firth
Mull of Galloway

0  100 Kilometers
0  75 Miles

"The Best Wee Country in the World" is what the Scots like to call their homeland. And for more than 250 years, countless numbers of English couples have had cause to agree. Since the 1750s, lovers too young to marry in England without their parents' consent have made for the "wee country" to the north, where the matrimony laws were less demanding. Skipping over the border, the first place they reached on the old London-to-Edinburgh road was the small Scottish village of Gretna Green.

Marriages in Gretna could be conducted by almost anyone, as long as there were two witnesses present. Village blacksmiths often performed the duty, and getting married "over the anvil" became part of the tradition. Today, thousands of couples, from farther afield than England, continue to travel to Gretna every year for this purpose, many getting married at the Old Blacksmith's Shop, which was built in 1712.

This region of Scotland is known as the Southern Uplands, the southernmost of Scotland's three major geographic regions—the other two being the more highly populated Central Lowlands and the more mountainous Highlands. Unlike its counterparts, the Southern Uplands boasts few mountains or people. What it does have, however, is a grand history of conflict and strife, dating back to Roman times and the great wall that Emperor Hadrian built to keep the Scots out of England.

**BATTLEFIELD SITE**
An inscribed stone marks one of the mass clan graves at Culloden. *Previous pages:* A farm cottage on the island of Canna.

## Scotland's Struggles

The terms "Scot" and "Scotland" can be both confusing and enlightening. They come from the Latin *Scoti,* the name the Romans originally gave to the Irish Celts. The Scoti had migrated from Ireland across the North Channel to settle in western Scotland. Eventually this part of Britain, together with the land occupied by the Picts in the east, would become known as Scotland.

During medieval times, the kingdom of Scotland began to emerge. By the late 1200s it had spread across roughly the same territory that it occupies today. The Southern Uplands and Central Lowlands—which are collectively known as the Lowlands—had become home to a mixture of peoples. Lowlanders intermingled with the English and Normans. And as was the case with the English, they developed a feudal society.

It was at this time that the Scots' royal line of succession was broken, and a number of rivals began vying for the crown. Seeing an opportunity, Edward I of England intervened and set himself up as feudal overlord of Scotland. For the country, a great era of turmoil began.

Sir William Wallace (Mel Gibson's "Braveheart" in the 1995 film of the same name) was an early leader in the Wars of Scottish Independence. So was Robert the Bruce, who seized the throne in 1306 and began a fight for Scottish freedom that would last for 20 years. Bruce, himself of Norman descent, won a great victory over the English at Bannockburn. This led to the Declaration of Arbroath in 1320, the world's first documented dec-

---

**IN ABERDEENSHIRE**

**Balmoral**—the sprawling, ivy-covered getaway for the royal family set amid sumptuous gardens and grounds—is dreamlike. The ballroom is the only part of the interior open to the public, as the rest of the castle is the well-used private quarters of Her Majesty the Queen.

---

laration of independence. "For, as long as but a hundred of us remain alive," it proclaims, "never will we on any conditions be brought under English rule. It is in truth not for glory, nor riches, nor honours that we are fighting, but for freedom—for that alone, which no honest man gives up but with life itself."

Although the country itself was now independent and unified, the divide between north and south remained very distinct. In the far north, a different type of society had developed. There, the Highlanders held on tightly to their Celtic traditions, and life and loyalty revolved not around a feudal master but around the clan. While Lowland Scots developed a distinctive dialect of English, known as Lallans, the Highlanders continued to speak the Gaelic of their Irish cousins. They also wore their own style of dress, a plaid wool robe that contained up to 16 yards of tartan and doubled as a sleeping blanket, of which today's tartan kilts are a knee-length reminder.

When the Reformation swept Scotland, another difference became apparent. In the 16th century, the

**RESIDENTS OF BALMORAL**

Unlike the vacationing royals who stay at the castle in summer, these Highland cattle are year-round Balmoral residents. Visitors of all sorts, and especially those with Scots heritage, flock to the area annually to attend the nearby Highland games at Braemar.

Lowlanders embraced Calvinism and its Scottish variant, Presbyterianism, which became the established faith of the nation. In the Highlands, however, Roman Catholicism remained strong—as did animosities toward Lowlanders.

The kingdoms of Scotland and England were ultimately united by the accession of James VI to the English throne. At the beginning of the 17th century, James, who came from the long-reigning Stuart dynasty of Scotland, was also crowned King James I of England. By the end of that turbulent century, his grandson and namesake, James II, would throw the kingdom into turmoil by attempting to reinstate the Catholic faith. He was eventually dethroned by his Protestant daughter and her Dutch husband, William, Prince of Orange.

James's successors would produce a line of pretenders to the throne. One of those Jacobites was Charles Edward Stuart, or as he is better known, Bonnie Prince Charlie. In 1745, he launched a rebellion in the Highlands, and the local clansmen flocked to his cause. Their defeat the following year, at the Battle of Culloden, ended the Jacobite hopes and way of life. It was the last pitched battle fought in Great Britain. After the failed rebellion, Highlanders were forbidden to carry arms or wear a tartan or kilt, symbols of Jacobite loyalty. The life of the clan, which had endured for a thousand years, was no more.

Yet the worst was still to come for the Highlanders. In the wake of Culloden, the Highlands were systematically emptied of people. Across the north, the glens and the moorlands and the islands were cleared. Cottages were burned, whole townships dispersed, all to make way for the lucrative raising of sheep. (The sheep were eventually replaced by deer, which today are hunted, along with grouse, by wealthy people from all around the world.) Many of the inhabitants were relocated to the Scottish Lowlands and the slums of Glasgow, others to the colonies in North America. In history, this is known as the Highland Clearances. Today, there are still fewer people living in the Highlands than there were before the Clearances began.

The depopulation of northern Scotland continued until the mid-19th century. But by then, the Highland ways and customs had made a comeback of sorts, thanks to the efforts of Sir Walter Scott. Edinburgh-born Scott was fascinated with the Highlands. His best-selling historical novels recreated the once thriving world of the clans and struck a chord with the Romantics of the era. *Rob Roy* was set during a Jacobite uprising in 1715, and *Waverly* took place in the time of Bonnie Prince Charlie's.

In 1822, Scott organized a visit to Scotland by the reigning British monarch, King George IV. For the occasion, he furnished

**SCOTTISH ICONS**
The bard and the bagpipes are both enduring symbols of Scotland and the Scots. Below, a statue of Robert Burns at the head of the High Street in Dumfries and, opposite, a piper in traditional dress.

ERECTED
BY INHABITANTS OF DUMFRIES,
(WITH THE AID OF MANY FRIENDS,)
AS A
LOVING TRIBUTE TO THEIR FELLOW TOWNSMAN,
THE NATIONAL POET OF SCOTLAND,
6TH APRIL 1882.

the Palace of Holyroodhouse in Edinburgh with Highland grandeur. He saw to it that the walls were draped with banners, bagpipers piped, and everyone wore kilts and weapons. He even persuaded the king to wear the tartan that the Scots had worn since Roman times.

And so the British royal family's love affair with Scotland began. Victoria and Albert bought Balmoral Castle in the Highlands as a summer home, the spot Victoria called her "dear Paradise." And every year, the Braemar Gathering takes place nearby: With the royal family in attendance, athletes toss cabers, hurl hammers, and compete in the other traditional sports of the Highland games, a faint echo of their independent, warlike forebears.

## The Beloved "Rabbie" Burns

To the northwest of Gretna is Ayrshire, "Burns Country." This is the region associated with Scotland's national bard, the Ploughman Poet—Robert Burns.

The eldest of seven children, Burns was born in 1759 in a cottage in Alloway, on the Firth of Clyde. (January 25, 2009, marked the 250th anniversary of his birth.) Young "Rabbie" had little by way of formal education. His family was poor, but the household was filled with songs and stories and laughter. His father, a tenant farmer, would read his children verses from the Bible or other books on his shelf. Then his mother would tell ancient tales about ghosts and fairies, witches and giants, haunted graveyards and enchanted castles, and sing them traditional ballads of love and loss.

Throughout his life, Burns identified with the common people and held on fiercely to his antiestablishment beliefs. He liked to mock the wellborn, satirize politicians, and glorify the nation's heroes, remembering its joys and sorrows. He also enjoyed recounting his whiskey-filled adventures and recalling the lassies he had loved.

Burns wrote in his Lowland Scots dialect. Among his most famous works are the comedic epic poem *Tam O'Shanter* and his poignant tribute to the ordinary man in the song "A Man's a Man for a' That." His other songs include "Robert Bruce's March to Bannockburn" and "Green Grow the Rashes."

**ROOM WITH A VIEW**
Much of Scotland is rugged terrain and sparsely populated. Ancient ruins dot the landscape, like those at left, which sit close to a modern home.

**GASTRONOMIC DELIGHT**

The centerpiece of Burns Night celebrations all over the world each January is the inimitable haggis. The traditional dish is complemented with the Bard's poetry and the country's whiskey.

His warmhearted words celebrate the joys of home, family, and friendship, and his works, translated into many languages—including English—are beloved by Scots and non-Scots alike.

Burns's love poems and songs like "Ae Fond Kiss" and "A Red, Red Rose" are world famous. And given Burns's reputation, they could have been written with any number of women in mind, among them "Highland Mary," "Handsome Nell," and "Sweetest May." But in poems like "To a Mouse," the Ploughman Poet could even show empathy for a "wee, sleekit, cow'rin, tim'rous beastie" that he considered his "earth-born companion, an' fellow-mortal."

## Burns Night

Few national figures anywhere can so well represent an entire country. Indeed, few are held closer to the collective heart than the man the Scots call "our Rabbie."

The Scots celebrate their patron saint on St. Andrew's Day and, to some extent, all things Scottish on their newfound Tartan Day. But neither compares to the celebration that takes place every January 25. Whether at home in Scotland or as part of the diaspora worldwide, the Scots gather to mark the birth of their national poet with Burns Night suppers.

The evening's festivities begin with the saying of the Selkirk Grace:

*Some hae meat and canna eat*
*And some wad eat that want it,*
*But we hae meat and we can eat,*
*And sae the Lord be thankit.*

Then guests stand to receive the haggis. To their accompanying rhythmic handclap, a kilted piper proceeds into the room followed by the chef, who carries the haggis to the top table. Haggis consists of sheep's heart, liver, and lungs minced with onion, oatmeal, suet spices, and salt that is mixed with stock and traditionally boiled in the animal's stomach for about three hours.

It is an impressive dish indeed, and thus, the person sitting at the head of the top table recites Burns's famous "Address to a Haggis" before slicing it open. The assembled guests then raise their whiskey glasses in a toast and the meal is served. The meal consists of traditional cock-a-leekie soup (a thin chicken broth with leeks and pepper), the main course of haggis, "neeps and tatties" (mashed turnips and potatoes), a dessert of Typsy Laird (a Scottish sherry trifle), and a cheeseboard with bannocks (oatcakes) and coffee or tea. Wine or ale is served with the meal. And throughout the meal, another "dram" of whiskey is always on hand.

As they eat, one of the guests gives a short speech about Burns and his continuing relevance today, called the "Immortal Memory." Next follows a lighthearted "toast to the lassies." The lassies then return the favor with a "toast to the laddies." The evening continues with more songs and poems. It concludes with the guests linking arms to sing "Auld Lang Syne," which translates as "old long since" or "long, long ago."

The other time of year when these words are sung, of course, is at the stroke of midnight on New Year's Day. For the Scots, this holiday is called Hogmanay. Hogmanay has traditionally been Scotland's main winter holiday. The Presbyterian church had long discouraged the celebration of Christmas, as had the Puritans of New England. They associated the excess with Saturnalia and other pagan festivals.

## [ Oldest Whiskey Distilleries ]

**1 Bowmore, Isle of Islay (1779)** This Hebridean island distillery's proximity to the sea is said to help the flavor of the whiskey—that, and the home-produced malted barley, rich Islay peat, and the icy waters of the River Laggan.

**2 Strathisla, Speyside (1786)** The most famous visitor at this beautiful distillery was Dizzy, a cat that arrived from Louisville, Kentucky, in 1993 after falling asleep between bourbon casks bound for Scotland. The cat survived the four-week transit and became the distillery's mouse-hunter.

**3 Balblair, Ross-shire (1790)** This distillery still uses its original water source—the fresh, clear burn (small stream) of Ault Dearg, which flows from the surrounding hills.

**4 Oban, Argyll (1794)** Oban has just two pot stills, making it one of Scotland's smallest distilleries. Unlike many of its rivals, which until recently only offered single malts during exceptional years, Oban has created a single malt since the 1880s.

**5 Glen Garioch (1797)** Garioch (pronounced GEE-ree) was deliberately sited more than two centuries ago in the Garioch Valley, said to produce the best barley in Scotland.

The Scots held out for a long time in their opposition to the holiday, with Christmas Eve and Christmas Day remaining as working days up until the 1960s. Instead, celebrations and gift giving have customarily been reserved for January 1 and 2.

One of the customs associated with Hogmanay is "first-footing." This practice involves being the first guest after midnight to cross the threshold of a neighbor's house. Often he or she brings a symbolic gift, such as a piece of coal or some Scottish shortbread. Food and drink are then plied on the guest, who is said to have set the luck for the household for the rest of the year. The "first-footing" may go on through the night and into the next day.

In Scotland, the drink in question is more often than not whiskey—called *uisge beatha,* or the "water of life." Today, most whiskey is a blend of malted spirit and grain spirit. Single malt, or unblended, whiskey is the connoisseur's choice, and these whiskeys vary by region. In the Scottish islands, for example, the malt is smoked over peat to produce a rich, tarry tang.

It takes years of maturing in oak casks to develop whiskey's golden color. Up to 30 percent of the precious liquid can be lost through evaporation during the aging process. This upward-drifting and invisible spirit is known as "the angels' share."

## Tour of the Highlands

The Lowlander Robert Burns loved the Highlands, the birthplace of his beloved "Highland Mary" (whose death prevented their planned marriage and emigration to the West Indies). He treasured the region's folk songs and traditional stories, collecting and preserving some and rewriting others. Much of these came from a trip he took to the Highlands in the summer of 1787.

Burns set out on his tour in a two-wheeled, one-horse post chaise. He headed first for the ancient town of Stirling, traditionally regarded as the "gateway to the Highlands." In 1567, King James VI of Scotland, the infant son of Mary Queen of Scots, was crowned here. He would go on to unite the kingdoms of Scotland and England when he was also crowned King James I of England in 1603.

But Burns was more interested in another Scottish hero with local

**HOME OF GOLF**

A favorite destination for visitors to Scotland is the Royal and Ancient Golf Club, St. Andrews. At right, the grand old clubhouse looks out over the course.

**PEERING INTO THE PAST**

A walker stops to ponder the mysteries of Ossian's Stone. Robert Burns himself stopped here more than 200 years ago, during his tour of the Highlands.

associations. For Stirling was where some of the great battles of the Wars of Scottish Independence took place, and Burns had come to pay homage to one of the country's greatest freedom fighters, William Wallace.

Today, the Wallace Monument stands outside Stirling, atop a hill from which Wallace is said to have watched the approaching army of England's King Edward I. Wallace went on to score a memorable victory against a much larger English army at the Battle of Stirling Bridge in 1297, making him Guardian of Scotland. After a later defeat, however, Wallace was captured by King Edward and executed—hanged, drawn, and quartered—for treason.

Nine years after his death, the Scots won a decisive victory against the English near Stirling, at Bannockburn. Robert the Bruce, who led the Scots in battle, strengthened his position as king, and ten years later he achieved full Scottish independence.

North of Stirling, Burns also visited Garrick, where the remains of a Roman camp testify to the fact that Rome had, in fact, tried to reach farther into Scotland. Indeed, the Romans had built another wall beyond Hadrian's, the Antonine Wall, which stretched across from the Firth of Forth to the Firth of Clyde. But this fortification was abandoned after only 20 years, and the legions withdrew behind Hadrian's Wall.

Burns continued heading north, to Comrie, where he passed through the Sma' Glen—considered the passageway from the Lowlands to the Highlands. There, he stopped at Ossian's Stone, a great boulder said to mark the burial place of one of Burns's predecessors, a bard of the Gaels.

At Dunkeld, Burns met acclaimed Scottish fiddler and composer Niel Gow. His tunes were played at the country dances and *ceilidhs* that Burns loved. During Burns's visit, Gow played for him "Loch Erroch Side," which the poet liked so much that he later set to it his song "Address to the Woodlark." The annual Niel Gow Fiddle Festival in Dunkeld celebrates the musician's memory. In Little Dunkeld Kirk yard his gravestone reads: "Time and Gow are even now, Gow beat time, now Time's beat Gow."

ON BURNS WENT, past Aviemore to the "capital of the Highlands," Inverness, and the Moray Firth. Just east of the city he visited the Culloden battlefield. It was there in 1746, on the exposed moorland, that Bonnie Prince Charlie had rallied the clans to fight one last time. The warriors were hungry and exhausted after invading England, having made it as far as Derby in the Midlands before turning back to Scotland. The English pursued them all the way to Culloden. There, 5,000 Highlanders charged an English army nearly twice that size—and suffered a momentous, historic defeat.

Heading east, Burns then traveled to Cawdor Castle and wrote that he "saw the bed in which King Duncan was stabbed" (although in Shakespeare's *Macbeth* the murder actually takes place in Inverness Castle). He listened to Highland ballads in the area and, heading along the coast, stopped at Forres to examine Sueno's Stone.

This mysterious 21-foot-high standing stone (the tallest in the British Isles) is probably a thousand years old and today is encased in protective glass. The monument has spawned a host of interpretations. Some say it commemorates a victory by King Malcolm II over a leader of the Norsemen named Sueno. Another theory claims that the stone commemorates the triumph of Christian Gaels from western Scotland over

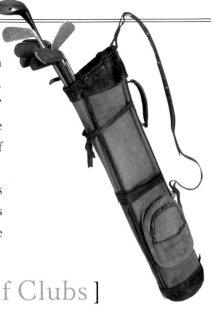

## [ Oldest Golf Clubs ]

**1** **Royal Burgess Golfing Society of Edinburgh** (founded 1735) A royal edict from His Majesty King George V commanded the world's oldest golf club to change its name from the humble Edinburgh Burgess Golfing Society to its present royal moniker on September 30, 1929.

**2** **Honourable Company of Edinburgh Golfers** (1744) This club started life in Leith, on Edinburgh's outskirts, but at the end of the 19th century moved to Muirfield, one of Scotland's most prestigious courses and occasional host to the Open Championship.

**3** **Royal and Ancient Golf Club of St. Andrews** (1754) This is Britain's most famous golf club, partly because it gave birth to the R & A—now a separate body—organizer of the Open Championship and, with the United States Golf Association, jointly responsible for the "rules" of golf.

**4** **Bruntsfield Links Golfing Society** (1761) Bruntsfield's 18th-century members played on a cramped links course in the shadow of Edinburgh Castle, but in 1898 moved to their current home, celebrated for its spectacular views of the Firth of Forth.

**5** **Royal Musselburgh** (1774) Members of the Royal Musselburgh play for the Old Club Cup, which dates back to 1774, making it the world's oldest competitive golfing trophy.

**6** **Glasgow Golf Club** (1787) Although this club dates from 1787, it is believed golf was being played in Glasgow almost 200 years earlier. The club still possesses the Silver Club, purchased in 1787, which has a silver golf ball attached for each club captain between 1787 and 1835.

**7** **Burntisland Golf Club** (1797) Burntisland members like to believe the historians who suggest golf may have been played here since 1688. Less contentious is the club's claim to have one of Scotland's most beautiful courses, with the view of Edinburgh Castle from the eighth hole its scenic star turn.

the heathen Picts. Others believe it may recall an ancient battle between local tribes.

Local legend has another explanation: It marks the spot where Macbeth originally met the three witches, one of whom proclaims him "Thane of Cawdor," and another, "king hereafter."

Nearby is Elgin and, just beyond it, the River Spey, which upstream becomes the beautiful Spey Valley whiskey region. The malts here are known for their lightness and sweetness, like Glenlivet and Glenfiddich. Burns did, however, cut across the shoulder of Aberdeenshire to the ruins of Old Deer Abbey. On the coast here is the fishing port of Peterhead and the "Bullers of Buchan," a 100-foot-deep collapsed sea cave filled with churning surf—"a monstrous cauldron," according to the 18th-century biographer James Boswell, who was here on a tour with his famous subject, Dr. Samuel Johnson, some 13 years before Burns.

The ruins of Slains Castle are nearby, perched on cliffs facing the North Sea. Bram Stoker, who is associated with Whitby farther down the east coast of Britain, visited here, too. He saw Slains as "the castle of the dead" and is said to have used it as one of his inspirations for *Dracula*.

Heading south along the coast, Burns arrived at Aberdeen, Scotland's largest fishing port, which he described as "a lazy town." Today the Granite City, as it is known, could not be more different, as it is the center of Britain's North Sea oil industry. The Scots have a wonderful word, "dour." It might have been invented here in Aberdeen, a place never known for its frivolity. A visiting American once remarked of the city: "It had all the extortionate high prices of a boom town but none of the compensating vulgarity."

From Aberdeen, Burns the Poet Patriot then would have made sure to pause in Arbroath, site of the signing of the famous 1320 declaration, which asked the pope to recognize the Scots' chosen king, Robert the Bruce. After Arbroath, Burns made his way to Dundee, then to the ancient capital of Perth, and finally to Dunfermline.

Had he taken a short detour after Perth, out toward the coast, Burns would have reached the small seaside town that all golf-loving tourists to Scotland make a point of visiting: the university town of St. Andrews. St. Andrews is elegantly situated on the North Sea,

**HIGHLAND REDOUBT**

In its splendid isolation, Dunagon Castle epitomizes the north of Scotland's remoteness and self-containment.

above broad sands and rocky bays. It boasts a cathedral and a castle from the 16th century. It is also home to Scotland's oldest university, with quadrangles—St. Salvator's and St. Mary's—that date to the 1450s and the 1530s, respectively. But the town's greatest claim to fame is as the Home of Golf.

It was here, during the Middle Ages, that Scots began knocking a small ball around with a stick, across the flat grass that overlay the sand dunes. Successive Scottish kings tried to ban the "unprofitable sporte" during the 1400s. Then, as now, it took time away from other activities: in the case of medieval Scots, archery and church. The royals eventually reconsidered the sport, though. By the time Mary Queen of Scots picked up a golf club at St. Andrews, the entire nation had caught the bug.

In 1754, a group of locals—who later took the name the Royal and Ancient Golf Club—decided to hold an annual competition. That competition would become known as the British Open Championship, which is regularly held at St. Andrews.

There are more than 500 courses in Scotland. Most tend to be integrated with the rugged and bracing landscape, combining at once daunting sporting challenges and spectacular vistas and views. Ever present is the weather, in the case of St. Andrews coming in the bracing winds off the North Sea. But as the Scots say, "If there's no wind and there's no rain then there's no golf."

But back to another national favorite: By the time Robert Burns got to the Abbey church in Dunfermline—which holds the tombs of ancient Scottish kings, including Robert the Bruce—he was nearing the end of his tour. Finally, Burns reached Edinburgh again, leaving behind him a part of the country that would be ever near. As he wrote:

*Farewell to the Highlands, farewell to the North,*
*The birth-place of Valour, the country of Worth;*
*Wherever I wander, wherever I rove,*
*The hills of the Highlands for ever I love.*

## The Northwest Highlands

The itinerary of Rabbie Burns's Highland tour in the summer of 1787 is an impressive one, touching upon many of Scotland's historic places and happenings. But it left out a vast swathe of the Highlands to the north and west of the Great Glen Fault.

As if cut by a huge Highland broadsword, the fault line is a gash that runs southwest from Inverness all the way to Fort William. The fault that left a deep, ruler-straight trench is mostly inactive today, though limited movement still occurs, as evidenced by occasional moderate tremors over the last couple of centuries.

**IN SCOTLAND**

Haggis is not the only uniquely **Scottish, "must try" food.** Shortbread, scones and bannocks (oatcakes), Arbroath Smokies (smoked and salty haddock), and Stovied Tatties or Stovies (a potato-based dish made of leftovers) are popular here and, in many cases, throughout the world.

**HOGMANAY**

With pipers piping, a traditional New Year's Eve celebration gets under way in Skibo Castle in the Highlands. The castle was once owned by the Scots-American industrialist Andrew Carnegie and today is a members-only club.

The weather is never "far away" in the Highlands. Here, storm clouds gather over the Old Man of Storr, a basalt rock formation on the Isle of Skye. Sightseers can reach the spectacular landscape after a mile-long walk along a well-constructed path.

A series of long, narrow lochs run the length of Great Glen Fault. Since the early 19th century, they have been linked by the Caledonian Canal, which connects the Moray Firth in the northeast with Loch Linnhe in the southwest. Only one third of the course had to be carved through land to complete the great canal, enabling small vessels to avoid the longer and often more treacherous journey up the coast and between the mainland and the Orkney Islands. In a feat of Victorian-era engineering, a series of eight locks known as Neptune's Staircase helped overcome the 93-foot climb that the canal had to make from sea level up to the highest loch, as the Scots call their stretches of inland water.

The most famous of the interconnected waterways is Loch Ness, at the northeast end of the Great Glen Fault, near Inverness. The loch is deep. Loch Lomond may be the largest in Scotland by surface area, but Loch Ness is the largest by volume. Reaching down some 754 feet, it contains more freshwater than all the lakes in England and Wales combined. Yet the waters of Loch Ness are not only deep and remote, they're also particularly murky (a result of the region's high peat content). All of this makes it a particularly good refuge for a camera-shy lake monster.

The Loch Ness Monster—"Nessie"—first came to the world's attention in the 1930s, identified variously as a monster-fish, a sea serpent, or a dragon. Eyewitness accounts described a creature with a large humped body, a long, narrow neck, and a small head, like the prehistoric aquatic reptile known as a plesiosaur. Indeed, there have been reports of a "water beast" in the loch since the sixth century, when St. Columba—here to evangelize the Picts—is said to have encountered it.

Considerably easier to spot than the elusive Nessie is Ben Nevis, at the other end of the Great Glen Fault. Ben Nevis, which rises 4,406 feet, is not only the highest mountain in Scotland but the highest in the British Isles. And near this Highland high point unfolded one of the low points of Scottish history.

It was here, close to the dark pass of Glencoe, that the massacre of the MacDonalds took place. Crown soldiers, under the command of Captain Robert Campbell, had been billeted with the MacDonalds in Glencoe for more than a week. But they had come with deadly intent: to stamp out these Jacobite clansmen.

The MacDonalds had recently sworn allegiance to William and Mary, the new monarchs of England and Scotland, albeit after technically missing a stated deadline

**NORTHERN DESTINATIONS**

Roman legionnaires could scarcely have looked forward to traveling north to man the defensive Antonine Wall, whose stone base is shown above. A more attractive proposition awaits modern-day travelers in the form of Scotland's many bed-and-breakfasts. The inviting B&B at right is on the Isle of Skye.

to do so. Nevertheless, this gave the Crown and a number of their allies from Clan Campbell—historic enemies of the MacDonalds—the pretext they needed. On the morning of February 13, 1692, after enjoying the hospitality of their hosts, the soldiers turned on the MacDonalds, slaughtering 38 unarmed men in their beds or as they tried to flee. Some 40 women and children later perished from exposure after their homes were burned. According to tradition, the order for the killing was written on a nine of diamonds playing card, ever since known as the Curse of Scotland.

The Campbell treachery was the most flagrant breach imaginable in Highland tradition, which had a special name for such a violation: "murder under trust." This event is commemorated every year, as descendants of the slaughtered MacDonalds conduct a wreath-laying ceremony in Edinburgh at the memorial to the Massacre of Glencoe. It is also recalled in the lament of a modern-day ballad:

*Cruel is the snow that sweeps Glencoe*
*And covers the graves o' Donald*
*O, cruel was the foe that raped Glencoe*
*And murdered the house of MacDonald*

Glencoe stoked Jacobite sympathies in the Highlands even further. Fifty-three years later, when Bonnie Prince Charlie raised his standard at nearby Glenfinnan, the MacDonalds flocked to the Jacobite cause, which ended, of course, disastrously at Culloden.

## Highlands to Islands

North of Inverness, the coastline angles toward John O'Groats. Traditionally, this marks the end of mainland Britain, the farthest point from Land's End in Cornwall—some 900 miles or so distant—and 250 from Gretna Green.

But it is not the end of the British Isles. Less than six miles across the Pentland Firth is the archipelago of the Orkneys and, beyond, the Shetlands. There are 67 islands in the Orkneys and more than a hundred in the Shetlands, although most of them are uninhabited. Fishing and sheep farming remain important on the islands. And the 1970s discovery of oil and gas off Shetland provided another source of income.

Evidence of the past is everywhere in the Northern Isles, as they are collectively known. These isles have everything from ancient burial chambers to Pictish defensive stone towers to villages abandoned during the Highland Clearances. Norse influence in Scotland is also strongest here, though it extends throughout all the islands as far south as the Isle of Man in the Irish Sea— places that the Vikings dominated for more than 400 years. In the Orkney capital of Kirkwall, the houses are built in Norwegian fashion, with small windows and gables facing onto narrow streets. Kirkwall's St. Magnus Cathedral, which was founded in 1137, resembles Trondheim Cathedral in Norway. It was originally the burial site of King Hako of Norway before his remains were removed to Trondheim. Twelfth-century Vikings carved runic graffiti on the wall of a chambered tomb here called Maes Howe, built around 250 B.C.

At the great Orkney anchorage of Scapa Flow, German sailors during World War I scuttled 70 of their surrendered ships to prevent them from falling into the hands of the Royal Navy. In World War II, a German submarine sank the *Royal Oak,* and with it more than 800 lives.

Some 54 miles long, the largest island in the Shetlands (often shown by necessity on maps in an inset box) is known as Mainland. The locals joke that their closest

---

**IN THE HIGHLANDS**

Chanonry Point, on the end of a spit of land that extends into the **Moray Firth** on Scotland's Black Isle, is one of the best places on the UK coast for observing dolphins, whales, and seals. Spectacular sightings and displays of wildlife have led to its designation as a Special Protection Area for wildlife conservation.

railway station is in Norway. It has so many fjords that no part of the island is more than three miles from the water.

The southern part of the island has the remains of a Viking house dating from the ninth century. Just off the coast here is the tiny island of Mousa. Uninhabited now, the island was evidently deemed worthy of dogged defense in the past, as evidenced by the best preserved Iron Age *broch,* or stone fort, in Scotland. The broch has a circumference of 158 feet and double walls, each five feet thick and 40 feet high. This strongpoint must have been

### IN THE HEBRIDES

Perhaps the most famous prehistoric site in Scotland is the **Callanish Standing Stones,** an impressive array of circles, rows, and other Neolithic megaliths beside a bleak and beautiful loch on the Isle of Lewis in the Outer Hebrides. It is believed to be an ancient calendar based on the moon.

virtually impregnable during prehistoric times. The remains of some 80 such brochs dot the Shetlands, and there are hundreds more along the other islands and the north coast, located at various strategic points on hills or beside bays.

Continuing north from Mousa for 175 miles would bring us to the Faroe Islands, an autonomous province within the Kingdom of Denmark, where Norse influence never waned. But we must retrace our steps now, back down the chain of islands to the Scottish mainland and then on around the coast.

Off the west of Scotland is a jumble of islands jammed up against the jagged coastline. The islands of the Outer Hebrides, or the Western Isles, are formed from some of the oldest rocks in the world, Precambrian gneiss. They include the island of Lewis, whose prehistoric stone circle, called the Standing Stones of Callanish, is among the most haunting Neolithic sites and may have been aligned to the sun, moon, and stars. Another is the island of Harris, where Harris Tweed is made. At one time, it was almost all hand-woven but now it is created in small factories, though some hand-weavers still practice the ancient craft.

**CALLANISH**
The standing stones on the Hebridean island of Lewis attest to settlement in this isolated spot dating to as long ago as 3000 B.C.

The Inner Hebrides include Jura, where George Orwell wrote the novel *1984,* and tiny Staffa, whose extraordinary basalt formation, Fingal's Cave, provided the inspiration for Felix Mendelssohn's *Hebridean Overture.* Iona is here, too, the cradle of the Celtic church and burial place of many Scottish, Irish, and Norwegian kings.

Nearby is the Isle of Skye. It was to Skye that Bonnie Prince Charlie fled after his defeat at Culloden in 1746. The fugitive was smuggled onto the island by young Flora MacDonald, who took him ashore in an 18-foot rowing boat and disguised him as her maid. Charlie eventually escaped aboard the French frigate *L'Heureux,* and spent the rest of his life in *un*happy exile, dying in Rome in 1788. Flora, who was imprisoned for a year in the Tower of London for her efforts, died in 1748 in faraway Skye. According to legend, she was buried in the bedsheet in which Bonnie Prince Charlie had slept.

IN THE ISLANDS and the Highlands, despite all past attempts to stamp it out, the Gaelic language remains a reminder of the ancient past. The bards that were once a vital part of each community, handing down Gaelic poetry and song by word of mouth, are now gone. But their language survives, and as Scotland reasserts its national pride and rediscovers its Celtic heritage, the language continues to undergo a rebirth.

Gaelic is soft on the ear, but has little in common with English. The latter has drawn thousands of words from French, German, and Latin but very few from Gaelic. Those that do derive from Gaelic tend to be evocative of Scotland. "Whiskey" is one, as is "clan." Another is "slogan," which originally meant a "war cry."

## [ What's in a Name? ]

**1 Balmoral** Her Majesty the Queen's Scottish estate probably takes its name from the Gaelic *baile* ("settlement" or "farm") and *morail* ("splendid").

**2 John o' Groats** Famous for its position near the northern extremity of the British mainland. Named after a Dutchman, Jan de Groot, who was awarded a charter in 1496 to run a ferry from the mainland to Orkney.

**3 Lewis** The Outer Hebridean island probably takes its Gaelic name, Eilean Leodhas, from the Old Norse *ljodhus* ("homes of the people") or the Gaelic *leoghuis* ("marshy"). The present anglicized name derives from the French Louis: Lewis is currently the most popular boys' name in Scotland.

**4 Muckle Flugga** Traditionally considered the most northerly point in Britain (though nearby Out Stack outcrop is farther north), this uninhabited island takes its name from a Shetland dialect word, *muckle,* which is derived from the Old Norse *mikla* ("big"), and the Norse *flugey* ("steep island").

**5 Orkneys** The Romans called these 67 islands the *Oracedes* in the second century; the Gaelic is *Insi Orc* ("Isle of Pigs"), but the Vikings changed *orc* to *okkn* ("seal"), hence *Oryneyjar*—Seal Islands.

**6 Roslin** This tiny village south of Edinburgh was propelled to fame by Dan Brown's novel *The Da Vinci Code* for its links to the Knights Templar. Some say the origin of the name is "Rose Line" (after a bloodline to Jesus and Mary Magdalene). But the derivation is actually from the Brythonic *ros* ("promontory") or *rhos* ("meadow") and *celyn* ("holly"), hence Holly Point or Holly Meadow.

**7 Scone** Renowned as an ancient Gaelic capital and for the Stone of Scone, Scone was a symbol of the coronation of Scottish kings, and said to have been the stone on which Jacob slept in Genesis. The word comes from the Gaelic *sgonn,* meaning "mound." The Scottish cake of the same name comes from the Gaelic *scon,* "flat."

## To the Bonnie, Bonnie Banks of Loch Lomond

Back on the Scottish mainland, the coast continues its broken way south. The Mull of Kintyre makes a particularly daring lunge out into the water, as if it would prefer to be one of the Hebridean Islands. From this great jutting peninsula the views are spectacular, and on a clear day they include sights of Burns Country in Ayrshire. More visible off to the southwest are the Antrim Plateau and Rathlin Island in Northern Ireland, just 12 miles distant.

**FOR PEAT'S SAKE**

These current Lewis residents take a pragmatic approach to what nature has bestowed on them. They are cutting peat that will be dried and then burned for heat.

It is believed that the Scoti traveled up the Mull of Kintyre on their migrations from Ireland into the Highlands. One of its more recent residents, however, has been Paul McCartney, who wrote a hit single about the Mull of Kintyre in 1977 that sold more than two million copies in Britain. "Mull of Kintyre, oh mist rolling in from the sea," he sang. "My desire is always to be here, oh Mull of Kintyre." (It's not too much of a stretch to suggest that Rabbie's lyrics, had he ever written about the place, would have been markedly better.)

By now, we are not far from the northern shore of Loch Lomond, another location famously celebrated in song:

*Oh, ye'll tak' the high road, and I'll tak' the low road,*
*And I'll be in Scotland afore ye;*
*But me and my true love will never meet again*
*On the bonnie, bonnie banks o' Loch Lomond.*

Various suggestions have been made about the author of the song and its original meaning. According to one, he was a Highland warrior from the 1745 Jacobite Rising, on his way home after the invasion of England. Another suggests that the song refers to the ancient belief that the souls of those who died in a foreign land would be transported home by the fairies along "the low road."

Whatever the purpose behind the author's travels, here we are nearing the end of our own journey, for the other end of Loch Lomond is within easy reach of bustling Glasgow. Behind us lies an ancient, Gaelic Scotland, and ahead a future to be played out in its two major cities: in Edinburgh, the hub of the Scottish Enlightenment, and in Glasgow, the powerhouse of the industrial revolution on the River Clyde.

Whenever Glaswegians get the chance, on weekends and on holidays, they desert the banks of the Clyde for those of "bonnie, bonnie Loch Lomond." Many, no doubt, are descendants of Highlanders forced to move south at the time of the Clearances. Perhaps that is part of the draw of the Loch, a hauntingly beautiful place where modern-day city folk can connect, knowingly or unknowingly, with the ghosts of the clans and the glories of their Jacobite past.

**GREAT SCOT**
A kilted accordionist provides the after-dinner music aboard the Royal Scotsman. Owned by Orient-Express Hotels, the luxury charter train takes travelers to the heart of the Highlands.

# Sites and Sights in Scotland

Scotland's southern border region, known as the **Lowlands**, has a long and contentious history with England, but for all its grim past, it's one of Britain's most beautiful regions. Here are great pine forests and heather moors, giving way as you go north to a greener and more pastoral landscape along the valley floors and around the little Scottish border towns.

Traveling north from Hadrian's Wall and the England-Scotland border, four great abbeys were founded within a short distance of each other in the 12th century. **Jedburgh Abbey** is the first of these. The abbey has an evocative monk's garden behind its cloister wall and a museum. The monastic buildings at **Dryburgh Abbey** are in excellent condition. The poet and novelist Sir Walter Scott is buried in the abbey's north transept. Not much remains of the ruined Benedictine **Kelso Abbey**, but the north transept's beautifully carved great facade is well worth visiting. Finally the Cistercian **Melrose Abbey**, also a ruin, is said to enshrine the heart of Robert the Bruce.

Robert Burns is Scotland's national poet, and **Alloway** and Ayr in Ayrshire are the heart of Burns country, both his real and his fictional life. Born into a poor family, Burns moved from farm to farm around the Ayr district, and a surprising number of his homes and haunts are preserved for posterity.
*www.burnsheritagepark.com*

**Burns Cottage and Museum**, the house where Robert Burns was born in 1759, was built by his father, William. Nearby are the heroic **Burns Monument** of 1823 and two places featured in Burns's comic epic poem *Tam O' Shanter*—the roofless shell of **Alloway Old Kirk** (burial place of the poet's father), where drunken Tam saw the devil playing bagpipes for a wild witches' and warlocks' dance, and below it **Brig o'Doon**, a late medieval single-arch bridge.

Stained glass window, Roslyn Chapel

In the town of **Ayr** stands the 13th-century **Auld Brig**, Burns's "poor narrow footpath of a street." The **Tam O'Shanter** pub is decorated with quotations from the poet. Five miles northeast of Ayr is **Tarbolton Village**, now a National Trust for Scotland museum, where Burns learned to dance, became a Freemason, and formed a Bachelors' Club. He lived at nearby Lochlea Farm from 1777 until his father's death in 1784.
*www.clydesite.co.uk/ayr/*

Robert Burns died in 1796 in the southwest Scottish town of **Dumfries**, and several sites there commemorate him: The **Burns House**, where he died, is now a museum, as is Ellisland Farm, outside of Dumfries, where Burns spent three years; the **Burns Mausoleum** is where he lies in St. Michael's Churchyard; the **Burns Statue** stands by Greyfriars Church; and the

**Robert Burns Centre**, tells of his life there and houses a popular film theater.
*www.rbcft.co.uk*
*www.ellislandfarm.co.uk*

In the Scottish Lowlands, the town of **Stirling** rises up the spine of a long volcanic crag, culminating in the famous castle perched dramatically at the 250-foot summit. **Stirling Castle** is the pride of the town, used by Scottish monarchs James IV, Mary Queen of Scots, and James VI as their royal court. Inside are spacious state rooms, most of them empty; the royal chapel; and the sumptuous great hall.
*www.stirlingcastle.gov.uk*

The upper part of the castle houses the excellent **Regimental Museum** of the Argyll and Sutherland Highlanders, ceremonial regalia, mementos from the regiment's service around the world, and remarkable photographs of the Crimean War.
*www.stirling.gov.uk/index/stirling/visitstirling/stirlingcastle/regimentalmuseum*

Best known as a mecca for golfers, **St. Andrews** is a charming little town set above broad sands and rocky bays. Well worth visiting are the cathedral ruins on their headland; the castle with its 16th-century mine tunnels, and the two university college quadrangles of St. Salvator's and St. Mary's, bustling centers of the University of St. Andrews, founded in 1450 and, after Oxford and Cambridge, the third oldest university in the English-speaking world.

Scene of the dramatic denouement of Dan Brown's blockbuster *The Da Vinci Code*, **Roslyn Chapel** (sometimes spelled Rosslyn or Roslin) is a richly carved 15th-century chapel crammed with myths and creepy stories. Nearby, in the rolling Border country farther south, the romantic ruins of 13th-century **Neidpath Castle** stand beside the River Tweed near Peebles.

The northeast region known as **Royal Deeside** has everything—woodlands; a noble river; high mountains; castles; and small, neat villages. It's no wonder that Queen Victoria fell in love with this "chocolate-box" valley and persuaded Prince Albert to buy the Balmoral estate. **Aberdeen** is a pleasant place to explore on foot, and nearby, two castles beckon: **Drum Castle**, a 13th-century keep with a 1619 mansion tacked on, and **Crathes Castle**, an L-shaped late 16th-century tower house with several turrets jutting from a solid base.

**Balmoral**—the sprawling, ivy-covered getaway for the royal family set amid sumptuous gardens and grounds—is the castle of everyone's dreams. The ballroom is the only part of the interior open to the public, as the rest of the castle is the well-used private quarters of Her Majesty the Queen. The simple **Parish Church of Crathie** is used for worship when they are visiting. Balmoral. *www.balmoralcastle.com*

Eight miles from Balmoral is **Braemar**, famous for its annual fall **Braemar Gathering**, where Scots toss cabers, hurl hammers, and participate in traditional games of all sorts in the presence of the royal family. *www.braemargathering.org*

The Grampian range of mountains form the central spine of Scotland—a spine with curvature, a bent bow springing from southwest Argyll, curving northeast until it dips toward the North Sea coast near Aberdeen.

The west coast of Scotland is known for its rolling hills, mountains, lochs, rugged coastline, and whiskey, to which it owes its nickname of the **Whiskey Coast**. Seven distilleries and one cooperage that make up the **Malt Whiskey Trail** are strung out along the River Spey. Most distilleries welcome visitors and even happily offer a free "wee dram" (a small glass of whiskey).

**Inverness**, known as the Capital of the Highlands, is a compact little place just the right size for exploring on foot. Behind the tourist information center is Inverness Museum and Art Gallery, with carved Pictish stones, Celtic jewelry, Jacobite relics, and much else. *inverness.highland.museum*

Once one of Scotland's largest castles, **Urquhart,** magnificently sited on the rocky banks of Loch Ness, was blown up in 1692 to prevent it from being taken over by the Jacobites. The ruin is a dramatic and impressive site and the most frequent spot at which sightings of Nessie, the Loch Ness Monster, occur.

Shaint Islands, breeding grounds for puffins and razorbills

The Inner Hebrides islands lie in a jumble off the west coast. Some are better known and more visited than others. **Iona** was the cradle of the Celtic Church and has been the center of Celtic spirituality for more than four centuries. It is still a spiritual beacon for contemplatives and fans of Celtic spirituality and, despite the time and effort it takes to get there, a very popular place. Here in sublimely peaceful surroundings are the restored abbey and chapels, and gravestones of ancient kings.

The **Isle of Skye**, one of the Inner Hebrides, is famous for its spectacular mountain scenery and beautiful transitions of rain, cloud, sun, and mist. Portree, the capital town, is strung around its bay 35 miles from the mainland bridge at Kyleakin. The **Aros Experience**, Skye's heritage center, displays the island's history. *www.aros.co.uk*

The **Outer Hebrides**, or the **Western Isles**, are wonderfully wild and beautiful and known for their friendly residents, who warmly welcome visitors. Birders around the world are drawn to many of the islands for the frequent sightings of rare birds. Lewis, the largest and most northerly of the islands, has two jewels. The 2,000-year-old Carloway Broch is the most complete Hebridean *broch* (stone tower) at 70 feet high. Perhaps the most famous prehistoric site in Scotland is the **Callanish Standing Stones**, an impressive array of circles, rows, and other Neolithic megaliths beside a bleak and beautiful loch. It is believed to be an ancient calendar based on the moon. *www.thewesternisles.co.uk*

The **Orkney Archipelago** is founded on warm sandstone, which gives these islets a pastoral, green fertility. Some of Scotland's most awe-inspiring prehistoric monuments are here. On the island of Hoy, 1,000-foot cliffs play host to peregrine falcons, arctic skuas, and a host of seabirds, while offshore rises the famous **Old Man of Hoy**, a 450-foot-high sandstone rock stack.

Twenty miles south of Mainland lies **Fair Isle**, the most isolated island community in Britain. But its remoteness does not stop the islanders from having fun; the Fair Isle dances, with music by the island band, are irresistible all-join-in affairs. Fair Isle is famous for its bird observatory and for its Fair Isle knitwear, still produced by the 60-odd inhabitants, some relative newcomers and some Fair Isle families established here for many generations.

**Chanonry Point**, on the end of a spit of land that extends into the **Moray Firth** on Scotland's Black Isle, is one of the best places on the UK coast for observing dolphins, whales, and seals. Spectacular sightings and displays of wildlife have led to its designation as a Special Protection Area for wildlife conservation. *www.undiscoveredscotland.co.uk/rosemarkie/ chanonrypoint*

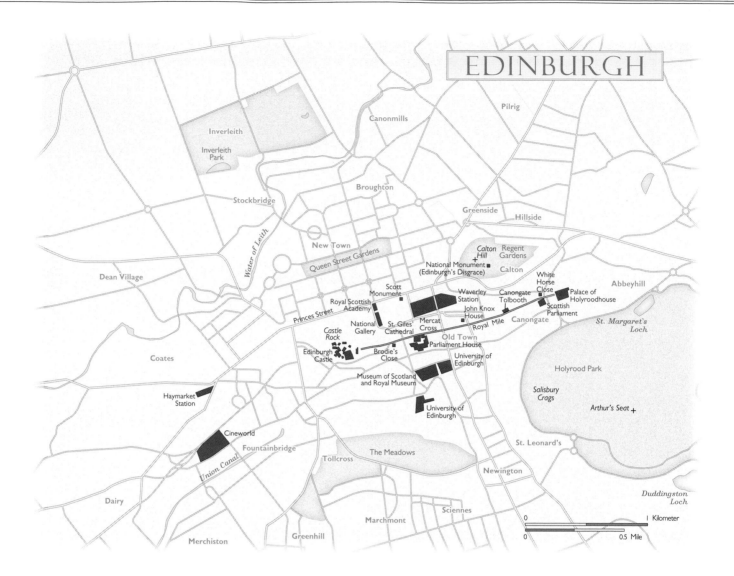

EDINBURGH

**GETTING
YOUR BEARINGS**

The map above shows the various districts of Scotland's capital, Edinburgh. Most famous are the Old Town, which stretches from Edinburgh Castle to the Palace of Holyroodhouse, and above it the New Town. *Previous pages:* Edinburgh from atop Calton Hill.

The British Isles contain great diversity, and Scotland is no exception. In the Highlands, the country has one of the last true wilderness areas of Europe. And in the narrow neck of land between the River Clyde and the Firth of Forth, Scotland boasts two of the great cities of the British Isles (which make up four-fifths of the entire Scottish population). One is the mighty manufacturing center of Glasgow, in the early 19th century considered the second city of the British Empire and a cradle of the industrial revolution. The other, just 40 miles away, is the refined and elegant Scottish capital of Edinburgh, the most visited city in Britain after London and known as the Athens of the North for its rich cultural traditions.

It is certainly true that Glaswegians and Edinburghers are very different. The people of Edinburgh have a reputation for gentility and, perhaps, a degree of stuffiness, their accent considered the only one in the British Isles to be as "acceptable" as the received pronunciation of the English home counties. Glaswegians have always been much more rough-and-tumble, their heavy accent almost incomprehensible to outsiders. Glaswegians are also renowned for their friendliness and black sense of humor. Says one travel writer, "They are resilient and wry—cheerful fatalists, convinced that life is basically a joke."

## City on a Rock

Few cities can boast so spectacular a setting as Edinburgh. Its castle sits upon a volcanic plug known as Castle Rock that looms over the rest of the city, a constant reminder of its geologic past. Millennia ago, as the last ice age came to an end and the glaciers retreated north, they left deposits of softer, eroded material behind the hard outcrop, thereby creating a distinctive "crag and tail" formation. Along the ridge of the tapered tail runs what is today known as the Royal Mile, a street that cuts right through both the city and the history of Scotland.

As its name indicates, the thoroughfare is a mile long. But in this case it is a Scottish mile, an old measurement that is one-tenth longer than the English mile that Parliament made standard in the early 19th century. Along the Royal Mile, the past is everywhere, in each of its dark courts and in the adjoining cobbled streets of the medieval Old Town. At one end of the thoroughfare, atop the crag and looming over the entire city, sits Edinburgh Castle. At the other, eastern end is Holyrood Palace, which over the years has often been preferred by the royal family to the windswept Castle. Much of Scottish history has been played out between these two residences.

The Picts were the first to seek the safety of the high ground that is Castle Rock. Over the centuries came a stream of challengers, determined to occupy the strongpoint and solidify their kingship and power. In the meantime, the city of Edinburgh grew in size and importance, and in the mid-1400s it replaced Perth as Scotland's capital.

Edinburgh Castle was always a coveted target—and several times a residence—for English invaders. Each time they lost the fortress, the Scots staged daring raids to recapture it. One famous example occurred in 1313, when Sir Thomas Randolph, Earl

## [ Edinburgh and Glasgow Firsts ]

1 **Chloroform** James Simpson (1811–1870), an Edinburgh physician, was the first to discover the anesthetic property of chloroform and introduce it (initially during childbirth) in general medical practice.

2 **Cloned sheep** Dolly, the world's most famous sheep, was the first mammal to be cloned from an adult somatic cell, and was born on July 5, 1996, at Edinburgh's Roslin Institute.

3 **Decimal points** First used by the Edinburgh mathematician, John Napier, who died in 1617.

4 **Golf** The rules of golf were first drawn up and followed at Edinburgh's Leith Links in 1744.

5 **International soccer** The first international soccer match (between Scotland and England) was played at Glasgow's West of Scotland Cricket Club in 1872.

6 **The teaching hospital** Glasgow surgeon Granville Sharp Pattison immigrated to the United States in 1816 and founded the Baltimore Infirmary, the country's first teaching hospital.

7 **The telephone** Western Union told Edinburgh-born Alexander Graham Bell (1847–1922) that the telephone he had invented was "an interesting novelty without any commercial possibilities."

8 **Steam power** Glasgow native James Watt devised the steam condenser in 1765, an invention that made the steam engine commercially viable.

9 **The television** John Logie Baird (1888–1946), inventor of the television, transmitted the first long-distance television pictures from the Central Hotel, Glasgow.

10 **The raincoat** Charles Macintosh (1766–1843), inventor of the first commercially produced waterproof coat (in 1824), lived and worked in Glasgow.

of Moray, and 30 intrepid followers scaled the rock in the dead of night to take the castle. Several decades later, Sir William Doubles led a band of Scots disguised as merchants up to the castle gates and convinced the English governor that their sacks of rocks contained edibles from England. As the gates swung open, the Scots threw down their bundles to hold back the gates and charged inside.

For some, the castle was not a prize but a prison. The Duke of Albany's escape from the castle's David's Tower in 1479 is a horrifying tale: After plying his guards with potent wine, he murdered them and piled them onto the open hearth to roast in their armor. By the time the guards were discovered, the duke was on his way to France.

The controversial Mary Queen of Scots occupied Edinburgh Castle in the next century. The daughter of King James V and his French wife, Mary of Guise, she became queen at just six days old, when her father died. Seizing the opportunity to get English hands on the crown, England's King Henry VIII tried to negotiate with Mary's regents to arrange for her future marriage to his son, Edward. The Scots refused, however, packing Mary off to France, and the jilted Henry twice reduced their capital to rubble.

In 1558, Mary married the French dauphin, who became King Francis II the following year. When he died in 1560, she returned to Scotland and married again. In a tiny bedroom in the castle's royal apartments, she gave birth to James, who would become king of both Scotland and England at the Union of the Crowns in 1603.

The strongpoint on Castle Rock is still garrisoned by the army. But today, the Castle is best known as a focus of the city's annual Edinburgh Festival, the world's biggest arts festival. Held every summer, it is really a series of festivals. The Edinburgh International Festival, which concentrates on the performing arts, includes theater, classical music, opera, and dance. The largest of the festivals is the Fringe, which features everything from jugglers and acrobats to stand-up comedians and avant-garde theater. Another famous event is the Military Tattoo, which occurs each night as hundreds of pipers march in front of the floodlit castle. (In this tattoo, the only skins that take a beating are those of the drums in the band.) Other events include a book festival, film festival, and a jazz and blues festival. During August, festival attendees double the city's population.

**RETAIL TRADE**

Princes Street, seen from Calton Hill, is Edinburgh's main shopping thoroughfare. Above, a seamstress makes up a kilt from a tartan in one of the capital's fabric shops.

VISITORS WHO CROSS the drawbridge to Edinburgh Castle are confronted by two Scottish heroes flanking the gate—the bronze figures of Robert the Bruce and William Wallace. Inside the castle walls is a monument to their successors: the Scottish National War Memorial. Its Gallery of Honour, which recalls the Scots who have died in battle since World War I, has been called "a cry in stone."

Another treasured stone at the castle is the Stone of Scone, the traditional place of coronation for Scots kings that was moved to London and eventually returned to Edinburgh in 1996.

The highest point of the castle is the citadel, which looks out to the north. St. Margaret's Chapel is here. Dating from the year 1090, it is the oldest surviving building in Edinburgh. Nearby sits Mons Meg, one of the world's oldest cannons. Built at Mons in Belgium in the mid-15th century, the gun weighs more than six and a half tons and fired stone cannonballs weighing about 330

> **IN EDINBURGH'S OLD TOWN**
>
> No one who experiences the **Edinburgh Military Tattoo** can possibly forget it—the sight or the sound. With the dramatic floodlit Edinburgh Castle as a backdrop, more than 1,000 performers, mostly playing pipes and drums, entertain hundreds of thousands of visitors every year.

pounds. At first, the great cannon was wheeled into battle, but it proved extremely cumbersome to move, covering just three miles a day. In the 1540s it was taken to its present home, atop Edinburgh Castle, and in 1588 it was fired to salute the marriage of Mary Queen of Scots to the French dauphin. A more modern counterpart, the One O'Clock Gun, is fired every day from the ramparts to mark the one o'clock hour.

## Down the Royal Mile

In the shelter of the castle, the Royal Mile descends east. On both sides are tall tenements, some rising up to 14 stories tall, the smoke from their chimneys earning the city the name Auld Reekie ("Old Smoky"). It was into these cramped buildings that Edinburgh's growing population squeezed. It was hardly the genteel picture it is today. From the upper stories, the Scots emptied their chamberpots directly onto the streets below, alerting passersby with the traditional warning, "gardyloo!"—a garbled version of the French term *garde à l'eau*, meaning "mind the water."

Along the way down the Royal Mile are "closes," courtyards sealed

**MILITARY TATTOO**
Every August, the performance of the pipers and drummers at the Castle is the high point of the Edinburgh Festival.

by gates at night that indent the street fronts. The most famous of these, not far from the Castle, is Brodie's Close. Here, the deacon who inspired Robert Louis Stevenson's *Dr. Jekyll and Mr. Hyde* lived by day and lurked by night. Stevenson, who also authored *Treasure Island, The Black Arrow,* and *Kidnapped,* was born in Edinburgh in 1850.

St. Giles Cathedral is a little farther, with its distinctive 15th-century crown tower. This airy cap is supported by eight flying buttresses that can be seen from all over the city. Inside, the Presbyterian reformer John Knox pitted church against state, roaring fiery sermons against the young Catholic Mary Queen of Scots. He was buried in the old churchyard in 1572.

Behind St. Giles is Parliament House, where the Scottish Parliament met until the 1707 Act of Union. With this act, the parliament effectively voted itself out of existence. Whatever the benefits, many Scots struggled to give up the independence their country had so long fought to win. Scotland's bard Robert Burns lamented its loss with the following words:

*What force or guile could not subdue,*
*Thro' many warlike ages,*
*Is wrought now by a coward few,*
*Fore hireling traitor's wages.*

## [ Five Edinburgh Novels ]

**1** **The Heart of Midlothian** (1818) Sir Walter Scott's finest novel is set in 17th-century Edinburgh and explores the theme of justice through the eyes of its heroine, Jeanie Deans.

**2** **The Prime of Miss Jean Brodie** (1962) The eponymous film, starring Dame Maggie Smith, brought Muriel Spark's novel about a charismatic teacher in a 1930s Edinburgh girls' school to a wider audience.

**3** **Trainspotting** (1993) A no-holds-barred portrayal by Irvine Welsh of hero Renton's decline into heroin addiction, offering a graphic account of the darker side of 1990s Edinburgh.

**4** **The Falls** (2001) One of series of crime novels by Ian Rankin set in Edinburgh, and featuring the hard-bitten, hard-drinking detective, Rebus.

**5** **44 Scotland Street** (2004) These tales, by the prolific Alexander McCall Smith, began life as a serial in *The Scotsman* newspaper, and detail the interwoven stories of the inhabitants of neighboring New Town apartments.

A century before, Edinburgh had "given up" its king when Mary's son, James, also took the throne of England. Now the capital had lost its parliament, too. But even so, the city retained a degree of authority as the seat of an independent church: While the established Church of England is Anglican, the Church of Scotland adopted the Presbyterianism of John Knox. Edinburgh also retained the infrastructure of Scotland's separate legal system, based in the Law Courts in Parliament Square. While the English common law system relies on precedent, Scottish law is based more on the Roman system, which relies on principle to resolve a case. The system has been renowned since the 16th century for its unusual verdict of "not proven"—sometimes translated as "not guilty, but don't do it again."

In addition, the University of Edinburgh continued to develop an international reputation in the fields of philosophy and medicine. Located just south of Parliament House, the university was founded in 1583. In the years ahead, it would be part of the remarkable flowering of intellectual life that became known as the Scottish Enlightenment.

Beyond St. Giles is the Mercat Cross, traditionally the spot where public announcements were made to the townspeople. The accession of a new monarch is still proclaimed here by herald, as is the calling of elections.

It was here too that a pretender to the throne, the Catholic Charles Edward Stuart—Bonnie Prince Charlie—staked his own claim to the throne in 1745 after arriving in the city with an army of Highlanders. The news would have quickly reached the Tron Kirk, just a hundred yards on down the Royal Mile. The church had been named after the tron that once stood outside it, the public weigh-beam where officials determined the true weight and measure of commodities sold in the city. After hearing of Bonnie Prince Charlie's arrival, the church's two Presbyterian ministers quickly and quietly made their exit from the city. However, the prince ordered that clergy should continue to conduct their Sunday services as before, except for one small change: In their prayers for the royal family, they should use no names.

On the first Sunday after the announcement, a minister from another church officiated at the Tron. A packed congregation waited to hear what the Reverend Neil

**ON A ROLL**
Street artists entertain the crowds on the Royal Mile as part of the Fringe Festival. Hugely popular, the Fringe features thousands of performances at venues all across the city.

Visitors find the view up to Edinburgh Castle from
Princes Street Gardens just as spectacular as the view from the
Castle down over the city. The gardens also include the Gothic
Sir Walter Scott monument and the Ross Fountain.

McVicar would say. During the prayers, the minister pointedly prayed for the reigning monarch, King George, by name. But then he went further. "And as for this young man who has come among us seeking an earthly crown," he prayed, "we beseech Thee that he may obtain what is far better, a heavenly one!" When reports of McVicar's prayers reached Prince Charlie, he laughed and declared his pleasure at the courage and "good wishes" of the minister.

Also on the Royal Mile is the home of John Knox, so keen an enemy of Bonnie Prince Charlie's great-great-great-grandmother, Mary Queen of Scots. The road then rambles past Canongate Tolbooth, its landmark clock jutting away from the wall. It served many purposes over the years, as an administrative building where tolls and other public dues were collected, and a prison where the clock ticked away the sentences of those imprisoned within its walls.

Near the bottom of the Royal Mile is White Horse Close. From an inn located on this site, stagecoaches departed for London. Officers from Bonnie Prince Charlie's army made their quarters here when they occupied the city.

Just beyond the site sits the anchor on the eastern end of the thoroughfare, the elegant Palace of Holyroodhouse, the British monarch's official residence when in Scotland. Bonnie Prince Charlie himself made full use of the facilities when he was in Edinburgh, and held a ball here for his short-lived Jacobite court. But the occupants of Edinburgh Castle—just one mile away—remained loyal to King George and his House of Hanover. They fired a cannon at the palace, but the cannonball fell far short, and is still embedded in a house along the Royal Mile.

Not far from the palace, and along this thoroughfare that is steeped so deeply in Scottish history, the Scots have constructed a building that symbolizes their future—the new Scottish Parliament. After an absence of nearly three centuries, the Scottish legislature was restored in response to a 1998 referendum. It provided a way for the country and its people to remain an integral part of the United Kingdom while retaining its distinct educational, financial, and legal systems, placing its own priorities on health, learning, economic development, and culture.

At the opening ceremony of the parliament in May 1999, one of the country's traditional singers reinforced the "everyman" nature of Scottish society and its egalitarian ideals with a moving performance of the Robert Burns classic "A Man's a Man for a' That."

## [ Hidden Edinburgh ]

**1 Blair Street Vaults** Shopkeepers with businesses on the city's North and South Bridges once used these damp (and reputedly haunted) 18th-century vaults as storerooms before they became slum dwellings for the city's poor. Several walking tours of the city visit the underground chambers, which were reopened in 1994.

**2 Gilmerton Cove** Mystery surrounds the purpose of this underground limestone cavern (which is open to tours) in the small former mining community near Edinburgh's southern city limit. Secret drinking den? Conspirators' hideout? The theories are many.

**3 Mary King's Close** When the City Chambers were built in 1753, they were constructed over some of the city's old closes, or streets, with the lower stories of their buildings used as foundations for the new structure. Today, the subterranean labyrinth of the old streets has been revealed, offering a spooky insight into life in 16th- and 17th-century Edinburgh.

**COBBLESTONE CHARM**
A lone figure casts a long shadow on Edinburgh's Victoria Street. During the weeks of August these and other streets in the Old Town are thronged with festival visitors.

And that is Edinburgh's Old Town. To the north of it stretches the New Town, which was designed in the second half of the 18th century to relieve the congestion and unsanitary conditions of the medieval city. Filled with graceful streets and squares, it is considered one of the most classic Georgian townscapes in Europe. Restrained, elegant, and ordered, it is a supreme achievement of 18th-century rationalism.

At the heart of this part of the city is Princes Street, which runs parallel to the Royal Mile. Lined with restaurants, stores, and hotels, it features a towering Victorian Gothic monument to Sir Walter Scott, who was born in the city. At its far end rises Calton Hill, site of a collection of several neoclassic monuments. Among them is "Edinburgh's Disgrace"—the fluted columns of the country's still unfinished National Monument.

The clear, rational planning of the New Town was very much a product of the burgeoning Scottish Enlightenment. Edinburgh in the late 1700s established itself as one of the leading intellectual centers in Europe. Figures like economist Adam Smith, philosopher David Hume, architect Robert Adam, and scientists Joseph Black and William Cullen helped make Edinburgh the so-named Athens of the North. Later pioneers such as Alexander Graham Bell, inventor of the telephone; John Logie Baird, inventor of the television; and Sir Alexander Fleming, discoverer of penicillin followed. It is little wonder, then, that Arthur Herman titled his 2001 best-selling book *How the Scots Invented the Modern World.*

The classically designed New Town stands in marked contrast to the dark closes and random arrangement of the Old Town. But together, they have been designated a UNESCO World Heritage site. Uniquely, the city that gave the world Robert Louis Stevenson, Sir Arthur Conan Doyle, and the Encyclopedia Britannica was also the world's first UNESCO City of Literature.

Edinburgh's literary tradition continues today. More recent luminaries include *Harry Potter* author J. K. Rowling, who famously wrote several chapters of her first *Harry Potter* book at an Edinburgh café, and Ian Rankin, whose *Inspector Rebus* mystery novels have done much to pry open the dark corners of the city's smart facades. And Alexander McCall Smith, a professor at the University of Edinburgh, has sold millions of books worldwide as author of the No. 1 Ladies' Detective Agency series.

**ELEPHANT HOUSE CAFE**
In this Edinburgh coffee house, J. K. Rowling wrote several chapters of her first Harry Potter novel.

## The Dear Green Place

Glasgow takes its name from the Gaelic *Glas Cau,* the so-called "dear green place." Here, the city's patron saint and first bishop, St. Mungo, founded a chapel in the sixth century that later became the site of a cathedral. Although the city's bishop often

had a powerful voice in Scotland's affairs, much of the national action centered on Edinburgh. Unlike Edinburgh, Glasgow has never been considered a handsome city, having spent much of its history as a soot-blackened center of industry. And while Edinburgh is "almost" a port city (Leith Docks and the North Sea beyond are visible from Edinburgh's high points), Glasgow is most definitely a port. Positioned astride both banks of the River Clyde, its development has been directly tied to its access to the sea.

For years, Glasgow has garnered a bit of a grim image, one of unemployment, slum housing, violence, and sectarian tensions. Much of the city's seamy underside has been captured in British television's hard-hitting detective series *Taggart,* said to be the world's longest continually running police drama. It is an image the city has been rapidly shedding, though. The city may never have the refined atmosphere of Edinburgh, but Glasgow—once called the greatest Victorian city in the world by Britain's poet laureate Sir John Betjeman—is now a transformed place.

**INDUSTRIAL MUSCLE**

Like giant prehistoric creatures, the cranes of a Clyde shipyard make a bold silhouette against the Glasgow sunset.

The eminent Enlightenment thinkers may have made Edinburgh great, but Glasgow's growth was due to its merchants. Until the late 1600s, Glasgow's main industry was salmon fishing in the River Clyde. Had it not been for the trade boom of the 18th century and the industrial revolution of the 19th, Glasgow would have remained a small cathedral and university town much like St. Andrews but populated by fishermen.

Although the Act of Union of 1707 that closed the Scottish Parliament was greeted by popular riots, Glasgow's merchants

> **IN GLASGOW**
>
> The **Glasgow School of Art** itself is a work of art, considered the architectural masterpiece of the pioneering art nouveau designer Charles Rennie Mackintosh, who designed it while still in his 20s.

soon realized the benefits of that union, which opened up free trade with the English colonies in the Americas. Gradually, the focus of Scotland's economy shifted from east to west—from Leith, and its trade with the Netherlands and the Baltic countries, to the Firth of Clyde.

## "Clydebuilt"

When trade with the Americas developed, cargoes of sugar, cotton, rum, and tobacco had to be offloaded some 20 miles down the river from Glasgow. In the city proper, the Clyde was so shallow it was possible to cross it on foot at low tide. In the 1760s, the shallow channel was dredged and lined by wooden quays, allowing sailing ships to float right up to the heart of the city. As the saying goes, "The Clyde made Glasgow, and Glasgow made the Clyde."

Although the American Revolution effectively ended one avenue of trade, the relationship with the colonies helped Glaswegians develop an entrepreneurial taste for doing business with the world. And new horizons in manufacturing were opening up, especially after James Watt's invention of the steam engine, the inspiration for which came to him during a stroll on Glasgow Green in 1765.

The growth of chemicals and dyeing followed in the early 19th century. These advancements went hand in hand with the cotton industry, and the skills learned in building textiles machinery were readily applied to marine engineering and shipbuilding. Production peaked around 1870, when 70 percent of British iron ships and two-thirds of all steamships moved down the slipways of the Glasgow yards. They included the two *Queen Elizabeths* and the *Queen Mary*.

"Clydebuilt" became a byword for quality and dependability. Ships that had been constructed on the banks of the Clyde regularly won Blue Ribands for their record speeds in crossing the Atlantic. By the eve of World War I, Glasgow's shipyards were turning out one-third of British tonnage, nearly one-fifth of the world's tonnage, and more than the total output of either Germany or the United States. Germany's sinking of the Clyde-built *Lusitania* in the second year of the war helped hasten U.S. entry into the European conflict.

Glasgow's growth was phenomenal. Shipyards lined the River Clyde, and iron foundries and heavy engineering works proliferated. During the 19th century, the city's population increased tenfold, reaching the one million mark by 1914. Rural Scots seeking a new life and Irish immigrants eager for work flooded the city, where the demand for cheap labor was insatiable. As a result, the city expanded to twice the size of Edinburgh.

GLASGOW'S EXPONENTIAL GROWTH was marred by the great extremes that the city exhibited, however. Rich Victorian bankers and insurance brokers had built handsome squares and terraces, and fine dwellings, grand offices, and spacious warehouses dotted the city. But Glasgow also had some of the worst slums in Europe.

In the 20th century, the armaments demands of two World Wars camouflaged the decline of heavy engineering and shipbuilding, which were Glasgow's main industries. In the postwar period, however, the intractable problems caused by uncompetitive industries, a congested downtown, and substandard housing were revealed. In

**WE ARE THE PEOPLE**

The flags of these Glasgow Rangers supporters—the British Union Jack and the Northern Ireland flag—identify not only their team loyalty but also their political and religious sympathies. Rangers fans are overwhelmingly Protestant with strong loyalties to their co-religionists in Northern Ireland.

**TEATIME**

The elegant interior of The Willow Tea Rooms in Glasgow's Sauchiehall Street—designed by Charles Rennie Mackintosh.

the 1960s and 1970s, zealous city planners tore apart the heart of the city, and whole communities disappeared under highways and multistory apartment buildings. Many Glaswegians wound up moving to housing developments on the periphery of the city.

Yet Glasgow—upbeat and optimistic—slowly turned things around. Eventually, urban planners switched from an emphasis on redevelopment to renewal. A massive promotional campaign was launched in the 1980s with the catchphrase "Glasgow's Miles Better," winning the hearts of the citizens and doing much to correct the image of the city. In 1990, Glasgow won the title of European City of Culture and less than a decade later, it was honored as a City of Architecture and Design.

Glasgow's once bustling shipyards are silent now. With the heavy industry gone, the River Clyde has been cleaned up for the use of its citizens. Tree-lined walkways and a new trade center grace its landscaped banks. Even the salmon are back: The water is getting so clean that in 1984 fish were sighted in the Clyde, provoking great excitement all over town.

Yet in the new millennium, some of Glasgow's old inequalities of wealth and employment remain. Another concern now is with depopulation and attracting modern industries like call centers and tourism. In both industries, the people's legendary friendliness has proved to be Glasgow's greatest asset.

One of the few times this attribute is *not* on display is during soccer games between the Glasgow Rangers and Glasgow Celtic—teams from different parts of the city, with supporters from different sides of the sectarian divide. Based at Ibrox Stadium in the southwest of the city, the Glasgow Rangers were founded in 1873 and have been traditionally identified with the Protestant community. Their great rivals are Glasgow Celtic, founded 15 years later in the east end and associated closely with the Irish Catholics who emigrated there in search of work. Matches between the two teams, collectively known as the Old Firm, are among the most intense sporting rivalries in the world. A famous Scottish coach named Bill Shankly once remarked: "Some people believe football is a matter of life and death. I am very disappointed with that attitude. I can assure you it is much, much more important than that." That's certainly the case in Glasgow.

The Protestant-Catholic divide can also be seen among local soccer rivals in Edinburgh and Dundee. But in Glasgow the animosity reaches red-hot proportions. The Glaswegian definition of an atheist continues to be someone who goes to a Rangers-Celtic match to watch the soccer. Both clubs have taken measures to tackle sectarianism, and there are signs of improvement. Even in recent years, however, deaths and serious injuries have occurred after Old Firm matches.

Yet whether Protestant or Catholic, supporters of Rangers or Celtic, all Glaswegians can relate to the story told about the local lady who paid a visit to Edinburgh. Her hostess was determined to make her feel cheap and unimportant.

"My dear," she said to the Glaswegian lady, "here in the capital we think breeding is everything."

To that the visitor replied, "Oh, really? In Glasgow we think it's fun, too, but we try to have a few outside interests as well."

## [ Buildings of Charles Rennie Mackintosh ]

1 **Glasgow School of Art** Mackintosh (1868–1928) studied at this art school and at the age of just 27 won a competition to design its new building. Today, it is his most famous work, celebrated for his quirky and geometric trademark lines and more ornate, often floral motifs.

2 **House for an Art Lover** Designed in 1901 as an entry for a German magazine competition, but only completed in 1996. The hand of his wife, Margaret, with whom Mackintosh worked closely, is evident in the recurrent rose motifs.

3 **Queen's Cross Church** Mackintosh produced designs for several churches, but this was the only one that was built. It is distinguished by its use of Gothic and Japanese-inspired stained glass. Today, it is home to the Charles Rennie Mackintosh Society.

4 **The Willow Tea Rooms** Designed in 1904 for a local restaurant owner, Kate Cranston. The willow tree is used as a recurring motif after the restaurant's address, 217 Sauchiehall Street (*sauchiehall* is derived from the Gaelic for tree). The tea rooms are open to the public.

5 **Scotland Street School** Mackintosh's last major work dates from 1906 and is dominated by two leaded-glass towers. Today, the building is a museum devoted to the history of education.

6 **Mackintosh House** An intimate reconstruction of the architect's demolished home, including his austere drawing room.

# Sites and Sights in Edinburgh & Glasgow

## Edinburgh

Edinburgh is an outstanding city, unquestionably the capital city of the Scots. The dark courts and cobbled streets of the medieval Old Town contrast with the grand Georgian squares, circuses, and crescents of the New Town.

The history of the city is closely bound to its most prominent building, perched on an extinct volcano, **Edinburgh Castle**. From castle walls you can see nearly a hundred miles of Lowland Scotland. Within the castle ancient regalia are displayed—the jeweled sword, scepter, and crown of the Ceremonial Honours of Scotland—which were discovered in 1818 sealed in the Crown Room, where they had lain forgotten for more than a century.
*www.edinburghcastle.gov.uk*

Here also is the **Stone of Destiny** on which all Scottish kings were crowned from the sixth century until the English king Edward I took it to Westminster Abbey in 1296. It was returned to Scotland in 1996.

For many actors, producers, and theater buffs around the world, the annual **Edinburgh Festival Fringe** (the Fringe) is the Holy Grail, a cutting-edge extravaganza and playground for the performing arts. The world's largest arts festival takes place for three weeks every August.
*www.edfringe.com*

No one who experiences the **Edinburgh Military Tattoo** could possibly forget it—the sight or the sound. With the dramatic floodlit Edinburgh Castle as backdrop, more than 1,000 performers, mostly playing pipes and drums, entertain hundreds of thousands of visitors every year.
*www.edintattoo.co.uk*

From the esplanade in front of the castle, the **Royal Mile** descends to Castlehill, Lawnmarket, High Street, and the tall houses of the Old Town. The Royal Mile is packed with bagpipe makers, whiskey sellers, kiltmakers, Highland crafts shops and weavers, and excellent museums and other attractions.

Covenanter Martyrs Memorial, Greyfriars Kirkyard

The **Whisky Heritage Center** celebrates Scotland's most famous export with barrel rides through a replica of a whiskey distillery.
*www.whisky-heritage.co.uk*

**Gladstone's Land**, a restored six-story "land" (tenement house) built for an Edinburgh merchant in 1620, allows a glimpse of home life in Old Town 400 years ago.
*www.nts.org.uk/Property/25*

The **Writers' Museum**, located within the elaborately decorated 17th-century Lady Stair's House, displays manuscripts, first editions, portraits, and personal effects of Scotland's best known writers, with emphasis on Robert Burns, Sir Walter Scott,

and Robert Lewis Stevenson. Robert Burns's writing desk is here, along with Scott's chessboard and the press on which some of his books were published.

**John Knox's House**, a beautifully carved and painted 16th-century town house, is where the fiery preacher and spearhead of the Scottish Reformation lived toward the end of his life. It was also the home of Mary, Queen of Scots' goldsmith. The stories of these men and the house are incorporated into the adjacent Scottish Storytelling Centre and Netherbow Theatre.
*www.scottishstorytellingcentre.co.uk*

**The People's Story Museum**, housed in Edinburgh's old Tolbooth (city jail), explores the work, fights, fun, and suffering of the city's citizens through the centuries.
*www.culture24.org.uk/sc000138*

The **Museum of Edinburgh** encompasses three 16th-century houses grouped together to tell the story of Edinburgh's history. A contemporary copy of the original 1638 National Covenant, the petition for religious freedom signed by Scotland's Presbyterians in 1638, is here, as well as the feeding bowl and collar of Greyfriars Bobby, the Skye terrier whose devotion to his dead owner won the hearts of the people of mid-19th-century Edinburgh.

Along this route, in between museums, are numerous wynds (narrow alleys) and closes (enclosed courts), hemmed in by tall lands that were built ever higher during the cramped Middle Ages. The 17th-century **Milne's Court**, above Gladstone's Land, gives a good idea of a typical close. There are various pubs full of character to enjoy along this walking route. **Deacon Brodie's Tavern** on the Lawnmarket is not only a cozy bar but also a mini-museum of the infamous William Brodie, the respectable Edinburgh citizen (by day) and burglar (by night). Robert Louis Stevenson is believed to have based *The Strange Case of Dr. Jekyll and Mr. Hyde* on Deacon Brodie's double life.

A five minute walk from the tavern leads to **Greyfriars Kirk**, in whose graveyard dissenting Presbyterians signed the National Covenant in 1638—some in their own blood. Greyfriars Bobby and his master are buried here, and a memorial drinking fountain topped with a statue of the beloved terrier stands outside the churchyard.

At the opposite end of the Royal Mile from Edinburgh Castle, behind imposing gates of intricate ironwork, stands the **Palace of Holyroodhouse**, the official home of the Queen when she is in Edinburgh. Originally a monastery, it was later the turbulent home of Mary Queen of Scots.

The imposing **National Gallery of Scotland** holds works from the 15th century to the 19th, including many of the major European artists, including Raphael, Rubens, Rembrandt, and Van Dyck. *www.nationalgalleries.org*

## Glasgow

Glasgow has come a long way in the past two decades, from a city known for unemployment, violence, and slum housing, to a much revived world-class city. Named U.K. City of Architecture and Design in 1999, Glasgow owes much of its depth of

George Square, Glasgow

character to the prosperous industrial era in the late 19th century, which bestowed on the city grand civic buildings and art collections funded by sons of Glasgow who had made it big.

**St. George's Square**, Glasgow's central plaza named after King George III, was laid out in 1781 in the Georgian central grid plan also employed in Edinburgh's New Town. Civic buildings of the late Victorian period dominate the square, chiefly the enormous 1888 **City Chambers**. Leading west is **St. Vincent Street**, lined with elaborate Victorian pomp-and-circumstance unicorns above the Old Post Office door, Ionic columns propping up the Old Bank of Scotland (now a pub), and the towering pink sandstone Royal Chambers and insurance buildings.

Many of Glasgow's artsy tearooms were the result of the entrepreneurial collaboration of designer Charles Rennie Mackintosh and Catherine Cranston, daughter of a tea merchant and an advocate of temperance. Glaswegians have enjoyed the most famous of these, the **Willow Tea Rooms** on Sauchiehall Street, for more than a century. *www.willowtearooms.co.uk*

The **Glasgow School of Art** is itself a work of art, considered the architectural masterpiece of the pioneering art nouveau designer Charles Rennie Mackintosh, who designed it while still in his 20s. *www.gsa.ac.uk*

The city of Glasgow owns an enviable cache of 13 museums, comprising one of the richest and most interesting collections in Europe, including St. Mungo Museum of Religious Life and Art, The Gallery of Modern Art, and the Burrell Collection. *www.glasgowmuseums.com*

Glasgow's leafy West End is a cluster of four fine galleries and museums centered on beautiful Kelvingrove Park. The **Art Gallery and Museum**, situated in a vast sandstone

pseudocastle of 1901, contains collections of British and Continental paintings, beautiful Flemish landscapes, and French works from Corot to Monet. Other sections of the museum include natural history, archaeology, and a magnificent display of arms and armor. The **Museum of Transport** contains enough locomotives, cars, trams, and ship models to gladden any child's heart.

Kelvingrove Gallery and Museum, Glasgow

On the other side of the park are two Victorian museum buildings of Glasgow University: **Hunterian Museum** and **Art Gallery**. The **Art Gallery** collection includes paintings, drawings, and prints by such artists as Pissarro, Corot, Rembrandt, and Whistler, as well as a reconstruction of principal rooms from the town house of art nouveau design genius Charles Rennie Mackintosh. The **Hunterian Museum** features zoological and archaeological treasures of Scotland such as coral, fish, mounted birds, invertebrates, reptiles, and mammals. *www.hunterian.gla.ac.uk/collections*

The **Burrell Collection**, in southwest Glasgow, is Scotland's finest individual collection of art and artifacts. This was the delight and obsession of Glaswegian ship owner Sir William Burrell, who gave it to his native city in 1944 and continued to add to it. It is a truly remarkable and eclectic collection including Rodin bronzes, Etruscan mirrors, Persian carpets, Tang dynasty tomb guardians, and paintings by Rembrandt, Cézanne, Degas, and Manet.

I t rises just 500 feet above the surrounding countryside, and is crowned with no buildings or grand ruins that testify to its glorious past. But the Hill of Tara, like no other place, looms large in the imagination of Ireland, a land where imagination often blends seamlessly with reality.

According to legend, a divine people known as the Tuatha Dé Danaan invaded the island, conquered its original inhabitants, and ruled from Tara. They ushered in a time of heroes and warriors, great deeds and quests, filled with tales of romance and valor and betrayal and loss. Some 142 high kings are said to have reigned here. And it was in "Tara of the Kings" that St. Patrick, the missionary to the Irish, confronted the leaders of pagan Ireland.

Tara sits in the Boyne Valley, the great crucible of Irish history and now a World Heritage site. The Boyne's prehistoric structures, like the neolithic passage grave at Newgrange, are older than the pyramids of that other valley, the Nile. It was here in 1690 on the "green grassy slopes of the Boyne" that one of the most pivotal events in Irish history took place, in which the Protestant King William defeated the Catholic King James, setting the course of Irish history right up until the present day.

More than a thousand years earlier, Patrick had come to the valley for his own battle. His, however, was a spiritual struggle with druidism and its supporters. One can imagine Patrick and a small band of followers arriving at the nearby Hill of Slane on the eve of Easter. At this time of the year in the pagan Celtic calendar, it was customary to extinguish all fires in anticipation of a new one being lit at Tara. To fail to do so was a capital offense.

As the druids gathered at Tara, they looked across to Slane, where Patrick had lit his own fire. Outraged, they demanded that the king—Laoghaire the high king over all of Ireland—summon the imposter to explain himself.

So summoned, Patrick walked over to Tara. As he did, he recited aloud the beautiful prayer for protection that has become known as St. Patrick's Breastplate. Patrick made his case atop Tara before the high king, who was so impressed with the newcomer that he granted Patrick permission to make converts throughout the four provinces of Ireland: Ulster, Munster, Leinster, and Connacht. Each of those provinces has traditionally

**GLASS ST. PATRICK**
The Irish patron saint in a detail of a stained glass window. *Previous pages:* Farmer and friends, Glenbeigh, the Ring of Kerry.

# IRELAND

**SCOTLAND**

Giant's Causeway
Malin Head
Tory Island
Rathlin I.
Portstewart
Portrush
Fair Head
Inishowen
Bushmills
Ballycastle
Coleraine
Cushendun
Lough Swilly
Limavady
Cushendall
Aran Island (Arranmore)
Ballymoney
Glenarm
Slemish Mt.
Antrim Mts.
Gweebarra Bay
Londonderry (Derry)
Ballymena
Larne
**NORTH CHANNEL**
Lifford
Strabane
Carrickfergus
Glencolumbkille
Magherafelt
Antrim
Newtownabbey
Donegal
Omagh
Cookstown
Lough Neagh
Belfast ★
Bangor
Newtownards
**NORTHERN**
**IRELAND**
Donegal Bay
Erne
Lower Lough Erne
Dungannon
Lisburn
**UNITED KINGDOM**
Belleek
Enniskillen
Portadown
Hillsborough
Strangford Lough
Ards Peninsula
Drumcliff
Upper Lough Erne
Armagh
Banbridge
Downpatrick
Sligo Bay
Sligo
Monaghan
Camlough
Newry
**ISLE OF MAN**
Erris Head
Slieve Gamph (The Ox Mts.)
Lough Gill
Mourne Mts.
Dundrum Bay
Slieve Donard 852
Mullet Peninsula
Lough Conn
Lough Allen
Shannon-Erne Waterway
Dundalk (Dún Dealgan)
Dundalk Bay
Achill Island
Castlebar
Carrick on Shannon
Cavan
Clare I.
Clew Bay
**CONNAUGHT**
Erne
Drogheda (Droichead Átha)
Croagh Patrick 765
Lough Mask
Longford
Hill of Slane
Slyne Head
Connemara
Roscommon
Navan
Hill of Tara 155
Lough Corrib
Lough Ree
Mullingar
Boyne
Swords
Lambay Island
Galway (Gaillimh)
**IRELAND**
Liffey
Dublin (Baile Átha Cliath)
Dún Laoghaire (Kingstown)
Galway Bay
Tullamore
Newbridge
Naas
Bray
Aran Islands
Burren
Shannon
Slieve Aughty Mts.
Lough Derg
Port Laoise
**LEINSTER**
Glendalough
Lugnaquillia 926
Wicklow
Ennis
**I R E L A N D**
Carlow
Wicklow Mountains
Arklow
Loop Head
River Shannon
Golden Vale
Kilkenny
Nore
Limerick (Luimneach)
Barrow
Tralee Bay
**MUNSTER**
Clonmel
Wexford
Wexford Harbour
Tralee (Tráighlí)
Suir
Blasket Islands
Dingle Peninsula
Dingle
Waterford (Port Láirge)
Dingle Bay
Killarney
Blackwater
Saltee Islands
Carrantuohill 1041
**ST. GEORGE'S CHANNEL**
Skellig Rocks
Lee
Cork (Corcaigh)
Kenmare River
Cork Harbour
Clonakilty
Skibbereen
Mizen Head
Roaringwater Bay
Fastnet Rock
Bantry Bay

**ATLANTIC OCEAN**

**IRISH SEA**

**CELTIC SEA**

0    75 Kilometers
0    50 Miles

**GETTING YOUR BEARINGS**

This map of the Emerald Isle shows the modern border between the Republic of Ireland and Northern Ireland, as well as the more ancient provinces of Ulster, Munster, Leinster, and Connaught.

been associated with its own particular quality: warfare in Ulster to the north, music in Munster to the south, affluence in Leinster to the east, and learning in Connacht to the west. Ireland as a whole, however, was about to be transformed—from a land of pagan power into the island of saints and scholars.

## St. Patrick's Country

Ulster is the county most associated with the missionary Patrick. Yet his first arrival in the province did not come as a result of missionary impulse. Kidnapped from his home in Britain by Irish pirates, he was sold into slavery in Ulster. There, he worked as a shepherd, tending flocks on Slemish Mountain in Antrim. After he escaped, he made his way back to Britain, but eventually he decided to go back to the land of his enslavement to bring the Gospel to the people.

Some believe that on Patrick's return to Ulster he landed on the shores of County Down and then moved inland to establish his principal church at Armagh. At that time, Armagh was the ancient capital of Ulster; today, it is the ecclesiastical capital for the Roman Catholic and Anglican churches of Ireland. Their cathedrals, both named St. Patrick's, gaze at each other across high ground, located less than half a mile apart. As Ulster poet John Hewitt has written of the two traditions:

*You say Armagh, and I see the hill*
*With the two tall spires or the square low tower;*
*The faith of Patrick is with us still;*
*His blessing falls in a moonlit hour.*

This part of the county, between Strangford Lough and the place where the Mountains of Mourne "sweep down to the sea," is known as St. Patrick's country. Tradition holds that he is buried at the cathedral in the nearby county seat of Downpatrick.

The Christianity that Patrick brought took quickly, rooting deeply in Ireland, one of the few places in pagan Europe where proselytizing was not accomplished with bloodshed and martyrdoms. Ecclesiastical communities soon sprung up across the island, and around these centers of scholarship small settlements grew. A notable example is the Abbey of Bangor in County Down, founded in A.D. 555. When Christian Europe descended into its dark age and barbarian tribes overran the old Roman Empire, places like Bangor kept the light of learning and faith aflame. It was from

## [ Ancient Sites ]

**1 Brú na Bóinne, County Meath** A thousand years older than Stonehenge, and predating the pyramids, this spectacular tomb complex is one of the world's most remarkable prehistoric sites.

**2 Cruachan Aí, County Roscommon** One of the most important Celtic royal sites in Europe, practically undisturbed for 2,000 years or more, with numerous standing stones, burrows, cairns, and 60 majestic megalithic tombs.

**3 Glendalough, County Wicklow** A strikingly beautiful and romantic site, Glendalough was first a Bronze Age tomb, then the home of a fifth-century hermit, St. Kevin, and then an important monastic center. Viking and English raids contributed to its eventual demise in the 17th century.

**4 Rock of Cashel, County Tipperary** A hill bristling with ancient fortifications, it was in the fourth century the base of the Eóghanachta clan, kings of the region, who made Cashel a rival to Tara (see below) as Ireland's main seat of power.

**5 Tara, County Meath** The sacred center of Irish myth and legend, home to the ancient Celtic priest-rulers of Ireland, and then the ceremonial capital of 142 high kings, who ruled until the arrival of Christianity in the sixth century.

**CASHEL OF THE KINGS**
The Rock of Cashel rises above the lush Golden Vale of Tipperary.

Under the watchful eye of the saint, pilgrims follow the various
shrines to the top of Croagh Patrick, Ireland's Holy Mountain.
Pilgrims have been arriving here from long before the time of
Patrick, and they continue to come from all over the world.

these remote spots, on the far edge of Europe, that missionaries set forth to take the Gospel back to the continent. In the process, to borrow from the title of Thomas Cahill's famous book, they "saved civilization."

## Leinster's Invaders

As Christianity took hold of Ireland, the arts of jewelry making and gold working flourished around its new monasteries. This had not gone unnoticed elsewhere. In the years ahead, Ireland's long coastlines became flooded with raiders eager to pillage the island's growing wealth—the Vikings. One Irish monk described the prospect of a rare night without terror:

*Bitter is the wind tonight,*
*It tosses the ocean's white hair;*
*Tonight I fear not the fierce warriors of Norway,*
*Coursing on the Irish Sea.*

**GLENDALOUGH MONASTIC SITE**

St. Mary's Church

Round Tower

the cathedral

St. Kevin's Church

**VALLEY OF THE TWO LAKES**

Glendalough has long drawn outsiders—from Norse raiders at the end of the first millennium to the tourists of today. The site is depicted in art form above, and its famous round tower is shown in the photo at far right.

The Norsemen were drawn to places like Glendalough in the province of Leinster, which they plundered in 922. Like many monastic settlements, Glendalough—or "the valley of the two lakes"—boasts a round tower, which rises some 110 feet and most likely provided a good vantage point to watch for approaching danger. These round towers are the only unique form of architecture found in Ireland. It was once thought that these distinctive and iconic symbols of medieval Ireland may have provided a refuge for the monks during raids, allowing them to scale a ladder to above-ground entranceways and then pull the ladder up behind them. But it is now believed that this was not their purpose: When their wooden doors were set on fire, these towers would have acted like giant chimneys, causing all inside to quickly perish. The structures were more likely to have been bell towers.

The Vikings had arrived in Ireland. But although they first came as raiders, they eventually stayed as settlers. To the Irish, the Vikings gave coinage and shipbuilding and towns, thus significantly altering a land where settlements were small, few, and far between. Viking towns popped up along the Leinster coast, including Dublin, Wicklow, Arklow, and Wexford. Founded in the ninth century, Wexford still has its original Viking street plan, with narrow covered alleyways that once connected its invaders to their jetties. Some, like Keyser's Lane, still have their Norse names.

Whether these newcomers had come to raid or to settle, the Irish continued to fight back. In 1014, King Brian Boru led an army against Dublin and defeated the Vikings at the Battle of Clontarf, effectively ending their reign of power.

But by now, the lines between native and newcomer had become somewhat blurred, and it became increasingly difficult to say where Irish influence ended and Viking ways began. In a nod to this development, archaeologists later created the term "Hiberno-Norse" ("Hiberno" meaning related to Ireland

---

**IN TIPPERARY**

The first sight of the **Rock of Cashel**—rising out of the Golden Vale of Tipperary—is unforgettable. With its domed top tightly packed with towers, spires, and pointed gables, it wields a power that, over time, acted as a kind of secular and spiritual capital, inspiring events both great and grim.

---

or Irish) for Viking currency and other artifacts discovered at sites across Ireland.

Soon other outsiders were arriving on the shores of Ireland. Strictly speaking, these too could be considered "Norse"—albeit Vikings who had long ago settled in Normandy, France, (which takes its name from these "Northmen"), before conquering England and Wales and making their way to Ireland. The first of these new settlers to Ireland were, strictly speaking, not "English," but Cambro-Normans from Wales. They came at the invitation of the King of Leinster, who was eager for allies to help him in his struggle against the High King of Ireland.

As they had in England, the Normans left their mark on the land, building strong castles to keep watch over their territories. Carrickfergus in Ulster boasts the best preserved Norman castle in Ireland, while Kilkenny in Leinster is the most complete Norman town.

**CATHEDRAL ON THE ROCK**
Although the remains of its 13th-century Gothic cathedral are almost deserted in the picture at left, Cashel is one of the most visited spots in Ireland.

By the 14th century, Irish parliaments were meeting in Kilkenny, and in 1367 they passed the famous Statutes of Kilkenny. This legislation was aimed at keeping the Norman

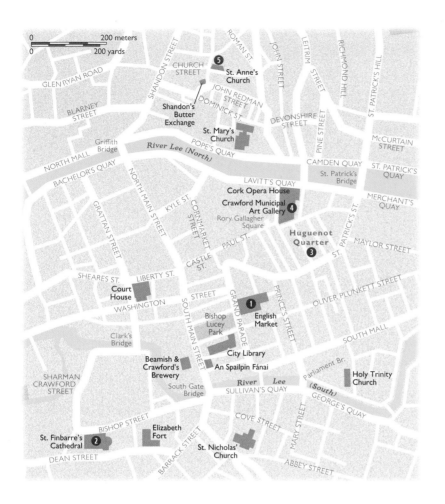

# Cork Walk

Although Cork is the largest conurbation in the southwest of Ireland, it is possible to walk around the whole city easily. Everything that makes for an enjoyable walk is contained within the island at the center of the city and the banks of the River Lee, north and south, above it. Highlights of the walk (two miles, half a day) include:

❶ **The English Market** is the heart of Cork's island center, a place of bustle and color.

❷ **St. Finnbarre's Cathedral** shows off High Victorian Gothic decor at its most extravagantly overblown.

❸ **The Huguenot Quarter** is now a chic part of the city, with small 18th-century houses.

❹ **The Crawford Municipal Art Gallery** is a good place to eat as well as enjoy the paintings.

❺ **St. Anne's Church** is the place to ring out a tune on the famous Bells of Shandon.

traditions and way of life free from being tainted by the Irish. Anglo-Normans, as they came to be known, were prohibited from intermarrying with the Irish, speaking their language, or playing their music or their sports. The laws were only sporadically enforced, however, and as happened with the Vikings and the Irish, the Normans and the native Irish began to merge. In the end, they became "more Irish than the Irish themselves," and Norman names like Fitzgerald—from the French *fils de Gerald,* or "son of Gerald"—became as Irish as O'Riley or McCann.

## To "the Dark Mutinous Shannon"

Following the coast beyond Wexford takes us into the province of Munster. There are more Viking towns here. They include Waterford (Vadrafjord), famous for its crystal, and Cork, the "city of tears" from whose port thousands of Irish left for new lives and new worlds as a result of the Great Famine of the 1840s.

The first Viking sailors to come upon this part of Ireland must have smiled as they navigated their way around its shorelines. Here, great fingers of seawater reach deep into the land, much like the fjords of their homelands. These flooded river valleys are known as *rias.* Their sides are lower than those of the fjords, but are remarkably similar to Scandinavia nonetheless.

The five peninsulas of Kerry and west Cork mark the beginnings of a more ragged coastline. As in Scotland, it is in the west where the land seems to fracture, breaking off to form rocky islands in the Atlantic. And here the names of towns roll off the tongue of those with soft Munster accents: Clonakilty, Skibbereen, Bantry Bay, Killarney, Skellig Michael, Tralee, Dingle.

The Dingle Peninsula has long been associated with St. Brendan. It was there that he and 17 monks set off into the western seas in a coracle, a round-bottomed, hide-covered boat. They sailed in search of the Promised Land of the Saints, and for seven years they discovered one fantastic island after another. On one occasion, they came ashore on a tiny isle, strangely bare of rocks or vegetation. As they gathered driftwood to build a fire for cooking, the ground beneath them began to tremble. They beat a hasty retreat in their coracle, finding that they had landed on the back of a whale.

**ST. COLMAN'S CATHEDRAL**

The cathedral towers over Cork harbor, the last port of call for the *Titanic* and the last view of Ireland for generations of Irish emigrants.

Far in from the Munster coast in the Golden Vale of Tipperary looms the Rock of Cashel. Also known as Cashel of the Kings, this was the traditional seat of the kings of Munster, the most famous of which was Brian Boru, scourge of the Vikings at Clontarf.

A popular tourist attraction, Cashel today is dotted with medieval structures. Visitors come to see the well-preserved round tower, built around the year 1100; Cormac's Chapel, constructed in the decades after the tower; and the remains of a cathedral completed in 1270.

---

**IN COUNTY CLARE**

Seabirds flap about O'Brien's Tower, the Victorian viewpoint stationed at the highest point of the mighty **Cliffs of Moher.** On a good day, the views span more than 100 miles in all directions, from the Kerry hills to the Aran Islands and the Twelve Bens of Connemara.

---

Tradition tells how St. Patrick came here to convert King Aengus, one of Brian Boru's royal ancestors, in 450. However, during a religious service to celebrate the king's conversion, Patrick got so carried away that he rammed his crosier into the ground, accidentally stabbing the king through the foot. Thinking this was some kind of test of his faith, Aengus bore the pain without flinching or uttering a word.

After the Dingle Peninsula—which is the most westerly part of Ireland—the coastline cuts back, making its way inland at the mouth of the River Shannon. The longest river in the British Isles, the Shannon marks most of the dividing line between the provinces of Munster and Connacht. Astride the Shannon sits Limerick, another Norse settlement, the Republic of Ireland's third biggest city and the one so unflatteringly portrayed in *Angela's Ashes* by Frank McCourt, who grew up in the city's slums.

Following the course of what James Joyce called "the dark mutinous Shannon" takes us into the Irish midlands. This part of the country is mostly flat, much of it Ireland's famous bogland.

**CLIFFS OF MOHER**
With the cliffs all to themselves, a couple lies on the rock to gaze down at the sheer drop and out to the Atlantic horizon beyond.

Bogs are generally concealed under a mat of living vegetation. They are composed of dead vegetation that has been naturally compacted over

The beautiful drystone walls that lace the green fields of
Inisheer testify to the barrenness of the soil on this, the smallest
of the three Aran Islands. Irish is the main language on the islands,
drawing schoolchildren as well as the many tourists who
arrive in the summer.

the millennia into a dense soil-like dark brown or black mass. Bogland holds vast quantities of water—about 95 percent water to 5 percent solid matter.

The natural resource produced by bogs is peat, which is known in Ireland as turf. Peat was for many years the only fuel available in rural areas. Until the 1930s, it was cut by hand with a turf-spade and laid out to dry. Only in 1934 did a state-directed board start using machines to cut it. Today it is used in power stations, and is sold in the form of peat briquettes.

At one bend of the River Shannon sits the monastery of Clonmacnoise, whose round tower, churches, and beautifully adorned high crosses rise next to the waters. The great Cross of the Scriptures at Clonmacnoise was carved from a single piece of sandstone around A.D. 900 and stands 13 feet high. It is adorned on all sides with scenes from the Bible, including the Crucifixion, Christ in the tomb, and the Last Judgment. Such crosses helped missionaries spread the Gospel to an illiterate populace and, on occasion, must have borne silent testimony to the Vikings who had come for another purpose.

Along its course, the Shannon links smaller rivers, lakes, and canals. Thanks to the reopening of the Shannon-Erne Waterway in 1994, it is possible to travel by water all the way from Limerick to Belleek in Northern Ireland, a distance of some 239 miles.

## Into the West

Back out at the mouth of the Shannon, the coastline arcs up the side of County Clare. The most spectacular point along the way is the mighty Cliffs of Moher, which rise straight up some 665 feet. The sheer rock face here is a prelude to the land inshore, the hauntingly beautiful region known as the Burren, which literally means "the rocky land." Few people live in this bleak spot now, which resembles a cracked limestone pavement, though ancient Celtic ring forts, fortified dwellings, tombs, and churches give evidence of past habitation.

This is now Connacht. As schoolchildren in the province are taught, after God had finished sifting the soil between his fingers over Ireland, he was left holding just the rocks, which he dropped onto Connacht. The dirt here has to be enriched with sand and seaweed from the shore. Yet as everywhere in Ireland, attachment to the land runs deep, no matter how poor it may be. Such is the poignant theme of the 1990 award-winning movie *The Field,* starring Limerick-born actor Richard Harris.

## [ Five Festivals with a Difference ]

**1 Bloomsday** Come to Dublin to adopt Edwardian dress, feast on the "inner organs of beast and fowl," and take part in other activities that celebrate the single June day on which James Joyce's *Ulysses* takes place.

**2 Lisdoonvarna Matchmaking Festival** Lovelorn Irish—and other—singles from around the world come to this west coast town in September in the hope of finding a partner.

**3 O'Carolan Harp Festival** The village of Keadue, County Leitrim, hosts a festival devoted to all things harp—recitals, workshops, lectures—in honor of blind harpist Turlough O'Carolan (1670–1738), best known for composing the tune to "The Star-Spangled Banner."

**4 Puck Fair** Three days of quirky festivities in Killorglin, County Kerry, which revolve around the crowning of a billy goat (the puck) in August.

**5 Rose of Tralee** Women with Irish links from across the world are eligible to enter this lighthearted beauty pageant in Tralee, County Kerry, held during the third week of August.

Two participants in the June 16 celebration retrace the route of James Joyce's character Leopold Bloom through the streets of Dublin.

The coast continues up to Galway Bay, with the lively town of the same name at one end and the fabled Aran Islands at the other. Originally a castle town built up by the Anglo-Normans, Galway stood in contrast to the wilds of Connemara where the Irish lived.

Just outside Galway's old city walls is an area called the Claddagh, initially a separate fishing village of thatched cottages, which had its own ancient history and a high concentration of native Irish speakers. Its most famous legacy is the traditional Claddagh ring, a small amulet shaped by two hands holding a crowned heart. Symbolizing love, trust, and friendship, it is used as a betrothal and wedding ring and is still commonly worn by both sexes in the west of Ireland.

Galway—in Irish *Gaillimh*—was known as "the place of the foreigners." It was an important port, and trade thrived here, especially with Spain. On their way out of port, the Iberian-bound vessels would have passed close by the Aran Islands, where traditional Irish life has, perhaps, changed less than anywhere.

**TALENT NIGHT**
Locals break out the instruments as well as the beer in a County Clare pub. For tourists, some of the best entertainment in Ireland is of this sort—free, spontaneous, and completely authentic.

In 1899, the Dublin playwright John Millington Synge spent the first of five summers on the Aran Islands, where he immersed himself in local ways and worked hard on his Irish. His 1904 play *Riders to the Sea* is set here, a one-act tragedy in which an island mother loses all of her sons to the sea. "No man at all can be living forever," she concludes at the end of the play, "and we must be satisfied."

Also set in the Aran Islands, Synge's most renowned work is the comic drama *The Playboy of the Western World*, which was famously staged at the Abbey Theatre in Dublin in 1907. The

**IN DONEGAL**

It is worth taking a whole day for the 75-mile clockwise drive on the twisty and switchback roads from **Donegal Town** around the bulge of County Donegal's most southwesterly peninsula. The celebrated quick and staccato Donegal style of traditional music wafts through the air from an abundance of homey pubs.

work was greeted with hostility, and much of the audience rioted against the perceived slight on the virtue of Irish womanhood when the play mentioned females in their "shift," the name for women's undergarments.

Another item of clothing more associated with the islands is the famous Aran jumper, or fisherman sweater, which features distinctive cable patterns on the chest. Traditionally, the sweaters were knitted with unscoured sheep wool that retained its natural oils, thus rendering the garment water-resistant. Some of the stitch patterns are said to have religious or symbolic significance, such as the diamond, which stands for wealth and success.

Tradition holds that these sweaters had their own distinctive family patterns and that drowned fishermen washed up on the shore could be identified by them. This is most likely an urban legend—or in this case an extremely rural one. Regarding this, the sartorially specific Synge might be partly to blame. In *Riders to the Sea*, a dead fisherman is identified by the stitching on his garment.

## Yeats Country

Back on the mainland, the broken, sea-battered coast makes its way around Galway to County Mayo. This is truly the west, a place on the edge of the map that blurs toward a mythical Irish Valhalla known as Tír na nóg, roughly, the "land of eternal youth."

It's also part of the Gaeltacht, the Irish-speaking region where traditional ways are preserved and promoted. When St. Patrick traveled to this remote region in 441, he was determined to undermine at least some of those traditional ways, namely the pagan beliefs of the locals. He climbed to a revered peak some 2,510 feet high that the people believed was inhabited by demons. Patrick fasted on the mountain for 40 days and 40 nights, battling the forces of darkness. It was here that he is said to have cast the snakes out of Ireland, repeatedly ringing a great bell and hurling it down from the heights, taking the serpents with it each time. Angels then retrieved the bell and returned it to him. Today, the hill is known as Croagh Patrick ("Patrick's Stack"), Ireland's Holy Mountain, a place of pilgrimage and retreat.

Continuing around the coast brings us to both the county and town of Sligo. This is Yeats Country—that of both the poet William Butler (W. B.) and his younger brother and postimpressionist painter, Jack. When he was a boy, young William steeped himself in local folklore. In the 19th century, educated society paid little heed to tales about the warrior Finn McCool or the deceitful Queen Maeve, deeming them fit only for children or peasants. But the man who would win the Nobel Prize in literature—for "inspired poetry" that gave "expression to the spirit of a whole nation"—reveled in it. W. B. Yeats celebrated a distinctly Irish culture, stirring what would become by the end of the century a Gaelic revival.

Throughout their lives, the Yeats brothers kept returning to Sligo, and Jack spent much time capturing in his paintings the local characters and what he feared was a disappearing way of life. One of their favorite spots was Lough Gill, where the wooded islet of Innisfree is immortalized in William's best-known poem:

*I will arise and go now, and go to Innisfree,*
*And a small cabin build there, of clay and wattles made;*
*Nine bean rows will I have there, a hive for the honey bee,*
*And live alone in the bee-loud glade.*

## [ Five Places to Meet St. Patrick ]

**1 Armagh, County Armagh** St. Patrick chose Armagh as the place from which he would disseminate Christianity across Ireland. He built the island's first stone church here, in A.D. 445, and decreed that Armagh should take precedence over all the churches in Ireland.

**2 Croagh Patrick, County Mayo** Thousands of pilgrims climb this 2,510-feet holy mountain on Reek Sunday (the last Sunday of June), partly in honor of St. Patrick, who is said to have fasted on its summit for 40 days and nights. It was from here that he banished all snakes from Ireland.

**3 Downpatrick, County Down** The town most closely associated with the saint, mainly because he is supposed to have died in nearby Saul. The traditional site of his grave is in the churchyard of Down Cathedral.

**4 Hill of Slane, County Meath** According to tradition, the saint lit a paschal (Easter) fire atop this hill in A.D. 433 to proclaim Christianity across Ireland—though some claim the fire was lit on the Hill of Tara.

**5 Slemish, County Antrim** The young saint is said to have tended goats and pigs on the slopes of this craggy peak. Thousands of pilgrims climb to the 1,457-foot summit every St. Patrick's Day.

**POT OF GOLD**
A rainbow arches over a thatched and whitewashed cottage and nearby fields in County Donegal. Many visitors remark on the frequency of rainbows in Ireland, but locals tend to take them more for granted in a country where, given the ever changing weather patterns and imminence of rain, they are a common sight.

TAKING PHOTOGRAPHS WITH A VIEW TO SELL OR MAKE COMMERCIAL USE OF ANY KIND IS STRICTLY FORBIDDEN

OFFICIAL PHOTOGRAPHERS TO BLARNEY CASTLE ONLY

REMOVE ALL HATS & GLASSES

NO STANDING ON THIS WALL

NO STANDING UP HERE

Yeats is buried as he directed, "under bare Ben Bulben's head," in the graveyard of the Anglican Church at nearby Drumcliff, where his great-grandfather had been rector.

North of Sligo is Donegal—part of Ulster and the most northerly county in the Republic of Ireland. This is Ireland's remotest county, yet it is a destination for many. Some people come for the beautiful shoreline, which includes Europe's highest sea cliffs. Others come to walk in the footsteps of the saints—to Lough Derg, which Patrick is said to have visited in 445 and which continues

### IN CORK

Everyone knows that those who kiss the **Blarney Stone** at Blarney Castle are magically endowed with the gift of gab. In fact, legends abound all around the castle. The Wishing Steps will grant your heart's desire if you can negotiate them backward with your eyes closed.

to be a place of pilgrimage, and to Glencolumbkille, "the glen of Columba."

Glencolumbkille is a sheltered valley that runs to the coast. It is named after the Ulster-born St. Columba, who founded the Christian colony of Iona in the Scottish Hebrides, along with a number of monasteries in Donegal. At midnight on St. Columba's Day, June 9, pilgrims undertake a barefoot walk to 15 stations in the valley that are associated with the saint.

From here, progress on around the Donegal coast is slow, requiring travelers to head west and north, and then south and east to round the many peninsulas. This is the Gaeltacht again, and Donegal has more Irish speakers than any other part of Ireland, its language sounding more like Scottish Gaelic than anywhere else in Ireland. From Bloody Foreland there are views across seven miles of the choppy Atlantic to Tory Island, which lies low in the water, as if hunkering down from the constant winds. In the Irish republic, this is the one spot still ruled by a king, a tradition that began when St. Columba appointed an islander to the position in the sixth century.

**KISS ME, I'M IRISH**
Standard drill at the Blarney Stone—one person to kiss, one to hold, one to photograph, and three to watch. Blarney Castle is about five miles north of Cork and boasts extensive gardens.

Passing around Inishowen, the great diamond-shaped peninsula in the far north, brings us to the shores of Lough Foyle and the border with Northern Ireland. Here, the landscape is marked most immediately by the city of Derry.

## Derry and Antrim

Originally a monastic settlement founded by St. Columba, Derry is one of Ireland's oldest continuously inhabited sites. However, the city is also known today as Londonderry, an indication of its later history, which is most obviously indicated by the magnificent walls that encircle the city.

The walls were built around the city in the early 17th century by English and Scottish settlers, and famously withstood a siege by England's King James II and his Irish Catholic supporters in 1689. The Jacobite army was unable to penetrate the walls, and intact they remain.

Derry today is one of the finest walled cities in Europe—and the only completely walled city in Ireland. The walls are between 12 and 35 feet wide and about a mile long, and visitors can follow a walkway around the entire length of the old inner city. From here, they can enjoy the city's spectacular views—the original grid pattern of the streets converging on the central square (the Diamond), the four original city gates, St. Columb's great Gothic cathedral that was completed in 1633, the Greek-revival courthouse, and the Victorian Guildhall.

Derry endured great turmoil and destruction during the Troubles that broke out at the end of the 1960s. The Guildhall was particularly badly hit, destroyed in a number of bomb explosions in the city. Derry, like its Guildhall, has been carefully restored and revitalized. The city provides the ideal backdrop for a number of festivals and celebrations. Derry's Halloween Carnival is the most famous in Ireland, dubbed the island's biggest street party. And every August, the 105-day Siege of Derry is commemorated during the Maiden City Festival, "maiden" being a reference to the fact that the city's defenses were never breached in 1689.

Following the coast around Northern Ireland takes us from County Londonderry to County Antrim, past the local seaside resorts

**LAND OF THE GIANTS**

Surf crashes against the Giant's Causeway on the north Antrim coast. A tourist draw since Victorian times, the Causeway is one of the top attractions of Northern Ireland.

of Portstewart and Portrush and their long sandy beaches. Royal Portrush Golf Course is home to the famous Dunluce Links, one of the world's great courses, with views west to Donegal and northeast to the southern Hebrides.

The coastline here grows more dramatic with every turn, moving from long sandy beaches to limestone cliffs that have been carved into a spectacular display of caves and arches. And then Dunluce Castle comes into view. Perched precariously on a basalt outcrop that is joined to the mainland by an arched

---

**IN SLIGO**

The **Yeats Country Drive** runs a meandering course for about 100 miles around the haunts of William Butler (W. B.) and Jack Yeats. Sites include the tiny inlet of Innisfree that W. B. Yeats made the subject of his best-known poem and the Church of St. Columba in Drumcliff, where he is buried.

---

walkway, it dates from at least Norman times, though an even earlier fort has occupied the site. In 1639, the castle's kitchen fell into the sea, taking the cooking staff with it.

One of the ships of the Spanish Armada, the *Girona,* also disappeared in these waters as it tried to make its way back to Spain in October 1588. The drowned crewmen are said to have been buried at nearby St. Cuthbert's Church. A local chieftain named Sorley Boy McDonnell promptly salvaged four of the vessel's cannons and mounted them on the castle walls. Today, the treasures of the *Girona* are on display in the Ulster Museum in Belfast.

As if constantly seeking to outdo itself, the north Antrim coast holds another wonder in store: the Giant's Causeway. Dubbed the "Eighth Wonder of the World," the causeway is a UNESCO World Heritage site—a collection of some 37,000 hexagonal columns of basalt, formed after a lava flow cooled and then fissured. Stretching out like an intricate mosaic pavement, the closely stacked columns rise up to 40 feet high and are set against a backdrop of 300-foot cliffs.

**PATCHWORK QUILT**

A byproduct of the abundant rainfall in Ireland is the greenness of the fields. Those at left are in a valley near the Slieve Gullion Mountains of County Armagh.

The geological explanation is interesting. But after a tipple at nearby Bushmills—founded in 1608 and home to the oldest licensed distillery in the world—visitors may be more taken with the traditional explanation. The Causeway, the story goes, was built out into the sea by Finn McCool, perhaps the most celebrated of all Irish heroes. Raised by a druid, Finn was a great warrior, leader of an elite band of fighters known as the Fianna, who guarded the high king of Ireland. Irish folklore is filled with his tales of valor in battle. But the Giant's Causeway is said to have been built not for warfare but for romance, a way for Finn to reach his girlfriend on the Hebridean island of Staffa.

Romantic troubles seem to have plagued Finn for much of his life. His most famous wife was turned into a deer. And when he was an old man, he fell in love with Gráinne, the beautiful daughter of the high king. But Gráinne had her own plans and the night before they were to marry, she ran off with a handsome young member of the Fianna, Diarmuid. Finn pursued them all over Ireland, finally catching up with them in the far west of the country.

IN WILD HEADLAND after wild headland, the Causeway coast makes its way around the top of Ireland. Along the way there are more ruined castles, like Dunseverick; what is said to be the smallest church in Ireland, at Portbraddon; Neolithic passage tombs overlooking Whitepark Bay; and a ruined friary just outside Ballycastle.

Every August, Ballycastle hosts the Ould' Lammas Fair, which it has done for the last three centuries. Today, the fair attracts visitors from all over the world. It is renowned for its traditional music, horse trading, and the sale of local food specialties like Yellowman candy and a reddish seaweed known as "dulse."

From Ballycastle, the ferry sets out for the offshore island of Rathlin, which sits in the Irish Sea like a stepping-stone on the way to Scotland. (The Mull of Kintyre is only 16 miles distant.) The waters here are extremely treacherous, and the 40-minute ferry ride to Rathlin can be a stomach-churning experience.

The wildlife finds no difficulty in reaching it, though. Seals bask on the rocks at Rue Point, and huge colonies of puffins and other seabirds nest at Bull Point. Robert the Bruce made his way here, too, and is said to have found inspiration from one

## [ The Irish-American Connection ]

**1 Carrickfergus, County Antrim** The hometown of the parents of Andrew Jackson, seventh President of the United States (16 U.S. Presidents to date have Irish ancestry), has a replica of their cottage home and a museum, the Andrew Jackson Centre.

**2 Cobh, County Cork** Cobh was the last glimpse of Ireland for the 2.5 million people who emigrated to the United States from its port in the 19th century. The heritage center, devoted to the Great Famine and the emigration that followed, is one of Ireland's best.

**3 Dergenah, County Tyrone** The Grant Ancestral Homestead re-creates the farm worked here by John Simpson, maternal grandfather of Ulysses Simpson Grant, before he immigrated to Pennsylvania in 1760.

**4 Dunganstown, County Wexford** The Kennedy Homestead is the birthplace of Patrick Kennedy, great-grandfather of John F. Kennedy, who immigrated to the United States in 1848. John F. Kennedy visited the homestead in 1963.

**5 New Ross, County Wexford** The Dunbrody Heritage Ship re-creates one of the so-called 19th-century Coffin Ships that took immigrants to the United States. There is also a database of Irish emigration between 1845 and 1875 with more than two million records.

of the island's humbler residents. After suffering defeat in battle at the hands of the English, the Scottish leader had fled to Rathlin, holing up in what is now known as Bruce's Cave. There, he reputedly was encouraged by watching a spider in the cave try to complete its web over and over again before finally succeeding. Vowing to show the same determination, he returned to Scotland and was eventually victorious over the English.

Back on the mainland, the land rises majestically at Fair Head, a 600-foot-high dolerite headland. From here, the coast angles down the western side of the Irish Sea. Charming villages like Cushendun and Cushendall, Camlough and Glenarm line the way, while the famed Glens of Antrim—with their glacial valleys and waterfalls, mist-draped hills, and remote forests—rise inland.

Only when it reaches Whitehead does the coastline shift. There, it turns sharply to follow the great indent of Belfast Lough all the way to the capital city of Northern Ireland. Belfast and its southern counterpart, Dublin, are particular Irish cities, part of the Irish story but with stories of their own—and the subject of the next chapter in this book.

# Sites and Sights in Ireland

**Note:** *A number of the places listed below do not have individual websites but rather have pages on Ireland tourism sites (see, for instance, www.irishtourism.com and www.discoverireland.com).*

The **Wicklow Mountains** are the Dubliners' country playground, rising enticingly in tall blue humps just a half hour's drive to the south. Hikers, birders, and shutterbugs claim that the terrain is more beautiful the farther into the hills you go.

County Kildare's 18th-century **Castletown House** is undoubtedly its finest country house, a no-holds-barred piece of Palladian architecture at its peak. The enormously long colonnaded facade is a breathtaking sight.
*www.castletownhouse.ie*

Whatever route you choose, all roads in the Wicklow Mountains seem to lead inevitably to **Glendalough**. This remarkable monastic site, tucked down in its lake valley among steep mountainsides, honors the humble miracle worker St. Kevin. It is not just the beautiful enclosed setting that makes Glendalough so special; equally remarkable are the quality of the monastery's dozen or more 10th-, 11th-, and 12th-century buildings.
*www.glendalough.connect.ie*

The small-scale town of **Kilkenny** is by far the most complete medieval city in Ireland. Set on the west bank of the River Nore, Kilkenny town lies between its two chief landmarks, the castle and the cathedral. Most visitors head straight for **Kilkenny Castle**, seat to the Earl of Ormond for more than six centuries. This three-sided fortress (the fourth side was destroyed) occupies a site over the River Nore that's both strategically superb and scenically outstanding.
*www.kilkennytourism.ie/eng/*

Best known around the world for its incomparable crystal, **Waterford** is not the elegant city one might anticipate. Rather it is a working port town with a lively student population. The Waterford Crystal factory is the town's main employer, and the tour—which allows the opportunity to see impossibly talented craftsmen and craftswomen whip up perfection—should not be missed.
*www.waterfordvisitorcentre.com*

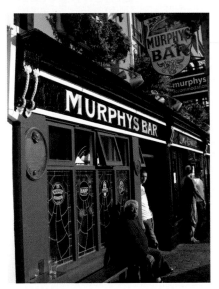

Pub in Galway

The first sight of the **Rock of Cashel** rising out of the Golden Vale of Tippery, its domed top tightly packed with towers, spires, and pointed gables, is unforgettable. Its power over time as a kind of secular and spiritual capital beckoned and inspired events both great and grim.
*www.cashel.ie*

Three picturesque and storied counties make up Southwest Ireland: **Cork**, **Kerry**, and **Limerick**. Here the land splits apart into five great peninsulas that jut out into the Atlantic. **Cork** is the most important city here.

The city center occupies a long island in the River Lee that is lined with fine old houses and connected by numerous handsome bridges to 19th-century suburbs on the steep hills to the north and south.

Kissing the **Blarney Stone** at Blarney Castle is one of Ireland's prime visitor activities. The stone, cloaked in legend, is set into the outer face of a gap in the battlements at the top of the castle. You'll have to lie on your back and wriggle your upper body outward and downward to kiss the stone. Make sure you don't have coins or other valuables in your pockets, and miniskirts are not recommended.
*www.blarneycastle.ie*

The glorious looping route around the coast of the Iveragh Peninsula, known as the **Ring of Kerry**, is Ireland's best-known scenic drive. Here are the mountains, craggy coasts, and charming small towns and villages depicted in chocolate-box photographs of the west of Ireland, up close and real.
*www.ringofkerrytourism.com*

The **Dingle Peninsula** is the connoisseur's choice among the five peninsulas of southwest Ireland. All around are beautiful sandpits, beaches, and mountains, and Ireland's greatest concentration of early Christian sites—not to mention the laid-back charm of **Dingle town** and the extraordinary literary hothouse of the remote and rugged **Blasket Islands**.
*www.dingle-peninsula.ie*

Aside from Dublin, western Ireland holds the greatest appeal for most travelers for its wild traditional music; spectacular coast; small-island scenery; vast, open tracts of ruggedly beautiful landscape, and the most laid-back approach to life in this notably relaxed country.

**County Clare** is the greenest, mildest, and gentlest of the three western counties. In the southwest are the old seaside towns Kirrush and Kildeee, while farther north is the strange and haunting landscape of the Burren region. Among its bare gray limestone hills lay hidden ancient tombs, churches, dwellings, and ring forts in a bleak setting jeweled with Ireland's richest flora.

Seabirds flap about O'Brien's Tower, the Victorian viewpoint at the highest point of the mighty **Cliffs of Moher**. On a good day one can view more than 100 miles in all directions from the Kerry hills to the Aran Islands and the Twelve Bens of Connemara. *www.cliffsofmoher.ie*

**Galway** is a lively city—one of the liveliest in Ireland, thanks to its university and colleges, and to a great revival in its economy and optimism over the past 20 years or so.

The **Aran Islands** are a byword for harsh, unforgiving landscape, and their Irish-speaking people have always epitomized hardy self-reliance. It is the wind-scoured, sea-bitten limestone that gives the three Aran Islands their extraordinary atmosphere, virtually treeless and more "out of this world" than any other landscape in Ireland.

Few place names in Ireland are more evocative than **Connemara**, and no region is more steeped in the romance of harshly beautiful, remote, and alluring country. The archetypal Connemara view is a line of craggy granite mountains forming the horizon between wide lake and bog waters and vast cloudscape skies. *www.connemaraireland.com*

**Sligo Bay** is forever associated with the Yeats brothers, who spent much of their childhood around Sligo town. The town itself is one of Ireland's most enjoyable, a lively but relaxed place of narrow streets and friendly, musical pubs.

Close to here lies **Innisfree**, the tiny wooded islet that W. B. made the subject of his best-known poem. You can reach the "Lake Isle of Innisfree" by boat from Parke's Castle on the north shore and wander where Yeats longed to live in dreamy seclusion.

**County Donegal,** northernmost and remotest of the Irish Republic's counties, throws dozens of peninsulas west and north into the Atlantic. The southwest corner of this ragged coastline bulges out the farthest, leading at its tip to Europe's highest sea cliffs and the beautifully enfolded sacred site of Glencolumbkille. *www.gleanncholmcille.ie*

Ring of Kerry, or the Iveragh Peninsula

**Strokestown Park House** retains the effects accumulated by one family over 300 years. The **Irish National Famine Museum** explores the disaster that befell rural Ireland in the 1840s. *www.strokestownpark.ie*

**Boyle Abbey** is a remarkably complete, very early Cistercian monastery. Very few monastic sites came through Ireland's bloody wars and repressions as unscathed as this abbey, where domestic and devotional buildings stand side by side. *www.heritageireland.ie/en/West/BoyleAbbey/*

It takes a full day to cruise the 40-mile Ballyconnell and Ballinamore Canal, better known as the **Shannon-Erne Waterway**, via boats—rented or chartered—that pass through 16 locks and under dozens of stone bridges past the picturesque villages and unspoiled countryside of central Ireland. *www.iwai.ie/nav/sew.html*

Beautifully situated on a bend of the River Shannon, **Clonmacnoise** is the most complete and evocative monastic site in the central region. With its exquisitely carved high crosses, multitude of ancient churches, and splendid round tower, many claim it as the best such site in all Ireland. *www.irishtourism.com/attractions-ireland/clonmacnoise_226738-attraction.htm*

The modest country town of **Kells** in the northwest of County Meath is famous for just one thing: the *Book of Kells,* often called "the world's most beautiful book." Kells is worth exploring for its magnificent high crosses and tiny oratory known as St. Columba's House.

The counties of Northern Ireland fan out like segments of a wheel from the central hub of **Lough Neagh,** the biggest lake in the British Isles. Lough Neagh covers an astonishing 153 square miles, and five of the six Northern Ireland counties touch its flat shores. *www.discoverloughneagh.com*

**Londonderry,** Northern Ireland's "second city" (after Belfast), is called Derry if the speaker is a Catholic and/or a nationalist, and Londonderry by Protestants and mainland Britons. Its superbly preserved 17th-century city walls offer a circular walk with truly memorable views over the city and hills beyond—by far the best way to appreciate the city. *www.irelandwide.com/regional/ulster/county_derry/coderry_main.htm*

East of Belfast is one of Ireland's most beautiful and haunting landscapes—the long southward-curving arm of the **Ards Peninsula** and the great bird-thronged sea inlet of **Strangford Lough**. This region has two fine National Trust houses, a spatter of beautiful islands, and dramatic coastline. *www.strangfordlough.org*

Dublin & Belfast

The Irish author James Joyce once famously said that if Dublin ever disappeared, it could be rebuilt, brick by brick, from the pages of his novel *Ulysses*. The great epic masterpiece, some 300,000 words in all, unfolds over the course of a single day, Thursday, June 16, 1904, in the life of a certain Leopold Bloom.

As Homer chronicled the journey of Odysseus (in Latin, Ulysses) around the islands of the Mediterranean, so Joyce follows the perambulations of Bloom through the streets of Dublin: past Peter Kennedy's hairdressers, the Burton Restaurant, "Trinity's surly front," through the shopping district of Grafton Street, and into Davy Byrne's pub at 21 Duke Street, where Bloom has a glass of Burgundy and a Gorgonzola cheese sandwich. Today June 16 is celebrated as Bloomsday, when Joyce devotees from far and near follow Bloom's fictional footsteps around the city. These have been helpfully marked by a series of bronze sidewalk plaques.

## [ Five Facts about St. Patrick's Cathedral ]

1 The cathedral is the largest church in Ireland.

2 It was supposedly built on the site of a well used for baptisms by St. Patrick himself, and there has been a church on the site since the fifth century, though the present church dates from 1191.

3 The cathedral's most famous dean was Jonathan Swift, author of *Gulliver's Travels,* who served here between 1713 and 1745. He is buried in the nave.

4 The phrase "chancing your arm" originated in St. Patrick's, after a 1492 dispute that ended with one Irishman putting his arm through a hole in the Chapter House door, unsure whether his foe would shake his hand or cut off his arm.

5 The choirs of St. Patrick's and the "rival" Dublin cathedral, Christ Church, came together in 1742 to give the first ever performance of Handel's *Messiah,* conducted by the composer himself.

Joyce left Ireland in 1904 for the broader horizons of the continent and published *Ulysses* in Paris in 1922. He was certainly aware of the impact his writing had on the city he loved from afar, describing his work as a "nicely polished looking glass" in which Dubliners could see themselves. "When you remember that Dublin has been a capital for thousands of years," he wrote his brother from the continent, "that it is the 'second' city of the British Empire, that it is nearly three times as big as Venice, it seems strange that no artist has given it to the world."

In *Ulysses,* James Joyce did just that. It took him seven years to capture the "dailiest day possible" in Dublin. And he did it from Paris, Trieste, and Zurich, cities where he poured over Dublin street maps and read and re-read Dublin newspapers. To fill in the gaps in his memory, he wrote friends and relatives still in the city for details about particular buildings and places, right down to particular species of trees. He even used a watch to time the movements of the characters in *Ulysses* from one Dublin location to another.

JAMES JOYCE WAS BORN one of ten siblings into a comfortable middle-class family on the south side of Dublin. When he was nine, though, his family fell on hard times and were forced to move north across the River Liffey to more humble, inner-city lodgings.

The family's travails and later relocations would all provide the raw material and characters for his future work. The Joyces were a Catholic, nationalist family, and

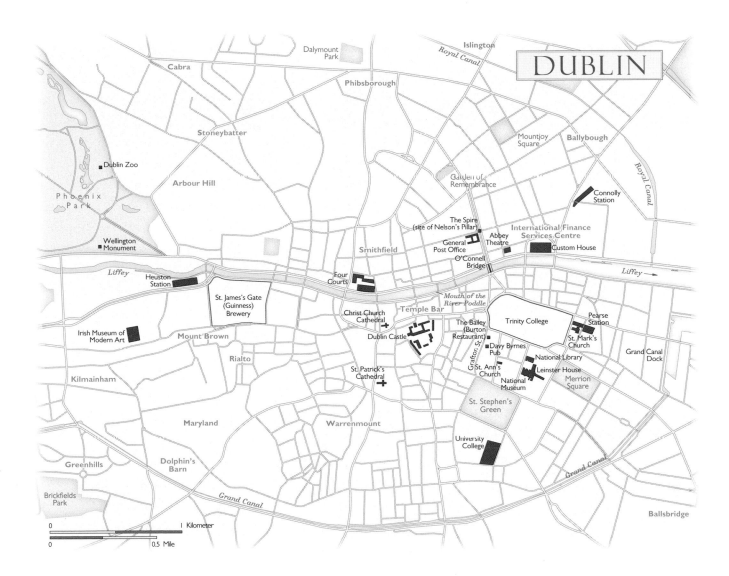

**DUBLIN**

Islington · Royal Canal · Dalymount Park · Cabra · Phibsborough · Stoneybatter · Mountjoy Square · Ballybough · Royal Canal · Dublin Zoo · Arbour Hill · Garden of Remembrance · Connolly Station · Phoenix Park · Wellington Monument · Smithfield · The Spire (site of Nelson's Pillar) · General Post Office · Abbey Theatre · International Finance Services Centre · Custom House · Liffey · Heuston Station · Four Courts · O'Connell Bridge · Liffey · St. James's Gate (Guinness) Brewery · Mouth of the River Poddle · Temple Bar · Trinity College · Pearse Station · Irish Museum of Modern Art · Mount Brown · Christ Church Cathedral · Dublin Castle · The Bailey (Burton Restaurant) · Davy Byrnes Pub · St. Mark's Church · Grand Canal Dock · Rialto · Grafton St. · St. Ann's Church · National Library · Leinster House · Kilmainham · St. Patrick's Cathedral · National Museum · Merrion Square · Maryland · Warrenmount · St. Stephen's Green · University College · Greenhills · Dolphin's Barn · Grand Canal · Brickfields Park · Grand Canal · Ballsbridge

0 | 1 Kilometer
0 | 0.5 Mile

were great supporters of Charles Stuart Parnell, the champion of home rule and the man known as "the uncrowned King of Ireland." Parnell, himself an Anglo-Irish Protestant, was a charismatic figure. British prime minister William Gladstone called him the most remarkable person he had ever met. But in 1890, Parnell faced political ruin when he was named co-respondent in a divorce case and the Catholic hierarchy issued a condemnation. The following year, Parnell delivered his last public speech during a downpour in County Roscommon. He died soon after of pneumonia, at just 45. The home rule movement had suffered a huge setback.

The nine-year-old Joyce was moved to write a poem in defense of Parnell. As he grew older, Joyce, like his father, came to associate Parnell's downfall and the political reversal that followed with his family's own hard times in a down-at-the-heels part of Dublin.

For a long time the north side of the city had been regarded as its less fashionable part, a place for the working classes. One explanation for this is the fact that

**GETTING YOUR BEARINGS**

The city, founded by the Vikings, is split by the River Liffey, which drew the Norsemen here in the first place. Highlights from central Dublin include St. Stephen's Green, Dublin Castle, and St. Patrick's Cathedral. Phoenix Park dominates the west of the city. *Previous pages:* Statue of labor leader James Larkin, O'Connell Street, Dublin.

trading ships sailing up the Liffey docked on the north bank of the river, and dock workers thus began to live on that side. The wealthier merchant and professional classes tended to live on the south side.

Today, Dublin writer Roddy Doyle, who won the Booker Prize in 1993, continues to draw on the blue-collar housing developments of north Dublin, especially in his fictional suburb of

### IN TRINITY

The requisite pilgrimage to view the glorious **Book of Kells,** held under glass at the Old Library at Trinity College, will not disappoint. On whatever page is exposed of the world's first illuminated manuscript, the beauty, humor, and force of imagination come shining through the patina of the centuries.

Barrytown. His "Barrytown Trilogy" is made up of *The Commitments* (1987), *The Snapper* (1990), and *The Van* (1991).

## A Walk on the South Side

Dublin, north or south, did not exist at all in 837 when a fleet of more than 60 Viking ships landed where the River Liffey flows into the Irish Sea. The Vikings began to explore the area, and four years later, they established a winter camp here.

The newcomers often clashed with the local Irish, but by 917 they had established the settlement that would become Dublin. They chose a spot on the south bank, at a pool where the smaller River Poddle flowed into the Liffey and where the Vikings developed a harbor for their ships. The Irish called the place *Dubh Linn,* or "dark pool," from which comes the name for the modern city.

The Viking town was a prosperous center of trade, some 15 acres in all and protected behind an earthen rampart and stone wall. As many as 10,000 people lived there, inhabiting houses of wattle separated by wattle fences.

By the 12th century, the Anglo-Normans had arrived, capturing Dublin and displacing the Viking

**INFORMATION SUPERHIGHWAY**

Trinity College's Long Room Library is one of the architectural wonders of Dublin. The most famous single item in the Old Library's collection is the *Book of Kells.*

settlers. It was the Normans who extended the settlement to the north bank of the river. As they did, they also strengthened their hold on Dublin by creating the Pale, a defensive territory surrounding the city. It ran in a great arc from Dalkey in the south to the garrison town of Dundalk in the north, defended by a series of castles and designed to keep at bay the native Irish who lived "beyond the Pale."

## [ Dublin's Guinness Trail ]

**1** **The Guinness Storehouse** Open to the public, this multimedia extravaganza devoted to Ireland's favorite drink is housed in part of the original St. James's Gate Brewery, which still produces 2.5 million pints of Guinness a day.

**2** **Number 1, Thomas Street** A plaque on the house at this address marks the home of Sir Arthur Guinness (1725–1803), the man who founded the St. James's Gate Brewery in 1759. He leased the premises for a £45 annual rent—the lease was signed for 9,000 years.

**3** **The pub** Dublin has more than 1,000 pubs where you'll be able to buy a pint of Guinness. Which ones are best? It's impossible to say, but among the more traditional are Long Hall (51 South Great George Street); O'Donoghue's (15 Merrion Row), known for its music; and Kennedy's (10 George's Quay), where nothing seems to have changed in 50 years.

For seven centuries, the focus of English rule in Ireland would be Dublin Castle. Completed in 1213 and added to over the years, the Castle, as it has always been known, was commissioned by King John to provide a "safe place for the custody of our treasures" and "for the administration of justice and if need be for the defence of the city, making it as strong as you can with good ditches and strong walls." The builders certainly got the last part right: Though it was besieged often over the centuries, Dublin Castle was never captured.

If the Castle represented royal power, Dublin's two Norman cathedrals were the embodiment of powers ecclesiastic. The first of them, Christ Church, sits just west of the Castle on a site where a Norse king of Dublin named Sigtrygg Silkbeard had built a wooden church. This was replaced by a more durable Norman version, which was in turn extensively renovated in 1875.

Just south of Christ Church is St. Patrick's Cathedral, founded by the saint himself in the fifth century. Like Christ Church, it has undergone significant restoration over the years. Jonathan Swift, who was dean of the cathedral from 1713 to 1745, is buried there.

WEST OF DUBLIN's castle and cathedrals is the huge Guinness Brewery, which in 2009 celebrated 250 years of stout-brewing and claims to be the country's top-ranked international attraction. The brewery produces half of all the beer consumed in Ireland, and Dubliners insist that the "black stuff" made here is the best because of the special taste it gets from Liffey water (though the Dublin brewery actually pipes its water in from the Wicklow Mountains, south of Dublin).

To the east of the castle and the cathedrals is Temple Bar. Once a rundown area, this is now the trendiest part of Dublin, and extends all the way to the "surly front" of Trinity College Dublin. Founded in 1592 by Queen Elizabeth I and a bastion of the Anglo-Irish ascendancy, Trinity has educated Catholics as well as Protestants since the mid-1700s. Even so, the Catholic Church forbade its members from attending until as recently as 1966.

Many of Ireland's greatest literary figures are Trinity alumni, including Jonathan Swift, Edmund Burke, Bram Stoker, Samuel Beckett, Oscar Wilde, and Oliver Goldsmith. But James Joyce, as a Catholic and a nationalist, was enrolled at the then-recently established University College Dublin.

In *Ulysses,* Joyce gave us a "modern" Irish masterpiece. In Trinity College resides an ancient one—the *Book of Kells.* An illuminated manuscript of the four Gospels, this 680-page book is thought to have been created by monks at the monastery of Kells in County Meath around the year 800 (although some claim it was made by monks on the Hebridean island of Iona). The manuscript has long been a must-see for visitors to Ireland. One 12th-century traveler from Wales, Giraldus Cambrensis, considered it "the chief glory of the western world."

## The Stage of Irish History

The O'Connell Bridge connects Dublin's south side to its poorer north side. Lining the northern quays are two of the city's architectural masterpieces, perched

**THE LIFFEY UPSTREAM**
Though not far from central Dublin and its outlet to the Irish Sea, the Liffey at Islandbridge seems every bit the rural river.

elegantly along the river: the great-domed Custom House, Dublin's grandest building, and farther upriver, the Four Courts, home to the High Court and the Supreme Court.

Continuing north of the bridge leads to O'Connell Street, Dublin's main thoroughfare and the site of modern Ireland's most momentous event. The street—one of the widest in Europe—is dotted with statues of Irish heroes, including Parnell, who led the cause of Irish nationalism at the end of the 19th century, and Daniel O'Connell, who championed it several decades earlier (and after whom the street is named).

The midsection of O'Connell Street is dominated by the General Post Office (GPO), where the drama of the Easter Rising played out its final acts. It was at the GPO that the 1916 rebels made their final stand and from whose steps they proclaimed the creation of an Irish republic. In 1922, O'Connell Street again took center stage when fighting broke out here at the start of the Irish civil war. And in 1966, republican militants would blow up the Nelson Pillar, a granite column topped by a statue of Admiral Lord Nelson, which had been erected in 1808 in honor of the Royal Navy hero.

Running east-west across O'Connell Street is Abbey Street, home to the famous Abbey Theatre where much drama—real as well as acted—has also played out. The theater was founded in 1903 by Lady Augusta Gregory and W. B. Yeats, who sought to stage works that reflected "the deeper thoughts and emotions of Ireland." These included, controversially, John Millington Synge's *Playboy of the Western World* and Seán O'Casey's *The Plough and the Stars.*

O'Casey was the first major playwright to write about Dublin's working classes. His pacifist drama, *The Plough and the Stars,* is set in the city during the 1916 Easter Rising and focuses on the role of ordinary Dubliners in the conflict. Like *Playboy,* the work elicited a strong reaction when it was first performed at the Abbey in 1926, prompting Yeats to address the rioting theater-goers: "You have disgraced yourself again. Is this to be the recurring celebration of the arrival of Irish genius?"

Yeats, though, had done his own part in rejecting Irish genius when he turned down for the Abbey the only play James Joyce ever wrote, *Exiles* (1918). By then, Joyce had been in exile from Ireland for 14 years. From the continent, he continued to watch as Ireland struggled for and then won independence, and set about creating the new Irish state. As he would for the rest of his life, Joyce continued to write about the city he had

## [ Dublin's Literary Landmarks ]

**1 Bram Stoker (1847–1912)** Number 36 Kildare Street was once home to the author of the gothic novel *Dracula,* which some say took its name from the Irish *droch fhola,* meaning "bad blood."

**2 Oscar Wilde (1854–1900)** Dublin-born and raised, at 1 Merrion Square East, but like many Irish writers, took his wit and talent abroad, to London and Paris.

**3 George Bernard Shaw (1856–1950)** The only man to win a Nobel Prize and an Oscar (for his play *Pygmalion,* which was turned into the film *My Fair Lady*). He was born at 33 Synge Street, now restored as a literary shrine open to the public.

**4 James Joyce (1882–1941)** Dublin is scattered with sites associated with this writer's famous novel *Ulysses* (1922), which is set in the city. It also features many from Joyce's *The Dubliners* (1914), a collection of short stories. The James Joyce Centre offers background, walking tours, and other information on the writer.

**5 Samuel Beckett (1906–89)** A Dublin native, but most of his most famous plays, including *Waiting for Godot* (1953), were written in French in self-imposed exile, mostly in Paris.

**6 William Butler (W. B.) Yeats (1865–1939)** One of the greatest Irish poets lived at 82 Merrion Square South before moving to 52 Merrion Square East—though he later professed to detest the square.

Note: The Dublin Writers Museum at 18 North Parnell Square offers much memorabilia and many insights into the city's literary heritage.

**LITERARY LOUNGE**
The parlor in the family home of another of Dublin's great writers, George Bernard Shaw

only ever left in a physical sense. In Dublin, however, the new leaders of the Irish state did not look at all favorably on the work of the self-imposed exile. *Ulysses* was banned, for alleged immorality and impropriety, in the city it had done so much to capture.

THE DUBLINERS WHO had just won their independence from Britain in the early 1920s were not ready to see the flaws of their politicians and priests reflected in Joyce's "nicely polished looking glass." The leaders of the new state were crafting a future. In the Irish constitution they drafted, they gave the Catholic Church the "special position" of being the state's "guardian of the faith." This provision would be mirrored in Northern Ireland, where the majority there created a "Protestant parliament for a Protestant people."

The new Irish nation adopted a tricolored flag of green, white, and orange, at once capturing affinities for the tricolors of revolutionary France and Catholic Italy. The flag was designed to reflect Irish Catholics (green), Northern Protestants (orange), and the aspiration for peace between the two traditions (white). The Ulster Unionists were concerned by the clause in the Irish Constitution that lay claim to the territory of the Northern Irish state, eloquent testimony to the cultural nationalism that remained central during the nation's early years.

Joyce found the movement to be narrow-minded, parochial, and stifling. He lamented in the following rhyme:

**NORTH AND SOUTH**

Above, a youngster holds aloft an Irish flag during St. Patrick's Day celebrations in Dublin. Opposite, a weaver works a loom at the Irish Linen Centre and Lisburn Museum just outside Belfast, the city once known as the linen capital of the British Empire.

*This lovely land that always sent*
*Her writers and artists to banishment*
*And in a spirit of Irish fun*
*Betrayed her own leaders, one by one.*

*'Twas Irish humour, wet and dry,*
*Flung quicklime into Parnell's eye . . .*
*O Ireland my first and only love*
*Where Christ and Caesar are hand in glove!*

Still, Joyce also looked back with tenderness and regret. In writing about Dublin, he admitted: "I have not been just to its beauty: for it is more beautiful naturally, in my opinion, than what I have seen of England, Switzerland, France, Austria, and Italy."

He would continue to draw inspiration from the city of his birth, his "dear, dirty Dublin." As he once declared, "If I can get to the heart of Dublin, I can get to the heart of all the cities of the world."

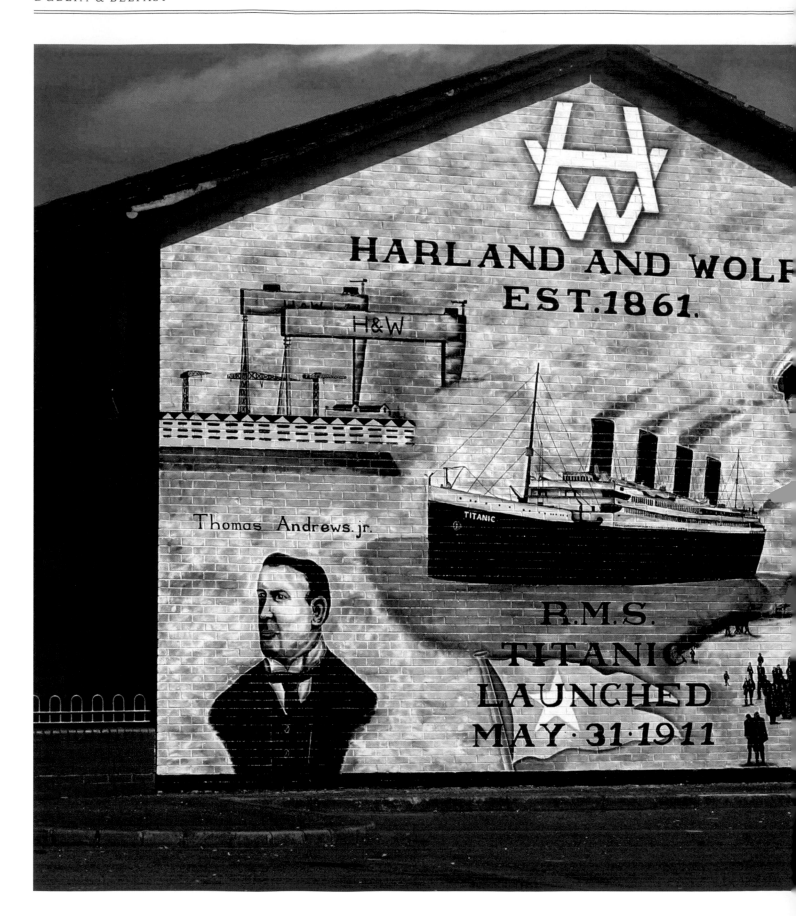

Captain,
Edward Smith.

**TITANIC MURAL**

A mural on the gable wall of a house off the Newtownards Road area of Belfast celebrates the ocean liner built at the local Harland and Wolff shipyards. Such murals are now replacing earlier ones featuring paramilitary groups.

## From Kilkenny Cat to Celtic Tiger

Independent Ireland has been poor for most of its short history, less affluent than Northern Ireland. In the 1950s, young people began seeking jobs and opportunities overseas. About half a million people left Ireland during the decade.

The country joined the European Union in 1973, as did the United Kingdom. Ireland has always been more enthusiastic

**IN WEST BELFAST**

There's no better way to experience Belfast than in a **Black Taxi.** A gabby cabby (and almost all of them are) can help bring the spirit and humor of Belfast to life. They are particularly knowledgeable about the city's murals, which they will gladly take you to.

about membership in the EU than the British, though. As one of the EU's poorest members, it initially received generous subsidies for much-needed infrastructure and development projects. In 1999, the Irish became one of the original members to adopt the euro, while the British decided to hold onto their pound.

Ireland's membership in the European Union soon helped transform it into one of the wealthiest countries in Europe. During the years of the so-called Celtic Tiger in the mid-1990s, the Irish completed the job themselves, as foreign investment soared and multinational corporations began doing business there. Dublin in particular underwent a boom. Disposable income reached record levels, and consumer spending skyrocketed accordingly. Unemployment plummeted from a 1980s high of 18 percent, and Ireland, which for so long had been a place of emigration, became a destination for immigrants seeking work.

In 2007, an estimated one in ten Irish residents was foreign-born. Most of the new arrivals came from Eastern Europe, from the new EU member states of Poland and the Baltic countries, seeking jobs in Dublin's retail and service sectors. Others came from China and West African nations like Nigeria and

Ghana. The Irish and U.S. governments even began talks about a new immigration policy between their two countries to meet the demands of Americans eager to relocate to Ireland.

By the time the world recession hit in 2007, Ireland was the fifth richest country per capita in the world. It was also the second wealthiest in the European Union, no longer a net recipient of the EU budget but a net contributor—and confident enough to (initially, at least) reject the EU-strengthening Lisbon Treaty.

Some believe, however, it has all come at too high a price. Various commentators have lamented Ireland's growing consumerism and the effect it has had on traditional culture. For the country has, to quote Yeats, "changed utterly," not least in the way that the Irish, now richer and more diverse, view the waning power of the Catholic Church.

What would Joyce have thought of the new Ireland, with its rampant Celtic Tiger, fabulously popular *Riverdance,* Maeve Binchy best-sellers, and world's biggest rock band, U2? More important, would its residents want to hear it?

THROUGHOUT THE BRITISH ISLES, a hundred miles is a long distance. That's roughly the distance between Dublin, capital of the Irish Republic, and Belfast, capital of Northern Ireland. The rail journey between Dublin's Connolly Station and Belfast Central Station takes about two and a half hours, passing through Drogheda, Dundalk, Newry, and Portadown—and through more history than most outsiders can imagine.

Belfast can be reached by rail or road. But the city, which has always been tied to the water, is best approached by sailing up Belfast Lough from the Irish Sea. Entering the great mouth of the lough takes visitors past two smaller towns that have an older pedigree than Belfast itself. On the north shore of the lough sits Carrickfergus, its castle evocative of Norman pride. It was here in 1690 that King William arrived with his Protestant army of English, Dutch, Huguenots, and Scots to take on King James and his Catholic army. The clash took place on the banks of the River Boyne, an event that is commemorated on the streets of Belfast every 12th of July.

Directly across the lough from Carrickfergus is Bangor and its famous abbey. From this and other remote Irish ecclesiastic centers, missionaries set out during the Dark Ages to take the Gospel back to Europe.

But ahead, the city of Belfast awaits. Its natural setting almost calls out for settlement, ringed as it is with high ground and split by the River Lagan. Inland, a ridge of

## [ Ships and Shipbuilding ]

**1 Belfast Maritime Festival** Held every June when a flotilla of sailing ships docks in the city.

**2 Connswater Shopping Centre** Occupies the site of the Belfast Ropeworks, established in 1873 to serve the shipbuilding industry, and in its day the world's largest rope manufacturer.

**3 Samson and Goliath** The names given to the great yellow dockside cranes, reputedly the world's largest, at the old Harland & Wolff shipyard in Belfast, which was founded in 1862 and once employed 30,000 men.

**4 Titanic** The most famous ship since Noah's Ark, this White Star behemoth was built in Belfast. Locals like to insist, "Well, it was all right when it left Belfast."

**5 Thomson Dry Dock** The vast basin in the Harland & Wolff yard where the historic White Star liners were built.

**NORMAN STRONGPOINT**
A train ride out from Belfast is Carrickfergus, home to the best preserved Norman castle in Ireland. Another way to see the castle is from one of the regular Scotland ferries that make their way up Belfast Lough.

hills—Black Mountain, Divis, Cave Hill, Squire's Hill—rise in a protective arc around the city. For this reason, Belfast has been called a "Hibernian Rio," though any who have visited will know that it shares nothing of the Brazilian city's climate.

## Titanic City

At the end of Belfast Lough, the city spreads out on two sides of the River Lagan. Guidebooks will focus on the city west of the river with its ornate city hall, St. Anne's Cathedral, and the Grand Opera House, perhaps. This area also contains the Linen Hall Library, Ulster Museum, and Queen's University, once attended by Nobel Prize–winner Seamus Heaney, who wrote about a peaceful Northern Ireland where "hope and history rhyme."

The city east of the Lagan is usually dismissed. But it is here that stand the biggest cranes in the world. Like two great colossi, these are the most visible reminders of the now silent shipyard of Harland and Wolff. "How many people work in the Belfast shipyard?" the joke used to go. "About half of them," would come the punch line.

Even with half its workers actually working, Harland and Wolff still would have dwarfed the area's other places of employment. At one time, it was the largest shipyard in the world. Here, legions of workers in flat caps, 30,000 of them, filed through the dark streets toward "the Yard," where they built ships like the *Titanic,* which slid out into the waters of the Lagan, the lough, the sea, and, eventually, the North Atlantic. Proud of the *Titanic,* if a little embarrassed at its fate, the locals shrug, "Well, it was all right when it left Belfast." Or, "It was built by Irishmen, but there was an Englishman sailing it."

**BELFAST ON FOOT**
Central Belfast is very walkable, from Queen's University (above) to the City Hall (opposite), which is also the hub for the city's buses, should the footsore need one.

The people of Belfast have been slow to capitalize on the fact that the most famous ship in the world was built here. But they are, finally, planning to celebrate the great vessel and incorporate it within the city, thanks to the creation of a *Titanic* quarter in the east of the city. The new quarter, featuring retail outlets, housing, and entertainment, will be developed around the site of the huge dry dock where the *Titanic* was built.

Such history is worth preserving. For generations, sons followed fathers into the Yard, working on the great liners that sailed to places they would never see, generating great wealth that they would never have. Most worked their whole lives at Harland and Wolff, raising families in their "two up, two down" row houses in the shipyard's shadow.

THE OVERLOOKED EAST of the city is also home to several famous figures. One is George Best, a star player for Manchester United in the late 1960s and early 1970s.

A tragic figure, Best led an extravagant lifestyle. He was a jet-setter, fashion designer, and often in the company of beautiful models. In the sixties Best was even dubbed "the fifth Beatle." One story tells how a room service waiter brought George several bottles of champagne, only to find him in the room with Miss World and thousands of pounds in casino winnings strewn on the bed. Look-

---

**IN EAST BELFAST**

One of the most popular C. S. Lewis sites is Ross Wilson's **"The Searcher,"** a bronze sculpture depicting the wardrobe from Lewis's classic novel *The Lion, the Witch, and the Wardrobe.* It was installed in central Belfast for the C. S. Lewis Centenary in 1998.

---

ing at the scene, the man turned to the soccer star and asked, "Mr. Best, where did it all go wrong?"

Though he undoubtedly wasted much of his talent, he is regarded by many as, in his day, the best player in the world. In recent decades, many others have been dubbed as such—Brazil's Pelé, Argentina's Diego Maradona, Holland's Johan Cruyff. But for Georgie's adoring fans in Belfast, the truth is summed up in the local saying: "Maradona good, Pelé better, George Best."

It's little surprise, then, that while Paris has named its airport after Charles de Gaulle, New York after John F. Kennedy, and Liverpool after John Lennon, Belfast's airport is now known as George Best Belfast City Airport.

George Best Airport is located near the birthplace of another famous local, C. S. Lewis. The great Christian apologist, who wrote *Surprised by Joy, The Screwtape Letters,* and *Mere Christianity,* grew up at the house in east Belfast known as "Little Lea." The house is now a private residence, but those wanting to explore Lewis's old neighborhood can take the local C. S. Lewis Trail, which also winds past St. Mark's

**MOURNE VIEW**
Though the sheep seem indifferent to the view, the Mourne Mountains are one of Northern Ireland's beauty spots. Distances are short here, and the Mournes can even be seen from Belfast.

Church (where his maternal grandfather was rector), his school, the 1998 Lewis sculpture "The Searcher," and other spots in surrounding rural County Down.

From hills near his home, the future Oxford scholar could see the distant Mourne Mountains, said to be the inspiration for his magical country of Narnia in his beloved children's stories. "Heaven," Lewis would say, "is Oxford lifted and placed in the middle of County Down."

The third of the famous East Belfast troika is George Ivan Morrison, better known as the singer-songwriter "Van the Man" or the "Belfast Cowboy." Morrison was born not far from Little Lea, though in a neighborhood more likely to house shipyard workers than Oxbridge scholars. In his own "echo" of *Ulysses,* Morrison's songs are filled with references to the parts of the city he knew— streets and avenues, movie theaters, bakeries, schools, and churches, even the local fish-and-chips shop. And like Joyce, Morrison has spent much of his creative energies writing about the city of his childhood, a place he has never truly ever left.

## Beyond the Troubles

At heart, Belfast is a Victorian manufacturing city, so different from anywhere else on the island of Ireland, its early claim to fame being ropemaking and tobacco production. This settlement on the banks of the River Lagan remained small up until the expansion of the textile and shipbuilding trades. It then became a great center of the textile industry, brought to the Lagan valley by French Huguenots, and earned for itself the nickname "Linenopolis."

Other differences mark this great city. Even the local accent is different in Belfast, harder and quicker, with a perceivable "Scottishness" to it. The humor of its people is dark but always matched by a spirit of generosity and friendliness.

The city's rapid growth in the 19th century is reflected in its acres of redbrick terraced houses, where industrial workers lived. It was essentially a Protestant city with a Protestant ethos, but Catholics began to arrive here, too, from the impoverished rural areas. They settled mostly on the west side of the Lagan. The Protestants and Catholics developed distinct neighborhoods in west Belfast, and they remain so today.

Tragically, some continue to be demarcated by the great snaking "Peace Walls," concrete reminders of communities still divided. During the Troubles that broke out at the end of the 1960s, neighborhoods all across the city suffered, especially those west of the

## [ Landmarks of the Belfast Divide ]

1 **Falls Road** The heartland of the Catholic and republican community in Belfast, and notable for its many large murals depicting characters involved in the city's religious and political history.

2 **Linen Hall Library, 17 Donegall Street** A beautiful library in its own right, established in 1788, but also a valuable resource, with a copy of everything written on Northern Ireland politics since 1966—more than 250,000 items.

3 **Shankill Road** Close to the Falls Road, and also with many murals, but a predominantly Protestant and loyalist area of the city, and part of the route of the summer "Orange" marches.

4 **The Europa Hotel, Great Victoria Street** Infamous during the Troubles for its reputation as the "most bombed hotel in the world," it is now one of the most sumptuous places to stay in the city.

5 **Milltown Cemetery, 546 Falls Road** Synonymous with Irish nationalism. Most of the ten Irish hunger strikers and many IRA members are buried here, including MP Bobby Sands. Also infamous as the scene of the Milltown Massacre (March 16, 1988), when loyalist Michael Stone killed three mourners.

**SIEGE MENTALITY**

The "No Surrender" message on this house in the Shankill area of West Belfast is understood locally in two senses. The first is a reference to the 1689 Siege of Protestant Derry by a Catholic army, the second to the armed campaign against Shankill Protestants by the IRA.

Lagan. There, two great parallel arteries, the Shankill Road and the Falls Road, run out of the city. These roads are now separated by the most famous of the Peace Walls. The wall is made of concrete, wire, and corrugated tin, parts of it more than 40 feet high, and the locals joke that anyone who can throw rocks or bottles over the Shankill–Falls Peace Wall shouldn't be in Belfast but in the Olympics.

The Shankill is the blue-collar Protestant heartland in west Belfast, the Falls Road its Catholic counterpart. At the height of the Troubles, tensions ran high here with gunmen roaming at night and bombers bombing by day. The conflict was also played out in political murals featuring various paramilitary groups that adorned the gable ends of row houses. The more antagonistic of these are finally getting artistic makeovers, though, and now also celebrate cultural heroes such as George Best or C. S. Lewis.

THOSE TRAVELING UP Belfast Lough toward the beckoning city cannot fail to miss one particularly striking section of the skyline. Napoleon's Nose is a great basalt cliff atop the Cave Hill, said to resemble a giant sleeping on his back. It is from this landmark that Jonathan Swift reputedly drew inspiration for *Gulliver's Travels*.

Long before he became Dean of St. Patrick's Cathedral in Dublin, Swift had been appointed minister at a Church of Ireland parish north of Belfast. There, he took up residence at Lilliput Cottage. The locals were Presbyterian, and Swift lamented that the only two Anglicans in the area seemed to be him and his horse. At the time, he was courting the daughter of a rich Belfast banker, who refused to allow the penniless preacher to see her. (In those days, ministers were paid according to their congregation's size.) Dejected, Swift was walking one summer evening when he looked up at the profile on the Cave Hill. Suddenly, the story of Gulliver came to him.

It is a sight a more recent writer has captured this way:

*Look up from the streets of the city,*
*Look high beyond tower and mast,*
*What hand of what Titan sculptor*
*Smote the crags on the mountain vast?*
*Made when the world was fashioned,*
*Meant with the world to last,*
*The glorious face of the sleeper*
*That slumbers above Belfast.*

**PADDY POWER**
Shamrock-winged clowns and their pom-pom–wielding followers take to the streets of central Belfast for the St. Patrick's Day parade on March 17, 2009.

# Sites and Sights in Dublin & Belfast

## Dublin

Dublin has come a long way from the days of James Joyce's sleepy city on the River Liffey into a place rattling with commerce—smart new businesses, chic eateries and wine bars, and popular dance clubs. Even so, it is also always easy to find the mythic Dublin where time runs slowly, the time-warp pockets of peace in traditional backstreet pubs and out-of-the-way gardens.

**Central Dublin** is small enough to visit almost everything on foot or via the light railway, and almost all of its celebrated attractions—Trinity College, St. Stephen's Green, St. Patrick's Cathedral, shops and cafés on Grafton Street, and the trendily renovated quarter of Temple Bar—lie south of the Liffey.

Dublin's **Trinity College** is best known for its fine architecture spanning four centuries and its long list of esteemed alumni, including Oscar Wilde, Jonathan Swift, Samuel Beckett, Dracula author Bram Stoker, and Ireland's first female president, Mary Robinson. An ideal way to approach Trinity is via College Street, where the low, modest entrance doorway belies the surprising grandeur of the buildings behind it. After the buzz of Dublin, the campus feels wonderfully peaceful.

The requisite pilgrimage to view the glorious *Book of Kells*, held under glass at the impressive **Old Library** at Trinity College, will not disappoint. On whatever page is exposed of the world's first illuminated manuscript, the beauty, humor, and force of imagination come shining through the patina of the centuries.

For playwrights, actors, and theatergoers worldwide, the **Abbey Theatre** is an icon. Founded in 1903 by W. B. Yeats and Lady Augusta Gregory to honor and celebrate Irish culture, the Abbey has hosted many world premiers and historic opening nights of plays by many of the finest 20th-century playwrights, including Yeats himself and Samuel Beckett, both Nobel Prize winners. *www.abbeytheatre.ie*

Wellington Testimonial, Dublin

The **National Museum of Archaeology and History**, known as the National Museum, holds the majority of Ireland's most significant archaeological finds, brought from the peat bogs, fields, and hillsides where they have been dug up or stumbled across over the years by turf cutters, ploughboys, and amateur archaeologists. The Treasury, the most popular permanent exhibition, boasts the bejeweled eighth-century Tara Brooch, a circular gold clasp and long pin that has become a familiar inspiration for modern Celtic jewelry. The brooch was found by chance in 1850 by a wanderer on the beach. *www.museum.ie*

The **Temple Bar** quarter on Dublin's River Liffey, the city's nerve center of nightlife and culture, was once seedy and rundown but escaped demolition in the 1980s. A group of young architects came up with some radical plans, designing a compact mix of galleries, theaters, and an arts center around a market square. Rooflines became fun, sprouting twisted rods like punk hair; balconies curved and snaked; buildings lost their drab brick and whitewash in favor of hot orange or Mediterranean blue. Temple Bar is now not only attractive and trendy, it's the place where folks of every age and interest gather. *www.templebar.ie*

**Meetinghouse Square**, the heart of Temple Bar, buzzes with activity largely centered around the arts: a school for acting, a children's activity center, the Temple Bar Music Centre, the Irish Film Centre and Archive, a center for photography, and scores of galleries and restaurants. The Saturday open-air market is a big draw, and in the summer Meetinghouse Square becomes an open-air cinema where films from a projector in one building are cast onto a shutter-style window shade on another.

In the heart of southside Dublin lies **St. Stephen's Green**, 22 acres of gardens where generations of Dubliners have strolled, sunbathed, and flirted among the flower beds and under the trees. Monuments here honor heroes of Ireland's long struggle for home rule. Elegant Georgian buildings surround the green, and the massive Shelbourne Hotel, a mid-Victorian extravaganza, dominates the north side.

For seven centuries the prime symbol of English dominance over Ireland, **Dublin Castle** has long had its medieval grimness dressed up in mellow Georgian brick. Built in the early 13th century, it served as the seat of power for the English rulers of Ireland for 700 years until the independent Irish Free State was formed in 1922. There are elaborate 18th-century **State Rooms**, an undercroft, and various towers to explore. The castle's **Clock Tower** is home to one of the world's great collections of Middle Eastern and Oriental manuscripts and art. *www.dublincastle.ie*

The real treasure of Dublin Castle resides in the gardens at the back of the castle, home to the incomparable **Chester Beatty Library and Gallery of Oriental Art**. The gift of Canadian mining tycoon Sir Alfred Chester Beatty, who moved to Dublin in his later years, this collection of treasures from world cultures and religions is considered one of the finest in Europe. *www.cbl.ie*

It took James Joyce seven years to capture the "dailiest day possible" in Dublin for *Ulysses*. Today, visitors to Dublin delight in tracing the exact steps of Leopold Bloom's day in James Joyce's novel, especially on June 16. The most popular stop remains **Davy Byrne's Pub** for a Gorgonzola cheese sandwich and a glass of Burgundy just as Leopold Bloom did.

Photographs, first editions, and other memorabilia commemorate Dublin's greatest novelist in the **James Joyce Centre**. Visitors can listen to tapes of Joyce himself reading from *Ulysses* and other works or take a James Joyce walking tour originating from the center.

The **Dublin Writers Museum** celebrates the many literary celebrities of Dublin from the past 300 years. They are brought back to life though their portraits, books, letters, and personal items and housed in a restored Georgian mansion on Farnell Square, a building that is itself a treasure. *www.writersmuseum.com*

The **Guinness Brewery** itself is not open to the public, but the **Guinness Storehouse**

offers the best pint and the best view in Dublin. It also provides an overview of the history and clever marketing of the iconic beer in a six-story exhibition in a giant atrium shaped like a pint glass. *www.guinness-storehouse.com*

**Phoenix Park**, the green lung of Dublin, is the largest walled city park in Europe, with 1,750 acres of open space—a vast oasis of trees and grassland, which grateful Dubliners use for walking, bicycling, and playing games. *www.phoenixpark.ie*

Cathedral of St. Anne, Belfast

## Belfast

Belfast is a friendly, gritty, interesting city that is undervisited and delightful to explore. It sits handsomely at the inner end of Belfast Lough, divided in two by the River Lagan, with a fine ridge of hills on the west—Black Hill, Black Mountain, Divis, Swuire's Hill, and Cave Hill.

There's no better way to experience Belfast than in a **Black Taxi**. A gabby cabby (and almost all of them are) can help bring the spirit and humor of Belfast alive. They are particularly knowledgeable about the city's murals, which they will gladly take you to.

**Donegall Square** is the heart of Belfast, with an electric, friendly energy and dramatic, beloved civic buildings. The

massive **City Hall,** a great white wedding cake of a building, exudes the Edwardian confidence it was designed to reflect. A memorial to the crew of the Belfast-built Titanic stands nearby.

One of the most popular C. S. Lewis relics is Ross Wilson's "**The Searcher**," a bronze sculpture depicting the wardrobe from Lewis's classic novel *The Lion, the Witch, and the Wardrobe* that was installed in central Belfast for the C. S. Lewis centenary in 1998.

Not far from Queen's University is Belfast's splendid **Botanic Gardens**, beautiful to stroll in and irresistible with their monstrous Victorian iron-and-glass greenhouses. The Palm House is a triumph of Victorian garden architecture in glass and cast iron and not to be missed. *www.fobbg.co.uk*

The walk up **Cave Hill**, popular with locals and visitors, is worth every step for the stupendous view over Belfast Lough and the city. The ideal launching point is **Belfast Castle**, where the **Cave Hill Heritage Centre** offers fascinating insights into the wildlife, geology, and history of the area. From here, the well-marked Blue Route footpath passes by the great basalt cliff called **Napoleon's Nose**, prehistoric caves, and **McArt's Fort**, where legend has it that a small band of friends met in 1795 to swear an oath that Irishmen of every creed should unite for independence. *www.belfastcastle.co.uk*

Large, colorful, sectarian **murals** of all kinds are ubiquitous and impossible to ignore throughout all of Northern Ireland, and in Belfast in particular. Many are highly political and even threatening, painted on houses, bridges, and the walls of any available building. Murals come and go as buildings are demolished or new developments inspire fresh commentary; thus, they reflect the spirit and story of Northern Ireland and the nature of Belfast's decades long struggles.

# [ Time Line of British & Irish History ]

**before A.D. 100**

**1640–1520 B.C.** Stonehenge is completed

**circa 480 B.C.** The Celts of mainland Europe begin migrating to Britain in large numbers

**55 B.C.** Julius Caesar visits southern Britain

**A.D. 100**

**A.D. 120** Emperor Hadrian orders a wall built in northern Britain to keep out the Picts

**400**

**407** Roman army leaves Britain

**432** Patrick takes Christian message from Britain to Ireland

**449** Anglo-Saxons arrive in southeast Britain

**500**

**563** The Irish monk Columba is exiled from Ulster, eventually founds Iona monastery

**589** St. David, patron saint of Wales, dies

**597** Augustine arrives in Britain, sent by Pope Gregory to convert the Anglo-Saxons

**598** The first English school is founded in Canterbury

**600**

**600** Saxons build Lundenwic, a mile west of Londinium

**601** Pope Gregory selects York as Christian center in northern England

**604** Original St. Paul's Cathedral opens

**627** Edwin of Northumbria accepts Christianity

**633** The Mercians defeat the Northumbrians

**635** Aidan, a monk of Iona, builds a priory on the island of Lindisfarne

**650** Scottish kings variously adopt Celtic Christianity or become subject to Rome

**664** At the Synod of Whitby, the English church decides to follow Roman instead of Celtic practices in Christianity

**670–870** Anglo-Saxons of Mercia control London

**700**

**732** Ecgbert becomes first archbishop of York

**757–796** Offa, king of Mercia, rules Wessex, Sussex, Kent, and East Anglia

**778** The poet Alcuin becomes headmaster of York Cathedral School

**793** Vikings raid Lindisfarne

**800**

**871** Alfred the Great becomes King of England

**871** Danes invade England and capture London

**876** York ("Jorvik") becomes the capital of Scandinavian Britain

**886** King Alfred recaptures London

**899** Alfred dies, and his son Edward the Elder takes the throne and continues to battle invaders

**900**

**917** Vikings found Dublin

**939–946** Edmund I succeeds as English king and establishes friendly relations with Scotland and Ireland

**954** Erik Bloodaxe, last Viking ruler of York, dies

**954** Eadred seizes York for the English

**959–975** Edgar the Peaceful consolidates the English kingdom

**1000**

**1000** The Danegeld is levied in England, a tax to protect against Danish invasion

**1014** Brian Boru defeats Viking forces at the Battle of Clontarf

**1016** The Danish king Canute becomes undisputed king of England and unites England and Scandinavia in 1019

**1040** King Duncan of Scotland is murdered by Macbeth, who becomes king

**1050** Building of Exeter and Winchester Cathedrals begins

**1065** Edward the Confessor consecrates Westminster Abbey

**1066** William of Normandy (the Conqueror) defeats King Harold and becomes king of England

**1068** York surrenders to William the Conqueror; York Castle built

**1086** The Domesday Book is completed

**1100**

**1106** King Henry of England defeats his brother Robert at Tinchebray and reunites England with Normandy, divided since the death of William I

**1110** Earliest record of a miracle play, at Dunstable, England

**1123** St. Bartholomew's Hospital is founded in London

**1124** The first Scottish coinage is made

**1133** St. Bartholomew's Fair takes place at Smithfield, London

**1151** The game of chess comes to England

**1152** Eleanor of Aquitaine divorces King Louis of France and marries the much younger King Henry II of England

**1154** Thomas Becket becomes Henry II's chancellor

**1171** Henry II claims Ireland

**1176** The stone-built London Bridge replaces earlier wooden bridge

**1189** Henry Fitz-Ailwyn becomes first mayor of London

**1190** Anti-Jewish riots in York

**1200**

**1209** Cambridge University is founded

**1200** Early Gothic architecture begins in England

**1209** King John of England invades Scotland and is excommunicated

**1212** York receives royal charter to govern itself

**1215** After the sealing of the Magna Carta at Runnymede, King John of England asks the pope to annul it

**1230** Leprosy brought to Europe by crusaders

**1240** The border is established between England and Scotland

**1233** Coal is mined for the first time in Newcastle, England

**1249** University College, Oxford, is founded

**1256** Henry III strips sheriff of York of power

**1258** The House of Commons is established as part of the Provisions of Oxford

**1269** The first toll roads are built in England

**1284** Wales comes under the English crown

**1297** William Wallace defeats the English at the Battle of Stirling Bridge

### 1300

**1305** Edward I of England standardizes the yard and the acre

**1306** Robert the Bruce is crowned king of the Scots and leads successful campaigns against the English

**1315** Robert the Bruce's brother, Edward, becomes king of Ireland

**1320** Declaration of Arbroath asserts Scottish independence

**1330** Edward III becomes king of England

**1332** The first record of English Parliament being divided into two houses

**1337** Edward III claims rights to the French throne. The Hundred Years' War begins

**1348** The Black Death reaches England

**1350** Edward III begins to rebuild Windsor castle

**1352** Tennis becomes an open-air sport in England

**1371** The death of David Bruce in Scotland brings the Stewart dynasty to the throne

**1373** Merchants in England must use tonnage and poundage weights

**1375** Robin Hood appears in English literature

**1381** English peasants revolt

**1387** Geoffrey Chaucer writes *The Canterbury Tales*

**1392** Foreigners in England are forbidden to sell goods

### 1400

**1405** The abbey in Bath, England, is erected

**1411** University of St. Andrews is founded in Edinburgh, Scotland

**1414** Henry V of England adopts French claims of Edward II and assumes his right to the inheritance of Plantagenets

**1419** All of Normandy comes under the control of Henry V of England

**circa 1430** Middle English gives way to modern English

**1455** End of Hundred Years' War

**1455** The Wars of the Roses begin in England between the House of Lancaster and the House of York

**1485** Henry Tudor of Lancaster defeats Richard III

**1486** Elizabeth of York marries Henry VII; Wars of Roses end

### 1500

**1500** The English navy begins building ships with double gun decks, carrying up to 70 guns

**1509** Henry VIII becomes king of England and marries Catherine of Aragon, his brother's widow

**1518** The Peace of London is agreed among England, France, Spain, the Holy Roman Emperor Maximilian I, and the pope

**1528** Henry VIII of England seeks a divorce from Catherine of Aragon

**1531** Henry VIII declares himself head of the English church

**1547** Henry VIII dies, succeeded by his nine-year-old son Edward VI

**1550** Cricket is first described in England

**1552** Mary Queen of Scots, plays golf

**1558** Queen Mary dies; Elizabeth I becomes queen of England

**1564** Galileo Galilei, Christopher Marlowe, and William Shakespeare are born

**1568** Bottled beer is first produced in London

**1574** James Burbage obtains a license to open a theater in London

**1579** The English and Dutch sign a military alliance against Spain

**1583** The University of Edinburgh is founded

**1583** Life insurance policies are first issued in London

**1588** Spanish Armada is defeated

**1590** William Shakespeare's career as a London playwright begins

**1592** Trinity College Dublin is founded

**1597–1598** The Elizabethan Poor Laws are enacted, providing relief for indigent children and the elderly and employment for able-bodied people in parish workhouses

**1599** The Globe Theatre is built in London

### 1600

**1603** Queen Elizabeth dies, leaving her throne to James VI of Scotland, her nephew. He will reign as James I of England

**1605** English Catholic conspirators, including Guy Fawkes, set explosives in Westminster, but their Gunpowder Plot is discovered

**1605–1612** Shakespeare writes his masterpieces *King Lear, Macbeth, The Winter's Tale,* and *The Tempest*

**1608** Bushmills Distillery founded north of Ireland

**1610** King James I discontinues a session of Parliament; disagreements between the kings and Parliament will continue for the next 50 years

**1611** King James Bible published

**1614** Scottish mathematician John Napier publishes tables of logarithms, arithmetical functions he invented

**1622** James I dissolves the English Parliament

**1625** James I dies; his son Charles I becomes King of England

**1629** Charles I dissolves the English Parliament. No Parliament will now be held until 1640

**1637** The introduction of a new prayer book in Presbyterian Scotland incites violence, precipitating the Covenanter rebellion against state authority

**1641** England produces cotton cloth

**1642** Puritans close all the theaters of London

**1645** Charles I is defeated by hostile Parliamentary forces led by Oliver Cromwell during the English Civil War

**1649** Charles I beheaded

**1650** The English begin the habit of drinking tea; the leaves are imported from China

**1651** Philosopher Thomas Hobbes publishes *Leviathan,* a defense of monarchy and political absolutism

**1653** The English and the Dutch begin sporadic fighting after the English Navigation Act (1651) restricts foreign trade

**1653** Oliver Cromwell becomes the First Lord Protector of the English Commonwealth. He reorganizes England into districts ruled by military governors

**1660** Charles II restored as King of England; the Commonwealth dissolves

**1660** The first female actors appear on stages in England

**1662** Robert Boyle publishes a description of the relationship between the pressure and volume of gas, known as Boyle's law

**1666** The Great Fire of London

**1667** John Milton publishes *Paradise Lost*

**1670s** Christopher Wren begins his most active period as an architect. He designs more than 50 London churches

**1684** Parts of London are equipped with street lighting

**1685** Charles II of England dies, succeeded by James II

**1687** Isaac Newton publishes *Philosophiae naturalis principia mathematica*

**1690** William III defeats followers of James II at Battle of the Boyne in Ireland

**1692** Massacre of Glencoe

### 1700

**1707** Edmond Halley predicts comet that would come to be called Halley's comet

**1707** Parliaments of England and Scotland united by Act of Union

**1710** The South Sea Company begins operations but goes bust due to fraud

**1715** James, son of the deposed James II, enters Scotland in an attempt to regain the British throne, but his attempt fails

**1717** The English Grand Lodge of Freemasonry is established in London

**1721** Regular mail service begins between London and New England

**1730** Methodist Church is founded

**1745** Charles Stuart, grandson of the deposed King James II, enters Scotland to regain the British throne

**1746** Jacobite rising is crushed at the Battle of Culloden, and the feudal clan system of the Highlands goes into decline. Many Scots emigrate

**1759** Robert Burns is born

**1762** Sandwiches are invented in England and named after the Earl of Sandwich

**1769** James Watt patents the modern steam engine

**1771** *Encyclopedia Britannica* is first published

**1790** Ninety percent of males in Scotland can read

**1791** Wolfe Tone forms the nationalist society of United Irishmen, which appeals to both Presbyterians and Catholics to rid themselves of English rule

**1796** Edward Jenner develops a smallpox vaccine using cowpox

**1798** Thomas Malthus argues that the population will always grow faster than the food supply

### 1800

**1805** Britain's Lord Nelson defeats the Franco-Spanish fleets at the Battle of Trafalgar, ending Napoleon's power at sea

**1815** An allied army, led by Britain's Duke of Wellington, defeats Napoleon at the Battle of Waterloo

**1824** The repeal of the Combinations Law allows British workers to form unions

**1831** Football, said to have existed in England since the 12th century, is revived at Eton

**1832** A cholera epidemic kills 31,000 people in Britain

**1838** Queen Victoria is crowned

**1840** First postage stamp issued in England

**1845** The Irish potato famine begins

**1859** Charles Darwin publishes *The Origin of Species*

**1878** First electric street lighting in London

**1898** C. S. Lewis is born in Belfast, Ireland

### 1900

**1900** The Labour Party is formed in Britain

**1901** Queen Victoria dies and is succeeded by her son Edward VII

**1901** The first British submarine is launched

**1903** The first motor taxis appear in London

**1903** Abbey Theatre opens in Dublin

**1904** John Fleming uses a thermionic tube to generate radio waves

**1904** Drinking license laws are enacted in Britain

**1905** The first buses operate in London

**1911** Winston Churchill is appointed First Lord of the Admiralty

**1911** Ernest Rutherford develops his theory of atomic structure

**1912** The Royal Flying Corps is established in Britain (later becomes the Royal Air Force)

**1913** The first English female magistrate is sworn in

**1914–18** World War I

**1916** Easter Rising in Dublin

**1918** Food shortage in Britain leads to the establishment of national food kitchens and rationing of butter and meat in London

**1919** Lady Astor becomes the first female member of Parliament in England

**1920** Oxford first awards degrees to female students

**1922** The Irish Free State is officially proclaimed

**1922** James Joyce publishes *Ulysses*

**1925** British troops pull out of the Rhineland after a seven-year occupation

**1935** Robert Watson-Watt of Scotland builds radar equipment to detect aircraft

**1936** BBC London inaugurates television service

**1939** World War II begins

**1940** Coventry Cathedral in England is devastated during the war's worst air raid

**1941** Britain and the USSR agree to a mutual assistance pact

**1944** Britain becomes a huge armed camp as Gen. Dwight David Eisenhower oversees Allied preparations for the D-Day invasion of Europe

**1945** The Big Three conference involving Franklin Roosevelt, Winston Churchill, and Joseph Stalin takes place at Yalta

**1945** World War II ends

**1945** Labour Party wins general election by a landslide

**1946** Winston Churchill warns of an "iron curtain" separating communist and noncommunist Europe

**1949** The Republic of Ireland is created

**1952** King George VI of England dies, succeeded by his daughter Queen Elizabeth II

**1953** British physicists unveil famous double helix of DNA

**1955** Commercial TV begins broadcasting in Britain

**1956** First nuclear power plant begins operating in Britain

**1957** Former British colonies begin to enter the British Commonwealth of Nations

**1957** Women are admitted to the House of Lords for the first time

**1960** British scientists invent a jet aircraft that can take off and land vertically

**1960s** The Beatles, the Rolling Stones, and The Who lead the English pop music scene

**1966** England wins the World Cup

**1966** Aberfan disaster takes place in south Wales

**1972** Britain imposes direct rule on Northern Ireland due to continued violence between Catholics and Protestants.

**1973** Britain and Ireland join the European Union

**1973** British scientists develop magnetic resonance imaging

**1974** Irish Republican Army terrorists bomb the Tower of London and the British Houses of Parliament

**1976** Britain suffers its worst drought on record

**1978** The first test-tube baby born in England

**1979** Margaret Thatcher becomes prime minister of Great Britain and begins privatizing state-owned companies

**1986** The final supplement (Se–Z) of the *Oxford English Dictionary* is published, more than a century after publication of the first edition

**1988** A Pan Am 747 explodes over Lockerbie, Scotland, killing all 270 passengers aboard

**1990** Glasgow wins the title of European City of Culture

**1991** British computer scientist Tim Berners-Lee puts the World Wide Web online

**1995** Britain establishes the world's first DNA-based crime database

**1996** The European Commission bans exports of beef from Britain because of an outbreak of mad cow disease

**1997** Diana, Princess of Wales, dies in a car accident

**1997** Labour Party leader Tony Blair wins the general election in Great Britain

**1997** Welsh vote in favor of their own Welsh Assembly

**1998** Scots vote in favor of setting up a Scottish parliament

**1998** Good Friday Agreement between Protestants and Catholics in Northern Ireland

**1999** Irish adopt the euro

### 2000

**2003** Britain joins the United States in an invasion of Iraq and the overthrow of Saddam Hussein

**2005** London is selected as host city for 2012 Summer Olympics

**2007** Liverpool celebrated as the European City of Culture

# [ Bibliography ]

Baedeker Guides. *Baedeker's Great Britain*. New York: Prentice Hall Press, 1987.

Beare, Beryl. *Ireland: Myths and Legends*. Bristol, England: Parragon Books Ltd, 1996.

Blackburn, John, ed. Gallery: *Poets Past and Present*. Edinburgh, Scotland: Oliver and Boyd, 1980.

Cahill, Thomas. *How the Irish Saved Civilization*. New York: Doubleday, 1995.

Editors of Time-Life Books. *What Life Was Like Among Druids and High Kings*. Alexandria, Virginia: Time Life Inc., 1998.

Green, Roger Lancelyn. *King Arthur and His Knights of the Round Table*. London: Puffin Books, 1994.

Hahn, Daniel, and Nicholas Robins, eds. *The Oxford Guide to Literary Britain and Ireland*. New York: Oxford University Press, 2008.

Lalor, Brian. *Blue Guide: Ireland*, 9th ed. New York: W.W. Norton, 2004.

Lehane, Brendan. *The Great Cities: Dublin*. Amsterdam: Time-Life International, 1978.

Levey, Michael. *Great Museums of the World: National Gallery London* (Great Museums of the World series). New York: Newsweek, 1969.

Lewis, C. S. *Surprised by Joy: The Shape of My Early Life*. London: Harvest Books, 1995.

McCluskie, Tom, Michael Sharpe, and Leo Marriott. Titanic *& Her Sisters* Olympic *&* Britannic. London: PRC Publishing, 1998.

McCourt, Frank. *Angela's Ashes*. New York: Scribner, 1996.

Morris, Jan. *A Writer's House in Wales*. Washington, D.C.: National Geographic Society, 1985.

Morrogh, Michael MacCarthy. *The Irish Century*. London: Weidenfeld and Nicolson Ltd, 1998.

National Geographic Society. *Discovering Britain and Ireland*. Washington, D.C.: National Geographic Society, 1985.

———. *This England*. Washington DC: National Geographic Society, 1966.

Nicholson, Louise. *Traveler: London*. Washington, D.C.: National Geographic Society, 2004.

Nuttgens, Patrick. *York: The Continuing City*. London: Faber and Faber, 1976.

O'Connor, Frank. *My Oedipus Complex and Other Stories*. London: Penguin Books, 1981.

Ormsby, Frank, ed. *Poets From the North of Ireland*. Belfast, Northern Ireland: Blackstaff Press, 1979.

Ousby, Ian. *Blue Guide: England*, 11th ed. New York: W.W. Norton, 1995.

Porter, Peter. *W. B. Yeats: The Last Romantic*. New York: Clarkson N. Potter, Inc., 1990.

Quindlen, Anna. *Imagined London*. Washington, D.C.: National Geographic Society, 2004.

Rankin, Ian. *The Hanging Garden*. New York: St. Martin's Press, 1998.

Richards, Mark. *The Cotswold Way*. Harmondsworth, England: Penguin Books Ltd, 1987.

Robinson, Adrian, and Roy Millward. *The Shell Book of the British Coast*. North Pomfret, Vermont: David and Charles, Inc., 1983.

Rogan, Johnny. *Van Morrison: No Surrender*. London: Vintage, 2006.

Scott, Ronald McNair. *Robert the Bruce: King of Scots*. New York: Peter Bedrick Books, 1989.

Shotton, Pete, and Nicholas Schaffner. *John Lennon: In My Life*. New York: Stein and Day Inc., 1983.

Somerville, Christopher. *Traveler: Great Britain*. Washington, D.C.: National Geographic Society, 2007.

———. *Traveler: Ireland*. Washington DC: National Geographic Society, 2004.

Stevenson, John. *Two Centuries of Life in Down: 1600–1800*. Belfast, Northern Ireland: The White Row Press, 1990.

Waterson, Merlin. *The National Trust: The First Hundred Years*. London: BBC Books and The National Trust, 1995.

Wills, Elspeth, and Michael Wills. *Scotland*. New York: W.W. Norton, 2001.

# [ Index ]

## U

Ullswater (lake), England 182
Ulster (province), Northern Ireland 38, 276, 279, 299
*Ulysses* (Joyce) 292, 310, 317, 318, 335
United Kingdom
  definition 9, 42
  European Union membership 321
United States
  Irish-American connections 304
  post-World War II powers 47
University College, Oxford, England 126, 133
University of Edinburgh, Edinburgh, Scotland 258
Urquhart Castle, Scotland 249

## V

Vale of Rheidol Steam Railway, Wales 213, 215
Vera Lynn, Dame 24, 49
Victoria, Queen (United Kingdom)
  reign 42, 174, 181
  residences 34, 69, 225, 249
Victoria & Albert Museum, London, England 70, 83, 138
*Victory,* H.M.S. **100,** 101, 102
Vikings
  in England 26, 172–173
  in Ireland 282, 285, 286, 313
  in Scotland 13, 241–242

## W

Wales **190–215**
  castles 204
  map 193
  mines and underground tours 208
  sites and sights 214–215
  steam railways 212, **212,** 213
Walking tours
  Bath, England 113
  Cambridge, England 134
  Cork, Ireland 286
  Covent Garden & Soho, London, England 75
  Knightsbridge & Kensington, London, England 83
  Oxford, England 130
  Westminster, London, England 60
  York, England 164
Wallace, Sir William 30, 220, 230, 254
*Warrior,* H.M.S. 101
Wars of the Roses 34, 184
Warwick Castle, Warwick, England 148, **148–149,** 157
Waterford, Ireland 286, 306
Watt, James 41, 147, 151, 253, 267
Weather 14, 20, 296, 303

Wedgwood, Josiah 148, 151
Wedgwood pottery 146, **146**
Wellington, Duke of 42, 60, 69, 116
Wellington Testimonial, Dublin, Ireland **334**
Wells, Allan 134
Wells, England 91, 121
Welsh, Irvine 258
Welsh language 195, 207
Welshpool & Llanfair (railway), Wales 213
Wesley, Charles 167
Wesley, John 166–168
West End, London, England 72, 75, 77–78
West Midlands (region), England 147–148
Western Isles *see* Outer Hebrides (islands), Scotland
Westminster, Palace of, London, England **62–63**
  architecture 60, 61, 86
  Cromwell statue **42**
  Houses of Parliament 47, 63, 65, 86
  location 63
  oldest portions 47
  State Opening of Parliament 65, 67, 69
  Victoria Tower 65
  *see also* House of Commons; House of Lords; Parliament, British
Westminster (village), London, England 60–61, 65, 67, 69, 86
  map and walking tour 60
Westminster Abbey, London, England **61,** 86
  Armistice Day service **46,** 47
  coronations 30, 47, 60, 67, 69, 86
  tombs and monuments 69, 70, 102
  Yeoman Warders **65**
Westminster Bridge, London, England 60–61
Wexford, Ireland 282
Whiskies 227, 228, 232, 249, 272
Whitby, England 20, 168, 171, 188
White Cliffs of Dover, England **9,** 98, 120
White Hart (pub), London, England 78
White Horse Close, Edinburgh, Scotland 263
White Horses (chalk figures) **14–15**
Whitechapel area, London, England 82
The Who 75, 98
Wicklow Mountains, Ireland 306
Wight, Isle of 121
Wilberforce, William 65, 168
Wilde, Oscar 82, 130, 315, 317
Wildlife viewing 241, 249
William I (William the Conqueror), King (England)
  Battle of Hastings 26, 94–95, **94–95**
  control of England 91, 152
  coronation 60
  Domesday Book 28–29, **29,** 91
  residences 34, 78, 119

William III (William of Orange), King (England) 41, 222, 238, 240, 276, 322
The Willow Tea Rooms, Glasgow, Scotland 270, **270,** 271, 273
Willy Lott's Cottage, Flatford, England 138
Wilson, Ross 326, 335
Wimbledon, England 84
Winchester, England 91, **96–97,** 97, 120, **121**
Windermere (lake), England 182
Windsor Castle, Windsor, England **32–33,** 116, **116–117,** 119, 120
Winston Churchill (pub), London, England **79**
Wodehouse, P. G. 77–78, 116, 119
Wool 142, 295
Woolf, Virginia 50, 72
Woolton, England 187
Worcester, England 156
Wordsworth, William 60–61, 182–183, 189, 214
World War I 24, 43–44, 47, 207, 208, 241
  Armistice Day memorial service **46,** 47
World War II
  Battle of Britain 65, 72, 83, 98, 101
  Blitz 60, 69, 72
  Cabinet War Rooms 60, 86
  colonial soldiers 47
  D-Day 101–102
  East Anglia airfields 137
  Japanese internment camps 134
  memorials 69
  Orkney Islands 241
  patriotism 24
Wormwood Scrubs, London, England 82
Wren, Sir Christopher 59, 60, 84, 130, 134
Writers' Museum, Edinburg, Scotland 272
Wye Valley, Wales 214

## Y

Ye Olde Cheshire Cheese, London, England 78
Ye Olde Mitre (pub), London, England 78
Yeats, Jack 296, 303
Yeats, William Butler
  associated sites 296, 299, 303, 307, 317
  founding Abbey Theatre 317, 334
  writings 24, 296, 322
Yeats Country Drive, Ireland 303
Yeoman Warders (Beefeaters) **64,** 65, 87
York, England 160, **162–163,** 163, **176,** 188
  map and walking tour 164
York, House of 184
York Minster, York, England 160, 163, 164, **166, 167,** 188
Yorkshire (county), England 160, 163–168, **184–185,** 186
Yorkshire Dales, England 166–168, 184, **184–185,** 188

# [ Contributors ]

## About the Writer

**ROBIN CURRIE** is an editor and writer whose books include Time-Life's *What Life Was Like in the Land of Druids and High Kings* and *Lost Civilizations: Anatolia*. He was an author of *National Geographic's Concise History of the World* and has edited National Geographic Traveler guides on New York, Hawaii, South Africa, and Greece. His writing has been published by the Smithsonian, McGraw-Hill, the National Endowment for the Humanities, and America Online, where he was senior editor of the AOL homepage. His most recent book, *The Letter and the Scroll: What Archaeology Tells Us About the Bible*, co-authored with Stephen Hyslop, was published by National Geographic in the fall of 2009. Currie was born in Belfast, Northern Ireland, and currently lives his wife and three children in Arlington, Virginia.

## Writer Acknowledgment

Thanks to **CANDEE CURRIE**, **GAVIN CURRIE**, and **STEPHEN GROSSMANN** for their help with this project—for their willingness to read and their readiness to talk.

## About the Contributors

**TIM JEPSON** is a writer and journalist. He has written many books on Italy and elsewhere, including five titles for National Geographic, and numerous articles for *Vogue, Condé Nast Traveler,* National Geographic *Traveler,* and other publications.

**KATHLEEN LINGLE POND** (travel tips and "sites and sights") is a writer and editor. She is the author of *The Professional Guide* and co-author of several guidebooks.

# [ Illustration Credits ]

2-3, Dennis Reddick; 4, Sam Abell; 6-7, Jim Richardson; 7 (UP RT), Wikipedia; 9, Britannia, c.1915, Kendrick, Sydney (1874-1955)/Private Collection/The Bridgeman Art Library; 10-11, Michael St. Maur Sheil/CORBIS; 12, Jim Richardson; 13, Linda Steward/iStockphoto.com; 14, Kenneth Geiger; 14-15, Kate Thompson/NationalGeographicStock.com; 16-17, Andrew Henderson; 18, Nik Wheeler/CORBIS; 19, Peter Macdiarmid/Getty Images; 21, O. Louis Mazzatenta/NationalGeographicStock.com; 22-23, David Hughes/Robert Harding World Imagery/CORBIS; 23 (UP RT), Wikipedia; 24, UK Alan King/Alamy; 27, Colin Monteath/Hedgehog House/Minden Pictures/NationalGeographicStock.com; 28, Susan Gadsby, Papilio/CORBIS; 29, Michael Freeman/CORBIS; 31, Gideon Mendel/CORBIS; 32-33, Patrick Ward/CORBIS; 33, The British LIbrary/Photolibrary; 34, Jonathan Blair/NationalGeographicStock.com; 35, Jeff J Mitchell/CORBIS; 36-37, Jonathan Blair; 37, Duncan Walker/iStockphoto.com; 38-39, Clive Nichols/CORBIS; 40-41, Steve Vidler/Eurasia Press/CORBIS; 41, Superstock/Getty Images; 42, Iain McGillivray/Shutterstock; 43, Catherine Karnow; 44-45, Murat Taner/Getty Images; 46, Richard Pohle/WPA Pool/Getty Images; 48-49, O. Louis Mazzatenta; 50, Len Green/Shutterstock; 50 (UP LE), Wikipedia; 51, Chris Jenner/Shutterstock; 52-53, Jason Hawkes/Getty Images; 53 (UP RT), Wikipedia; 54, Tischenko Irina/Shutterstock; 56-57, George Rose/Getty Images; 58, Leon Neal/AFP/Getty Images; 61, Annie Griffiths Belt; 62-63, Lazar Mihai-Bogdan/Shutterstock; 64, Indigo/Getty Images; 65, Morozova Tatyana (Manamana)/Shutterstock; 66-67, Jason Hawkes/Getty Images; 68, Adrian Dennis/AFP/Getty Images; 69, Pawel Libera/CORBIS; 70, Greg Dale/NationalGeographicStock.com; 71, Hazel Stuart/Robert Harding World Imagery/CORBIS; 72-73, Thomas Sztanek/Shutterstock; 74, Ted Spiegel/CORBIS; 76-77, Derek James Seaward/CORBIS; 78, Carlos E. Santa Maria/Shutterstock; 79, Will van Overbeek/NationalGeographicStock.com; 80-81, Richard Waite/Shutterstock; 82, Catalin Petolea/Shutterstock; 84-85, Catherine Karnow; 86, Shutterstock; 86 (UP LE), Wikipedia; 87, Vladimir Korostyshevskiy/Shutterstock; 88-89, Brian Lawrence/Aurora Photos; 89 (UP RT), Wikipedia; 91, Angelo Hornack/CORBIS; 92, Martin Gray/NationalGeographicStock.com; 93, Bo Zaunders/CORBIS; 94-95, Hulton Archive/Getty Images; 96-97, Nick Lewis/Loop Images/CORBIS; 99, Martin Gray/NationalGeographicStock.com; 100, Adam Woolfitt/

# BRITAIN & IRELAND

ROBIN CURRIE

## PUBLISHED BY THE NATIONAL GEOGRAPHIC SOCIETY

JOHN M. FAHEY, JR., *President and Chief Executive Officer*

GILBERT M. GROSVENOR, *Chairman of the Board*

TIM T. KELLY, *President, Global Media Group*

JOHN Q. GRIFFIN, *Executive Vice President;*
    *President, Publishing*

NINA D. HOFFMAN, *Executive Vice President;*
    *President, Book Publishing Group*

## PREPARED BY THE BOOK DIVISION

BARBARA BROWNELL GROGAN, *Vice President and*
    *Editor in Chief*

MARIANNE R. KOSZORUS, *Director of Design*

SUSAN TYLER HITCHCOCK, *Senior Editor*

CARL MEHLER, *Director of Maps*

R. GARY COLBERT, *Production Director*

JENNIFER A. THORNTON, *Managing Editor*

MEREDITH C. WILCOX, *Administrative Director, Illustrations*

## STAFF FOR THIS BOOK

GARRETT BROWN, *Project Editor*

CAROL FARRAR NORTON, *Art Director*

KEVIN EANS, *Illustrations Editor*

KATHY POND AND TIM JEPSON, *Contributing Writers*

MATT CHWASTYK AND GREG UGIANSKY, *Map Research and Production*

MARSHALL KIKER, *Illustrations Specialist*

AL MORROW, *Design Assistant*

## MANUFACTURING AND QUALITY MANAGEMENT

CHRISTOPHER A. LIEDEL, *Chief Financial Officer*

PHILLIP L. SCHLOSSER, *Vice President*

CHRIS BROWN, *Technical Director*

NICOLE ELLIOTT, *Manager*

RACHEL FAULISE, *Manager*

The National Geographic Society is one of the world's largest nonprofit scientific and educational organizations. Founded in 1888 to "increase and diffuse geographic knowledge," the Society works to inspire people to care about the planet. It reaches more than 325 million people worldwide each month through its official journal, *National Geographic,* and other magazines; National Geographic Channel; television documentaries; music; radio; films; books; DVDs; maps; exhibitions; school publishing programs; interactive media; and merchandise. National Geographic has funded more than 9,000 scientific research, conservation and exploration projects and supports an education program combating geographic illiteracy. For more information, visit nationalgeographic.com.

For more information, please call 1-800-NGS LINE (647-5463) or write to the following address:

National Geographic Society
1145 17th Street N.W.
Washington, D.C. 20036-4688 U.S.A.

Visit us online at www.nationalgeographic.com

For information about special discounts for bulk purchases, please contact National Geographic Books Special Sales: ngspecsales@ngs.org

For rights or permissions inquiries, please contact National Geographic Books Subsidiary Rights: ngbookrights@ngs.org

ISBN: 978-1-4262-0627-6
978-1-4262-0628-3 (deluxe)

## LIBRARY OF CONGRESS CATALOGING-IN-PUBLICATION DATA

Currie, Robin, 1948-
  Britain and Ireland : a visual tour of the enchanted isles / Robin Currie.
    p. cm.
  Includes bibliographical references and index.
  ISBN 978-1-4262-0627-6 -- ISBN 978-1-4262-0628-3 (deluxe)
  1. Great Britain--History. 2. Ireland--History. 3. Northern Ireland--History. I. Title.
  DA27.5.C87 2010
  941--dc22

               2010001705

Printed in U.S.A.

10/RRDW-CML/1